Maximiliano

LIFE

OF

MAXIMILIAN I.,

LATE EMPEROR OF MEXICO,

WITH A SKETCH OF

THE EMPRESS CARLOTA.

BY

FREDERIC HALL,

ONE OF HIS MAJESTY'S LEGAL ADVISERS.

"*Fiat justitia ruat cœlum.*"

NEW YORK:

PUBLISHED BY JAMES MILLER,

522 BROADWAY.

1868.

PREFACE.

TWO great events of the last half of the Nineteenth Century will stand out like embossed inscriptions on the pages of American history, all crimsoned with the blood of the murdered. And the advancing waves of Time will not efface them, nor the names of those who prominently figured therein. President Lincoln was the victim of the one, and Ferdinand Maximilian of the other. The essential difference characterizing the two is, that the tragedy of the latter followed a judicial farce, and was performed by a Nation, while that of the former, unaccompanied by a farcical show, was perpetrated by a private individual.

The trial and execution of an Emperor are not of so frequent occurrence as not to produce excitement, and attract attention all over the civilized world. The history of such events, and of the life of him who formed the great subject thereof, cannot fail to be observed with more than ordinary interest, although recorded in a homely style.

The meeting in that tragical scene of Republicanism

and Imperialism will somewhat heighten the desire to scan with a piercing eye, to probe to the bottom the feelings, the passions, the seething hate, that actuated and governed the whole act.

I have endeavored to portray succinctly, in the first chapter, a history of the leading events which mark the Austrian nation and the House of Hapsburg, that the reader may carry in his mind that picture of the past, while he surveys the portrait of one of the late descendants of that ancient line of Imperialism.

It has not been my purpose to give a history of the Mexican Empire during the reign of Maximilian, but to detail his personal qualities and actions; and to concisely state the facts and law pertaining to his trial; adding thereto a short biographical sketch of his affectionate and talented spouse, the Empress Carlota.

The biography of a ruler necessarily includes many important facts that peculiarly belong to the historical records of his nation. But the main subject of the one excludes the bulk of the other.

It has not unfrequently been observed that the biographies of Sovereigns and Statesmen usually contain too much of State documents to interest the general reader, and not sufficient of the minutiæ of their private life. In other words, the majority of the reading community wish to see the person live, as it were. I have sought to weave both herein. The most of the documentary statements are contained in the chapter which relates to the trial of the Emperor; and in this instance will perhaps be, to many, the most interesting portion of the work, particularly to those of the legal profession, and to statesmen.

I gathered my materials and nearly completed the work while in Mexico, and was most diligent in my exertions to collect facts. And the task of sifting the truth from the many false rumors, in my researches, was not an easy one. The variety of statements placed in circulation during battles and sieges is great; and many incorrect and improbable stories are related by honest persons, believing them to be authenticated facts. Those who have observed criminal proceedings in a court of justice, and have heard half a dozen or more witnesses relate their conflicting stories as to what occurred at the time of the committing of the alleged crimes, will readily understand all this. Scarcely any two individuals hear or see alike all of the actions and sayings in a conflict of arms between either small or large forces.

I trust I shall not be charged with either vanity or egotism in recording the many brief conversations between His Majesty and myself. To most persons, the exact expressions of an emperor, under the circumstances in which I met Maximilian, are fraught with greater interest than the chronicle of events which transpired while he swayed with full power on the imperial throne.

What I have written in regard to the relative value and progress of the Empire and Republic of Mexico, has not been prompted by any tincture of taste for Imperialism, nor by any personal enmity to the President or Cabinet of the Republic, with whom I have had none but amicable relations.

The engraving of the place where the execution of the Emperor occurred is taken from an excellent drawing made for me by my friend, Mr. JOHN M. PRICE, an English gentleman, and engineer on the Vera Cruz Railroad. It is a far better view than any photograph ever taken of that ground. None were taken at the very time of the execution.

If I have failed to embalm the name of that good man, MAXIMILIAN, in a pleasant style, I hope that the value and interest found in the materials of this work will compensate for the poverty of their dress.

FREDERIC HALL.

RUTLAND, Vt., December, 1867.

MAXIMILIAN.

CHAPTER I.

Austria—Her accessions—House of Hapsburg—Its origin—Descendants thereof.

COULD we count backward the notches on the long measure of Time, for ten centuries, and by a magic wand bring up the then living from their subterraneous dwellings, in a certain part of the territory watered by the Danube, the ear would catch the sound of *Oest-reich* (east country), as the appellation of Austria. That territory was the nucleus around which, subsequently, has been formed the great Austrian empire.

If we carefully view that empire through the long vista of ages, we shall not fail to observe that its political and territorial phases have been more diverse than the number of the centuries.

If we now examine it in a geographical, ethnographical, and linguistic point of view, we shall consider it a curious piece of Mosaic work. It has been observed that the ethnographical map of Austria exhibits one hundred and twenty different groups of nationalities, and the number of linguistic groups nearly two thousand. It suggests itself to one's mind that the workers on the Tower of Babel might have settled there. If, by a vote of those different races, the pieces of that artistic work could be disunited, what great political artist would be able to replace them?

If the diversified lands of that empire have long been illuminated by the gladsome light of peace, they, too, have had their share of the blazing light of camp-fires. And as their mighty hosts clashed the glittering steel, they counterfeited the stars of heaven.

If we glance at the variations made by the finger of Time, as it has traced the exterior lines of that empire, we shall see that it has been as meandering in its course as the winding Amazon.

As we review the history of Austria, in all its points, we shall be unmistakably impressed with the fact, that, with its governing power, there has been talent, genius, great foresight, and indomitable will. And if its rulers have given value and importance to things according to their dimensions, it is only what political history will attribute to every other powerful nation. The charge of the aggrandizement of territory would bring more than Austria into the culprit's box. And if the culprits were to be tried in the order of the magnitude of their crimes, Austria might not be first upon the list.

If, among the various groups of her subjects, and the diversity of their interests, there has been much complaining against the throne, the same has been witnessed by every other nation, at different periods, although the cause of the one may not have been that of the others. Still some cause has existed, in the estimation of the malcontents, for the complaint.

During a long period of time, the dukes of Austria sprang from the House of Bamberg. The governors of Austria received the title of dukes in the 12th century. Death, that never-failing visitor, at his appointed time walked in, and drew a notable mark on the family record of that house, in the year A. D. 1246. That visitor then carried away the last of the male line thereof. Soon thereafter the main study of the inhabitants of that empire was skill in the use of the sword, the battle-axe, and the spear. There was a long struggle with the contending elements of war. The times, the circumstances, did not fail to present a man of powerful mind, a leader of men, who shaped events according to his will. That man was RUDOLPH OF HAPSBURG, Emperor of Germany, who was born in 1218, and son of Albert IV., Count of Hapsburg.

He placed his son Albert upon the throne of Austria, in the year 1282. Thus dates the beginning of that illustrious House of Hapsburg, as connected with Austria, which has so long, so powerfully, and so successfully swayed the destinies of a vast portion of Europe; although, as has been observed, not without its terrible struggles, its alternate losses and gains.

As the years rolled on, the circle of its territorial jurisdiction extended wider and wider, by the force of marriage, purchase, and inheritance, until its superficial area had expanded far beyond that of any other State in the German Empire. This vast accession of territory necessarily elevated the rank of its sovereign head. Rodolph IV. assumed the title of Archduke Palatine in 1359; and he further marks his reign by the acquisition of Tyrol, in 1363. To the Archdukes thereof was allotted the high position of Emperor of the mighty Germanic Empire. As we trace back its history, we observe that on the list of emperors taken from among those Archdukes, the first was Alfred II., who acknowledged the receipt of that imperial crown in the year 1438.

The holy link of matrimony that united the exceedingly ambitious Maximilian I., at the age of eighteen, to Mary, daughter of Charles the Bold, Duke of Burgundy, in 1477, became as it were an extension of

Austria's territorial chain, which enclosed Flanders, Franche Conté, and all the Low Countries. Likewise the ceremony of marriage of Ferdinand I. with Ann, sister of Louis, King of Hungary and Bohemia, in 1521, was but the seed sown for another national harvest for Austria. That harvest became effectual on the death of the said king, which event transpired at the battle of Mohaez, in the year A. D. 1526; when Ferdinand gathered the two latter kingdoms into the great storehouse of his empire.

Upon the history of the sixteenth century, the bold, the enterprising, and ambitious Charles V. left his mark indelibly stamped. His own ambitious designs roused up the internal vigor of other nations more than the influence of any other sovereign head in Europe. His success was startling, and viewed with jealousy. The acquisitions of Austria, in his day, were unequalled by those of any other power. He was the great captain of the age, in whom was embodied the advancing spirit of the times. He was the ruler of half the world. He was the great shining light among crowned heads, and he shed his lustre on the surrounding kingdoms. His knowledge of men was remarkable. He adapted their talents and abilities to their proper sphere, as readily and as appropriately as a joiner fits his various pieces of work together.

He was born at Ghent, on the 24th day of February, in the year 1500. He was the son of Philip the Handsome, Archduke of Austria, and grandson of Maximilian and Mary,—the latter being the only child of Charles the Bold.

The blood of Charles V. trickled down through the veins of the late Maximilian, Emperor of Mexico, who was not the only Maximilian that suffered imprisonment. The grandfather of Charles V. attempted, with an inadequate force, to take the city of Bruges, in 1488; the result of which was, that he became imprisoned, but afterward favored with his liberty by giving hostages for his fidelity.

The increasing fear of other European States, occasioned by the territorial aggrandizement of Austria and the feuds between Protestants and Catholics, produced the Thirty Years' War, that commenced in 1618. The result of its termination was the treaty of Westphalia, in 1648, which secured the independence of the German States.

By the treaty of Utrecht, Austria gained the Italian provinces, in 1713.

The power, the wealth, the lustre of Austria could not protect its crowned heads from that fate which is reserved for all mortals. The last of the male line of the House of Hapsburg answered the summons from the grave, in the year A. D. 1720. That summons was served on Charles II. In consequence thereof the succession to that throne fell to his daughter Maria Theresa, who was succeeded by her son, Joseph II.

Francis II., at the age of 24, became Emperor of Germany, King of Bohemia, Hungary, etc., having succeeded his father, Leopold II., in 1792. Some of his claims and pretensions were contested, and the field of battle became the forum of trial and decision. After three unsuccessful campaigns, at different periods, against the French, he lost much of his territory. The decision thereon, made by the sword, was registered by the pen, in the treaty of Presburg. In 1804, he assumed the title of Francis I., Emperor of Austria; and in 1806 yielded up that of Emperor of Germany. Thus, through an unbroken line, male and female, did the House of Hapsburg hold the dignity of the title of Emperor of Germany from 1437 until 1806, when the dissolution of that great Germanic empire was recorded as an historical fact.

Francis doubtless thought that he had taken out a

policy of insurance when he gave the hand of his daughter, Maria Louisa, to Napoleon I. in 1810. But the premium paid produced no security. Francis found it necessary to array himself against his son-in-law, in 1813, on account of the unbounded ambition of the latter. He united with Russia and Prussia, entered the field himself against France, and there remained with his forces until peace. The darkness which then overhung Europe, was only dispelled by the glimmering light of the sword; and the gleaming thereof guided the pen that recorded the treaty of 1815. By which treaty, not only did Francis I. regain the greater part of his lost territory, but cemented firmer than ever the contending elements of the Austrian Empire.

Francis I. died in 1835, leaving the throne to his son Ferdinand I., who, in consequence of the political revolution in 1848, the fatigue of State affairs, added to an enfeebled state of health, decided to abdicate, at Olmutz, the 2d of December of that year, in favor of his brother, Archduke Francis Charles; who on the same day transferred his right to that throne to his eldest son, who was declared to be of the age of majority at 18, and who is the present Emperor of Austria. The storm then gathering over the house of Hapsburg was threatening, and augured danger. Hungary refused to recognize the new monarch, and constituted a Republic, under Kossuth, April 14th, 1849, which was short in its duration. By August, the superior force of Austria became victorious, and Hungary a conquered province. Fickle-handed Fortune was not more constant to Austria than to others. The Empire has lost beautiful Venice—the territory over which His Majesty Maximilian governed a short period, with leniency, receiving on his departure evidence of affection and regret on the part of the subjects therein.

Such is a brief outline of some of the noted changes

and conditions of the Austrian Empire and its rulers, during a long period of centuries. This roll of Austrian history we will here tie up.

The foregoing has been written that the mind of the reader may be refreshened by a glance at some of the prominent characteristic features of the history of that country and family whence sprang the main subject of this work.

If it may sometimes be said that, among the numerous streams that flow from the same pure source, some, whose waters are not limpid, may be discerned, it cannot thus be stated of that branch of the Hapsburg fountain which wound its way into the North American Continent. That branch has dried up. The drying up thereof caused millions of human tears to gush forth. But whilst it ran it was crystal clear, and beneath its radiant surface were seen the shining pebbles of Truth, Honor, Justice, and Charity.

Let us drop the curtain over long-past events, and bring up in review scenes of a nearer date.

CHAPTER II.

Maximilian—His birth—Family—Imperial robe—Personal description—Education—Travels—Marriage—Letter from Estrada to Maximilian, 1861—His reply—Farewell of Trieste to Maximilian—His answer.

> "His life was gentle; and the elements
> So mixed in him, that Nature might stand up,
> And say to all the world, *This was a man!*"
>
> SHAKSPEARE—J. CÆSAR

FERDINAND MAXIMILIAN, late Emperor of Mexico, who could trace a blood connection for nearly six centuries with the ruling monarchs of Austria, and who at an early period of life made the last move on the great chessboard of nations, has been the subject of much thought and the topic of much conversation. Alas! to many, the subject of sad thoughts, in mournful silence.

It may be said that leaving the ancient grounds of Imperialism, to found a new dynasty in the New World, while the tide of Republicanism was rolling up to the confines of the American Continent, was a great error into which he fell; but if so, it was an error of the head and not of the heart.

Whatever may be the odium which some of the inhabitants within his new territorial sphere may have heaped upon him, it cannot dim the lustre in which his name will appear, not only to thousands of Mexicans, but to the candid people of every other nation. His character, like that of every other man of position, will doubtless be traced in opposite colors; for who has not some enemies? And who is perfect?

> "No human quality is so well wove
> In warp and woof, but there's some flaw in it."

It was not his sin, but his misfortune that he was caught in the eddy of betrayal, in which, by a breeze from the atmosphere of vengeance, he was carried down. From those who knew him well, he will receive a righteous judgment. Let the now living read the evidence, before their sentence shall be recorded.

"According to his virtues, let us use him."

Whatever posterity may say, we can only surmise. Let us hope that the present age will furnish them only with the proper materials.

"The form of thought
Goes with the age—the thought is for all time."

Maximilian was born in the palace of Schönburn, near Vienna, on the 6th day of July, A. D. 1832. He was the second son of Francis Charles, Archduke of Austria, and of the Archduchess Frederica Sophia. His father was born on the 7th day of December, 1802: his mother, on the 27th day of January, 1805. They were married November 4th, 1824. They are now living, to mourn the loss of their renowned and affectionate son.

The eldest brother of Maximilian is Francis Joseph I., present Emperor of the Austrian Empire, who was born August 18th, 1830. The younger brothers are Charles Louis, Archduke of Austria, born July 30th, 1833; and Louis Victor, Archduke of Austria, born May 15th, 1842.

In the first engraving we see Maximilian mantled in his imperial robe of purple, united with the white ermine. He has on a coat of dark blue, bearing the uniform of a Mexican general with decorations; a scarf with the Mexican eagle; a sabre; high military boots; his sceptre in his right hand, and crown resting on the table behind it. That robe was never worn except for the purpose of having his portrait taken in it; which portrait was painted in Mexico, and from which photographs were made; and the engraving herein was copied from one of those photographs. No State occasion ever occurred on which it became necessary for Maximilian to present himself in that imperial splendor of purple and white, with crown and sceptre. Had any event required that regal pomp, he would have graced in stately style the robe, with all the dignity of Charles V., united to far more gentleness of manner. But in truth he had no anxious desire to dress in gorgeous pomp. He dressed plainly, and the insignia of rank were only exhibited when time and place, by the rules of etiquette, demanded it.

Maximilian was about six feet and two inches in height, well-proportioned, light complexion, large blue and penetrating eyes, high and broad forehead, and rather large mouth; his hair was light flaxen-color, and rather thin in quantity, which he parted in the centre of his forehead, and also in the middle of the back part of his head, brushing the same forward. His whiskers, moustache, and goatee, were lighter colored than his hair, and very long; particularly the goatee, which he parted in the centre of his chin and twisted each half to its respective side, turning the same under, thereby making its length not clearly observable. He possessed a fine, intelligent, and commanding look; stood straight, and withal had a pleasantness of expression. He was favored with a natural kindness of temper—an urbanity, elegance, and refinement of deportment, which, it may be said, would be expected from one who had received the advantages of a familiar intercourse with the highly polished personages of the European Courts. Yet it may well be remarked, that Nature gave him a greater share of mildness of temperament than is allotted to the majority of mankind. That quality was apparent on all occasions, and it made him troops of friends.

He spoke German, English, Hungarian, Slavonic, French, Italian, and Spanish. Prince Esteraze was his teacher in the Hungarian language; Count de Schnyder, in mathematics; Baron de Binther, in diplomacy; Rev. Mr. Myre, in religious instructions; and for some time by Vice-Admiral Thomas Zerman, in naval tactics and the Italian language. All of said teachers, except the latter, are now living.

If it be true, as generally remarked, that the influence of the mother shapes the mind of the child, more than that of the father, Maximilian had a very superior instructor in every point of view. His mother possesses a mind of rare endowment; great natural qualities combined with extraordinary and varied attainments, acquired by attentive observation, and a severe training of her mental faculties. Her great ambition, and the pride that would naturally spring from her position, could not have failed to stimulate her to extend an ever watchful care over the physical and mental being of her son.

Maximilian, although surrounded by royalty and wealth, was not the associate of idleness. His youthful mind was exceedingly active; and no less so were his bodily movements. He was accustomed to perform those athletic feats that strengthen the muscles, and which are requisite for great mental vigor. His mother had not forgotten that nature provides that in the earlier growth, the frame-work must be well constructed, in order to support the later growth in harmony and health.

It was observed in him at an early age, that he possessed a strong relish for books. The rapidity with which he garnered up knowledge into the storehouse of his mind, gave conclusive evidence of talent, of clearness of thought, and of great ambition. And as he became of that age when he was able to discern his own position, he began to fix his attention upon a future fraught with the elements of success, and to mark out a road that might lead safely to it. Although he could only conjecture as to his future destiny, he cherished exalted views, and resolved to so adorn his mind that it would be able to reflect lustre in any position that might perchance fall to his lot. He looked back along the line of his ancient family, and saw the bright intellectual lights at their respective stations: then ambition flamed his own mind as he wheeled about and fancied he saw posterity gazing at him, in the regular order of that same line.

He was most laborious with his books; his knowledge was varied; he delved into the abstruse sciences, familiarized himself with ancient and modern history, and, as has been stated, his attainments in linguistics were of a high order, having been well instructed in the dead as well as the living languages. As he had determined to prepare himself for the navy, he made the science and art of navigation special studies. He entered the Austrian navy at an early age, and received a most severe training in the tactics and practice pertaining thereto. His proficiency soon became remarkable; and he was made a lieutenant at the age of eighteen. Although thoroughly drilled in solid studies, he was possessed of the love of æsthetics; he admired the beauties of art, and for them, he cultivated, with an increasing appetite, his taste.

At an early age he acquired a desire to travel—to compare what fancy had drawn, with the originals in other lands. It was a pleasant relish to feed his mind upon the beauties of statuary, architecture, poetry, and painting. His mind was such a storehouse of ancient and modern learning, that he was prepared to drink in the exquisite beauties of art. He thought of Greece and Rome as great galleries of fine arts. At the age of sixteen he visited Greece. And there he could spend hours gazing on those ancient statues modelled to deify the human form, and trace their well-defined outlines, their beauties; and then pause for a moment and contemplate the character of the race, which so long ago so exquisitely used the chisel.

Leaving Greece, he visited Italy, Spain, Portugal; thence he travelled to the island of Madeira, crossed the African provinces, studied the character of the country, the people, their colonization system, and their forms of government. He had a keen perception, a polished mind, such as is ready to take correct impressions of what he saw. He had sufficient knowledge to travel with: so that he was able to bring back more. The richly colored tales that had been woven about fair Italy, her arts, her entombed artists—the land of the Cæsars—had fascinated and charmed his youthful mind; and it was with eagerness, with enthusiasm, that he held the ideal picture beside the real. He well knew that while curiosity was excited, his knowledge was increased. If he had been in error concerning the realities, he now dropped the errors as he detected them.

After his return home, he applied himself more to the study of marine duties. In 1854, he sailed as commander in the corvette *Minerva*, on an exploring expedition along the coast of Albania and Dalmatia.

While riding out one day at Trieste, his horse fell down with him, bruising him considerably, causing the blood to flow rather profusely, and rendering him for a time senseless. After recovering his proper state of mind, and feeling about a little, and finding that he was in the house of a ship-caulker, where he was kindly treated, he wished to pay the occupiers of the house some compliment; and in perfect keeping with his good nature, he observed to them that he would like to remain there until he became well, adding that in no other place would he be so well cared for.

Afterward, while on the *Minerva*, he received a commission as Vice-Admiral and Commander-in-chief of the Austrian navy, which caused him to return immediately to Vienna.

The summer of 1855 found Maximilian ready for another pleasure-tour. He boarded the Admiral-ship, *Swartzenberg*, and accompanied by a fleet of seventeen sail, steamed for Candia, the Archipelago, and coasted along Syria; traversed Lebanon, the Holy Land, to Jerusalem. Thence he sailed for Alexandria, in Egypt. After a short visit there, he proceeded to Cairo and the Pyramids; thence to Memphis and the Red Sea,—not failing to closely observe the preparatory works of the then contemplated canal across the Isthmus of Suez. And as he stood gazing upon the apex of the mighty Cheops, viewing on the one hand the vast desert, and on the other the luxuriant vesture of the Valley of the Nile, the view might have suggested to his mind, that it was emblematical of royalty and poverty side by side.

After bidding farewell to the sandy desert, he returned home.

In 1856, he visited the Emperor of France, spending over two weeks at the palace of St. Cloud. The time there was doubtless passed most agreeably; and their mutual friendship increased with the visit. Whether ten years' time produced the snapping asunder of the chain of friendship that bound them, is not for me to say, as I wish to do no injustice to Napoleon, nor the memory of the departed, nor his friends. Some are of opinion that while Napoleon sat comfortably and securely in Paris, and Maximilian on the weak throne of Mexico, the cord of friendship would have been greatly strengthened by threads of silver—an article so much needed and expected by the latter.

After that visit with Napoleon had been finished,

Maximilian proceeded through Belgium and Holland to Northern Germany; also to Southern Germany and the banks of the Rhine, admiring with intense interest the beauties presented to the view in those densely populated regions, where art and nature had combined in forming the useful and the beautiful.

That Maximilian was excessively fond of travelling, we have already had ample proof: that he profited by it, is equally clear. While the scenes of Belgium and the Rhine were still freshly pictured in his memory, he returned again to glance at the originals. In 1857, he glided upon the beautiful waters of the Rhine, where the works of the ancients and moderns stand out in bold contrast. His eyes caught this and that ancient castle; and while thus closely viewing the footprints of Time, he turned his thoughts inwardly and looked upon a page of memory, and read the date, the history of the walls and grounds of many a contest that lay before him—the lords and knights all steeled in armor, who mingled there in the affray. And may he not have said: "What one of Hapsburg was there?"

He passed thence into Lombardy and Central Italy, and then to Merry Old England, where he passed an exceedingly pleasant time, judging from the manner in which he spoke of Queen Victoria. He never mentioned her name but in the greatest kindness in my presence. When there, he felt that he was among true friends. Taking his departure therefrom for the second time, he found himself in Belgium. That busy land soon came to be the centre of his attractions. He had before observed there the works of art with much interest: that densely thronged country, where nearly every foot of land is cultivated, had agriculturally drawn his attention. But now there was something of more importance than all those. The object was not the skill of art—No! art could not adorn it. It illuminated his whole being. He felt the heart-strings pull. They led him always to the house of royalty. It might be said that his rank and position would lead him there; that is true, but his stays were longer. If he left, his heart prompted him to return forthwith. The great charmer was there. To him, all that was lovely, divinely beautiful, were embodied in the Princess Maria Charlotte Amalia. On the 2d of July, 1857, Count Arquinto, imperial ambassador, in solemn audience, in behalf of Maximilian, asked King Leopold I. for the hand of his daughter, Princess Charlotte. The request was granted, and during that same month they were married. That ceremony was not merely an imperial tie—it was a linking together of two happy, loving hearts. The waters of two meeting streams do not more harmoniously mingle into one, than did those two hearts.

The brightest jewel in his crown was her love. It threw its dazzling rays all over and around him. Its brilliancy never lessened. If darkness was apparently about to cast a shade over his path, the lustre of that jewel dispelled it. In the summer of 1857 he was made Governor-General of Lombard-Venice, in which position he remained until July, 1859; still holding that of Superior Commander of the Austrian navy. No man ever reigned over that country more beloved by its people than Maximilian. He suggested many reforms in the administration of affairs in that kingdom. He was remarkably liberal in his views, and he exhibited there high qualities as a statesman. His keen foresight, his plans, his real desire to benefit the people, and their attachment for him, were not unobserved by Count de Cavour, who once remarked that "Archduke Maximilian is the only adversary I fear, because he represents the only principle that can forever enchain our Italian cause."

Whenever any great affliction fell upon the people, or

any part of them, he was the first to render succor. At the great fire in Chigrenlo, he cheered up the men, lest they should sink back in despair at the progress of the frightful elements. And when the Po, the Ambro, the Ticino, came surging over their banks, spreading devastation around, he darted off in a frail bark to give aid to the unfortunate who had neither food nor shelter. Nor did the cold snows and icicles of the Alps deter him from ascending thereon to visit Valtelina, as hunger was gnawing away at human hearts. When disease carried death to the silkworms, with such fury that the silk-looms of Lecio stopped their motion, and left willing workers idle and in want, Maximilian did not forget to perform works of charity, which, to him, were always a pleasure.

On the sixteenth day of September, 1857, he and the Archduchess Carlotta made their grand entrance into the city of Milan. The populace were wild with excitement; shout after shout, mingled with music, were deafening to the ear. Scarcely ever did that city give such a universal shout of welcome to mortal man. His residence there did not lessen their affection for him, but only increased it.

The Italians watched him with pleasure, mingled with surprise; for no Austrian, in their judgment, had ever extended so generously the hand of charity, or viewed them with so much good-will. His own generous heart was his bodyguard. He needed no other, even in times of political excitement, although he had some enemies from his position. He was always shielded with the armor of generosity. About the time of the contemplated assassination by Orsini, he was told that some parties would seek an opportunity to throw a bombshell under his carriage; and many of his friends begged him not to attend the theatre. Although thankful for the interest those friends had taken in his welfare, their entreaties he considered of the same importance as the threats of the public agitators. As he entered his carriage with Count de Stromboli, having no escort to guard them, he remarked, "If we jump, it will be in good company."

He showed the populace what confidence he had in their friendship. It was not misplaced. They felt a pride in sustaining it. Among the aristocracy some hostile feelings were fomenting against him. An organization had been made to vent their spleen upon him in the Piazzetta. He made up his mind to stem the current, that he might learn its force. He, with the Archduchess Carlotta, walked among the group of malcontents, with a firm step; the crowd parted like the Red Sea when the Israelites passed through. After about an hour's promenade they returned to their palace of San Marcos, followed by an immense crowd, that cheered them with great enthusiasm. No living man, not an Italian, could have governed there without having enemies; and, probably, no foreigner could have reigned with as few enemies as he.

The desire of the Italians and Maximilian to preserve the works of the fine arts was mutual. The works of those great masters, their ancestors, were the artistic and historic monuments of the Lombards and Venetians. And he whose pride and pleasure mingled with their own in that work of preservation, was their friend, and they his.

The cities of Venice, Milan, Como, and other places, bear test of his beneficial improvements in their streets, canals, public gardens, and their cleanliness.

The city of Pola is greatly indebted to Maximilian for its resuscitation. He caused several edifices to be constructed there, planted gardens, built a large dike, an aqueduct, an arsenal, and three docks. After the expiration of the term of his governorship in Italy, he paid much attention to the improvement of the navy, and made the fleet of Austria, in proportion to its size, not inferior to any in Europe.

After the war in Italy, and about the middle of November, 1859, he made a voyage to Brazil, and returned home in the forepart of the month of April following.

It is apparent from my foregoing observations, that Maximilian's range of study and reading was extensive. And while he thus drew from so many well-springs of knowledge, he considered that he himself might impart to others from his well-moulded thoughts, ideas of interest and of value. His linguistic attainments showed an aptness for the learning of languages; and this fact itself, is some evidence that the expression of his thoughts in writing would be in no inelegant form. He has presented the proof of my assertion, in the various works which he wrote in the German language; although not written for the purpose of public distribution and sale, but for his own use and gratification, and the pleasure of his particular friends. A few copies were printed by the government of Austria, at Vienna; some of which were circulated among his friends and acquaintance. Since the death of Maximilian, it has been decided to extend their publication, for the purpose of sale to the public. Those works are the following: Sketches of travels, known as "Italy," "Sicily," "Lisbon and Madeira," "Spain," "Albania and Algiers," "Voyage to Brazil," "Aphorisms," "Objects of a Navy," "The Austrian Navy:" also two volumes of poetry, which I believe have never been published. German scholars, who have had an opportunity to peruse some of the foregoing books, have pronounced them works highly creditable to the author, not only as to the principles advanced, the deep thought and argumentative style in some of them, but also for the elegance of diction in which they are clothed.

It appears that some of the Mexican people had, at an early date, and long before their deputation first presented themselves at Miramar, addressed His Imperial Highness Maximilian upon the subject of his occupancy of a throne in Mexico. The following letter was the first correspondence upon that subject, and was written by Señor Gutierrez de Estrada, on behalf of himself and many other Mexicans:

"PARIS, October 30th, 1861.

"PRINCE:

"With profound respect, the undersigned have the honor to address Your Imperial and Royal Highness, in testimony of the deep feeling and sincere gratitude which they have felt, on learning that Your Imperial and Royal Highness was animated with the most generous sentiments toward our unfortunate country.

"Mexico, the spoil of intestine convulsions, renewed without cessation, and of disastrous civil wars, in consequence of the rigid adoption of a political system diametrically opposed to the customs, traditions, and dispositions of her people, has never enjoyed, so to speak, a moment's repose since the day in which, forty years ago, she occupied her place among independent nations. So then, her people will bless, from the bottom of their hearts, whoever shall have contributed to extricate the country out of the horrible state of anarchy into which it fell many years ago, and shall give it again life and happiness.

"What would, then, be their joy if they should behold in such a glorious undertaking the co-operation of a Prince a descendant of one of the most noble, illustrious, and ancient dynasties of Europe, and who, with the prestige of such an elevated origin, of so eminent a position, and of such personal qualities universally acknowledged, should so powerfully support the great work of the regeneration of Mexico!

"The undersigned have expressed their wishes, because they believe that work might be realized soon, under the auspices of Your Imperial and Royal Highness, and because such may be the will of the Almighty.

"The undersigned have the honor to subscribe themselves, with the most profound respect,

"Your Imperial and Royal Highness'

"Obedient servants, etc."

The foregoing letter was answered by the Archduke, with the response which here follows, directed to Señor Estrada:

"Sir:

"I received the letter signed by you, for yourself and various others of your countrymen, and which you sent me, bearing date the 30th of October last. I hasten to express to you, and beg you to transmit to those gentlemen, my gratitude for the sentiments of respect to me, which that letter attests.

"The welfare of your beautiful country has always interested me, certainly; and if, in effect, as you appear to suppose, its inhabitants, aspiring to see founded among them an order of things which, through its stable character, could restore internal peace to them, and guarantee their political independence; and should they believe me able to contribute in securing these advantages, I should be disposed to take into consideration the wishes they might present me, with that view. But for me to think of assuming an undertaking surrounded by so many difficulties, it would be necessary, before all, that I should be very certain of the will and co-operation of the country. My co-operation in favor of the work of governmental transformation, on which depends, according to your convictions, the salvation of Mexico, could not be determined, unless that a national manifestation should prove to me, in an undoubted manner, the desire of the nation to see me occupy the throne.

"Then, only, would my conscience permit me to unite my destinies with those of your country, because then only could be established, from its beginning, my power, in that mutual confidence between the government and the governed, which is in my eyes the most solid basis of empires, next to the blessing of Heaven.

"Lastly, whether or not I may be called to exercise the supreme authority over your noble country, I shall not cease to treasure a very agreeable recollection of the step which you and the other signers of the letter to which I refer have taken towards me.

"Receive, Sir, the proof of the
"sentiments of estimation, etc.

"Castle of Miramar, December 8th, 1861."

The mind of the reader will doubtless continually have in view two questions, pertaining to the acts of Maximilian concerning Mexico. First, whether, in his heart, he desired to act in harmony with the will of a majority of the Mexican people; and second, did he *believe* that such a majority were in favor of his occupying the throne of Mexico?

Every declaration which he made upon the subject of accepting the crown, clearly and unmistakably stated that no such consent could come from his lips, unless there was satisfactory evidence produced, showing emphatically that a majority of the Mexicans desired him as their ruler. And in further support of that position on his part, I will here call the attention of the reader to a fact, unknown to but a few persons.

In March, 1864, Maximilian, while at Brussels, procured a gentleman to proceed to Mexico, and to communicate certain facts to Mr. Juarez. In order that there should be something more certain than oral declarations appertaining thereto, Baron de Pont, counsellor of Maximilian, at the request of His Imperial Highness, wrote a letter addressed to the above-mentioned gentleman, bearing date March 16th, 1864, Bellevue Hotel, Brussels, wherein was set forth the following facts: That Maximilian did not wish to force himself upon the Mexican people by foreign troops, against the will of the people; that he did not wish to change or make for them any political system of government contrary to the express wish of a majority of the Mexicans; that he wished the bearer of the letter to say to Mr. Juarez, that he, Maximilian, was willing to meet Mr. Juarez in any convenient place, on Mexican soil, which Mr. Juarez might designate, for the purpose of discussing the affairs of Mexico, in an amicable manner; and that doubtless an understanding and conclusion might be reached wholly in unison with the will of the people.

The said gentleman went to Mexico, saw Mr. Juarez, stated his mission, and gave a copy of said letter to him. Mr. Juarez replied that he could not consent to any meeting with Maximilian.

The letter to which I refer was written in French, and I read it; and unless it is a forgery, which I do not believe, it is strong evidence in favor of Maximilian's good faith. I have been unable to ascertain any facts which in the slightest degree disprove an honesty of intention upon his part.

In April, 1864, after the word "farewell" had been exchanged between the two august princes and their families, and particular friends, the people came in large numbers to the palace of Miramar, on and after the 10th of the month, to say a parting "good-bye." Commissioners from the neighboring provinces also came to tender an affectionate adieu to their majesties. The true feelings of the inhabitants of Trieste, on that important departure, was happily expressed in one of the journals of that city, of the date of the 10th of April, wherein the Emperor was tenderly and sympathetically addressed as follows:

"Sire:

"The word '*adieu*,' which was said, resounds in every heart, and is on the lips of all the good citizens of this city. If adieu—adieu to the best of princes. Citizen of Trieste! by your noble and magnanimous will, these shores, this port, and these delicious villas have been the objects of your predilection.

"You have given all your heart to this people, who love you as a father loves his son, with all the power of his soul. This people is the one who gives the most painful adieu—this people, whose love will follow you on the waves of the ocean on which you are going to place yourself, will accompany you with all its feelings of gratitude to the other side of the sea; this people, who is saying *adieu*, feel a pain in losing you, after having had the pleasure of your company so many years.

"When you are far from here, Sire, when the imperial crown circles your brow, which was given you by a nation full of enthusiasm and hope; when, after the cares of the throne, and the perturbation of politics, shall be seen to flourish, in their order, peace, work, and prosperity, the fruits of your efforts and your wisdom, may it please Heaven, Sire, that there shall resound forever in your ears this *adieu* which accompanies Your Majesty to the other side of the seas—this adieu, which is that of a people who have loved you; an adieu from the country that weeps your absence—an affectionate adieu of a noble city where you leave such sweet and pious recollections.

"Here, you leave brothers in arms, intrepid mariners, soldiers, who have learned from you how to serve and love their country. On the other side of those mountains which separate us from the empire, beyond those seas, everywhere, you will leave tender and noble recollections. All the Austrians say with us this adieu to the excellent prince, to the loved brother of our beloved emperor. Here is remembered your charity, there your greatness, and everywhere your magnanimity.

"There is no heart that does not treasure your qualities, and those of your august companion, who is called to participate with you in the love and the blessings of a whole people; to second you resolutely in the work of your regeneration; to cultivate your happiness, and to conquer your affections.

"The inhabitants of Trieste will continue their peregrinations around Miramar; and at the sight of its groves, of its splendid habitations, of its magnificent terraces, which command this sea so often furrowed by your ships, they will remember your receptions, so full of grace and affability; and they will bring to memory the thousand times that they have been your honored guests.

"Miramar, your cherished retreat, is reflected in the waters that bathe Trieste. Between Miramar and this city exist bonds of affection that can never be broken: this affection runs in the blood of the people, and will be transmitted to our sons.

"He who has been an excellent prince, will be an excellent sovereign. Mexico has just extricated herself from sad discords; that people feel sensitive still, perhaps, on account of the asperity of their origin; being haughty and affected, even from ancient national pride, they have something of the virgin nature of their vast territory. The task undertaken by Ferdinand Maximilian is difficult, arduous, great; he will know how to accomplish it.

"This victory, O generous Prince, will be the most glorious, and the most enviable, and its value to you will be the gratitude of a whole regenerated people. You will place quietude on the passions; your virtues and your heart will secure your triumph.

"Adieu, then, in the name of all the people of Trieste. May the heavens be propitious for you, and may they promote the accomplishment of your ardent desires, making the country prosper that has selected you to preside over its destinies. You carry with you the benedictions of a people that will never forget you in their hearts; who will associate themselves with your glorious enterprise, and will ask God to assist you with His inspirations. We never could have desired to give you this adieu; we should always have preferred to keep you, tranquil and happy, in our midst. But since Your Majesty is called to pacify a people, to regenerate a vast country, to help it to fulfil its high destinies, may the hand of God guide you; may the work of Your Majesty be holy and blessed.

"Adieu! May the heavens protect you and your august companion! May they concede to you, and to the people that await you, all the fortune that you have known how to give to those who, for the last time, say to you from the bottom of their hearts, Adieu!"

As we read such a *farewell* to His Majesty, from the people of a great city that have known him long and well, what must be our conclusions as to the character of the man?

Not only did they know him as a man, but as a prince, as a governor. A man placed in his position, with his power, over that same people, must have acted wisely, humanely, and justly, as is evidenced by their united voice. Had he acted otherwise, no such burst of affection could spring forth from their hearts. The words themselves make it self-evident that they came not from the surface, but from the very depths of the Austrian heart.

Those words of love and affection escaped not the mind of Maximilian; they touched the cords of sympathy, and they vibrated. And as they moved in harmony with his gentle thoughts, he wrote to Dr. Charles Porenta, the Podesta (or mayor) of Trieste, as follows:

"My dear Podesta:

"In the moments of parting, full of confidence in the assistance of Heaven, to place me at the head of a distant empire, I cannot do less than send a sad and last adieu to the dear and beautiful city of Trieste. I have always professed profound affection for that city, which in a certain manner has become my country; and on abandoning Europe, I know how dear are the recollections of gratitude which link me to that city. Never shall I forget the cordial amiability of its inhabitants, nor the proof of adhesion which has been given to my house and to my person. This recollection will follow me to the foreign land as a strong consolation, and as a happy augury of the future. It will always be grateful to me to know that my garden of Miramar is visited by the inhabitants of Trieste; and I wish that it may be open for that purpose, whenever circumstances may permit it. I desire that the poor may preserve a memorial of my affections; and I have placed the sum of twenty thousand florins, so that the interest thereon may be distributed every year, on Christmas Eve, among the poor families of the city; which distribution will be made by the City Council. As to you, Sir, Dr. Charles Porenta, I decorate you with the cross of Commentator of the Order of my Empire.

"Maximilian."

Thus cursorily have I chronicled the European life of Maximilian. As we trace it through, we are not unconscious of the fact, that the construction of his mind well fitted him to please. And though moving beneath the robes of royalty, he so pursued his course of life, that the light of friendship threw its cheering rays all around him.

We will soon follow him across the trackless ocean.

CHAPTER III.

Carlota—Her birth—Genealogy of family—Education—Personal description—Marriage—Life in Italy—In Mexico—Her derangement—Cause of it—Late residence in Belgium—Palace of Tervueren.

THE frame that includes the biographical portrait of His Majesty Maximilian, would present a blank space if the characteristic features of his august spouse, the lovely, the beautiful, the accomplished, and much-beloved Carlota, were not portrayed by his side, in their true colors. We cannot think of His Majesty without having the vision of the Empress rise up before the mind's eye, as though she were a part of the same being. Scarcely one of her sex has attracted equal attention in the present age. The dazzling splendor of her virtues has caused unbounded praises to be lavished upon her, while her misfortunes have grieved the hearts of millions.

She is a descendant of Henry IV. of France, who perhaps was one of the best rulers France ever had, since Louis IX. He fell by the hand of the assassin, the fanatical Ravaillac, May 14th, 1610. Her father was Leopold I., of Belgium, who was born December 16th, 1790, and was the son of the Duke Francis of Saxe Cobourg Saalfelde. He was naturalized in England, March 27th, 1816, and married May 2d of the same year to Princess Charlotte Augusta, daughter of George IV., of England. He received at that time a pension of fifty thousand pounds sterling, the title of Duke of Kendal, and the rank of a prince of the blood.

It was not long thereafter before he was deprived of that lovely companion. She died in childbirth, Nov. 5th, 1817,—the child non-surviving.

In 1832, August 9th, he again married, uniting himself to Louise Maria Theresa Charlotte Isabella de Orleans, daughter of Louis Philippe, King of France. It was his fortune to enjoy the companionship of the second far longer than that of the first wife; but before a score of years had rolled away, she, too, bid farewell to all there is of earth, on the 11th of October, 1850.

He had by his last wife the following issue: Leopold, Duke of Brabant, now King Leopold II. of Belgium, who was born April 9th, 1835; Prince Philippe Eugene Ferdinand Marie Clemente Bandonin Leopold George, Count of Flanders, born March 24th 1837, and was Major-General and Honorary Commander of the Regiment of Guides; and the Princess Maria Charlotte Amelia Auguste Victoire Clementine Leopoldino, born June 7th, 1840, and who is Carlota, ex-empress of Mexico. Her father, Leopold I., was a man of rare scholastic attainments; and was not ignorant of that science and that art requisite to make skilful moves on the military chessboard. He was termed *the Nestor of kings.* He expired in December, 1865. He was then the oldest sovereign in Europe.

The mother of the Empress Carlota was known by the appellation of the *Holy Queen.* As she died in 1850, it was not her pleasure to long watch over the advancing years of her lovely daughter, who, nevertheless, became a bright ornament even among princesses.

Carlota was born at the palace of Laeken, which is about fifteen miles from Brussels, on the 7th of June, 1840; and never passed over six months of her life in France, although she is called French. The French tongue is her vernacular.

Nearly eighteen years ago, the promenaders that sauntered through the public park of Brussels, frequently observed a charming and attractive little girl, the picture of beauty and loveliness, accompanied by her two little brothers, a preceptor, and governess. She was plainly dressed, wearing a broad-brim straw hat, a short dress, and white pantalettes; and under her *coiffure*, on each side, could be seen her neatly braided hair. That her appearance of beauty and innocence should not be lost to memory, the skill of the artist was brought into requisition, and her portrait, as she was then dressed, was taken; which may now be seen in one of the private apartments of the palace of Brussels. She was usually then seen, when promenading, with a little hoop in her hand, which she never rolled. The little bright-eyed and rosy-cheeked girl wishfully looked upon the various groups of children which she chanced to meet, anxious to join them in their innocent pleasures. But, no, that was not allowed,—the governess said, *No.* She then doubtless wished that she had no teacher to control her, as she saw no good reason why the freedom of others should not be allowed to her. Her little party never seemed to stop nor run, but gravely walked on with a measured tread.

The former part of the life of those children was not a gay one. At home, in the palace, during the lifetime of their mother, they were taught to pray, and all the principles of religion which their youthful minds were capable of receiving, were instilled into them. The days of reception were not play-days to those youths;—the lessons of Christianity were dispensed with, only to let those of etiquette be given in their stead. As visitors entered, they found the little princess by her mother's side; and as salutations were given and received, the bright-eyed daughter did not fail to act her part. The rank and dignity of the different personages were soon known to her, and the respective salutations due to each.

The young princess never seemed to have a playmate of her own age. She saw no one around her save the ladies of honor, whom her father had chosen for her mother. Their conversation was principally upon religious topics, or matters of importance. And yet with all the apparent severity and strictness of her mother, the princess was the object of that parent's deepest affection, who doted upon and idolized that daughter. It was the Christian virtue, the honest pride of that good mother's heart, that caused her to watch with a jealous care every act and word of that young and tender heart, that was destined to attract the world. But while that young princess was in the bud of life, the genial rays of that mother's affectionate heart ceased to shed their holy influence over her. She saw that mother on the couch of death, and heard her last affectionate farewell, which fell upon her ear like the music of a sad dream, mournfully sounding, long after that Spirit of Love had entered the heavenly portal. After that sad bereavement, the broken-hearted princess lived as it were alone in the midst of the ladies of honor.

It was quite observable, that from the age of eleven to fifteen she was less child-like in her manners and conversation than most children of that age, even including those of royalty. It must be attributed to her continual companionship with those of maturer years. She always possessed a marked gravity and dignity even in the ballroom. At the age of sixteen she was allowed to attend balls; but only four times a year, when they were given by the king in the winter season. None but those of royal blood were honored with her company in the dance; and none were permitted to embrace her in the waltz but her brothers. And while she gazed upon others that whirled in the round dances, it was apparently with indifference; and as they glided briskly in the circle, she promenaded in a dignified manner, yet with a pleasing air.

She was fine-looking—her stature tall, majestic, not haughty, graceful in her carriage; and with her air of majesty there was mingled a gentleness and mildness of disposition that won and attracted all who chanced to meet her. Her face is oval; complexion bright, and readily flushed; her nose is a little aquiline; her mouth is pretty, and beneath her rosy lips is a set of regular pearl-white teeth; her eyes are not large, but very bright, and when she becomes excited, they flash like fire. She has a heavy head of hair, of a beautiful dark auburn shade. Nature formed her for an empress, and her acquirements not less fitted her for the station. As she rose above the horizon of childhood, she appeared in all the splendor of the morning star, bright, beautiful.

The photographer, the painter—all the powers of art, have failed to do her justice, in attempting to transfer her beauty on paper or canvas. Her beauty, her goodness, her Christian virtues, will ever defy the pen.

She inherited the talents of her father. Her mind was deep, and exceedingly well cultivated. If her native powers were not more than ordinary, it would be remarkable, since her father and mother were both of superior intellect. At an early age she was placed in the presence of the ministers of State, while matters of importance were discussed; and therefore her opportunities for forming her judgment and training her logical powers of thought, were more than those usually allotted to princesses,—of which she gave conclusive proof in after years. She spoke and wrote, with great perfection, the French, Spanish, German, English, and Italian languages. As has been before observed, she was married in the year 1857, being then of the age of seventeen years. She never became a mother.

Not long after her marriage, in the month of August, a multitude of the people of Brussels might have been seen in front of the palace, as though attracted by something unusual. It was so to them. Upon the balcony of that palace stood the enchantress of that house, Archduchess Carlota, in bridal robes; and by her side stood, arm in arm, a tall, fine-looking man, in the uniform of an admiral. That personage was the then Austrian Governor-General of Italy, Archduke Maximilian. Three days after, the new Archduchess bid farewell to her native home. The then gathered concourse of people had often seen her; but that pleasure was about to be taken from them, and they gazed lingeringly upon her with admiration mingled with regret.

Early deprived of her mother, surrounded by no female blood-relatives (whose affections are always deeper than those of any other persons), they almost wondered at her remarkable qualities, her intelligence, her Christian virtues, and, above all, her charity.

She was fortunate in her marriage, for love tied the knot that bound the two. She seemed to entirely forget her passed hours of loneliness, and thought of the future, which was portrayed by her in bright colors. Nothing thwarted her for a while in her desires. Her husband was all kindness, and his feelings of affection never for a moment slackened.

As she arrived at Milan, she was delighted with her change—with the land of Italy, which was to be her new home for some time to come. She saw in the Archduke perfection, a man of intelligence, of dignity, of power—brave to a fault, and the personification of affection. She was complete mistress of herself. She might almost have believed herself an absolute sovereign, at least while the Archduke held the position of Governor-General of Lombard-Venice.

Her advice was listened to with the utmost attention by the Archduke; for one possessed of such a fund of knowledge, with such a keen sagacity, might well be considered as having a judgment based upon reflection, which would be entitled to much weight, and far too important to pass unheeded.

Carlota

Her mind was deeply engrossed with the affairs of State. She sought the welfare of Italy while there, rather than parties, balls, and fashionable entertainment. The poor of the cities where she visited, and where she resided, will bear ample evidence of her generosity. She was desirous of possessing the good-will of the people. She was always kind to those around her; even to her servants, she rarely made use of any bitterness of tone in language, under even the most provoking circumstances. She was impressed with the idea that the hearts of the subjects were the true throne of a sovereign. Her ambition was exceedingly great,—but withal, an ambition to do good. The Christian principles instilled into her youthful mind never forsook her. In her studies she gave undeniable testimony of energy and great determination. In some of the voyages made by the Archduke she accompanied him; also on the various trips made in Italy. She sailed to the island of Madeira, and there remained while her husband was on a voyage to Brazil. After her return from that island, she wrote a work in French, entitled, "A Voyage to Madeira." The work has been highly spoken of by those who have had the opportunity of perusing it. It bears evidence of a cultivated mind, of reflection, refinement, and elegance of taste, clothed in a pleasing diction.

If her heart swelled with pride, as she was called to sustain the dignified position of Empress, it was an honest pride—a pride to fill the station with honor to herself, her husband, her adopted country, and with honor and virtue in the judgment of the world.

She seemed ever watchful for the progress and improvement of Mexico—the advancement of education, and the protecting care of the poor and needy. The same generosity which she exhibited in Europe was made manifest in the New World, even to a greater degree. She has often been observed walking through the mud, holding up her skirts, in order to visit the poor in the hospitals, and also others that were needy, in their own desolate homes. She established schools, and visited them in person. If she visited a town, only for an hour, the first inquiry made by her was as to the condition of the schools. She was not satisfied with the answer of any one as to the state of the houses of instruction, but would visit them in person. The bad condition of the weather and roads never prevented her from so doing. She examined the scholars in their lessons, gave them kind advice, and not unfrequently pieces of money, to encourage them in their studies. Never in the history of Mexico was the number of beggars so small in the capital as during her presence there. The poor never had such another friend in all Mexico.

While she was in the city of Puebla, on her way to the capital for the first time, on the 7th of June, which was the anniversary of her birthday, she presented to that city the sum of seven thousand dollars out of her own private purse, for the benefit of the poor. On that occasion she wrote the Prefect of that city the following letter:

"Señor Prefect:

"It is very pleasing to me to find myself in Puebla, the first anniversary of my birthday which I have passed far from my old country. Such a day is for everybody one of reflection; and these days would be sad for me, if the care, attentions, and proofs of affection, of which I have been the object in this city, did not cause me to recollect that I am in my new country, among my people. Surrounded by friends, and accompanied by my dear husband, I have no time to be sad; and I give thanks to God because he has conducted me here, presenting unto him fervent prayers for the happiness of the country which is mine. United to Mexico long ago by sympathy, I am to-day united to it by stronger bonds, and at the same time sweeter—those of gratitude. I wish, Señor Prefect, that the poor of this city may participate in the pleasure which I have experienced among you.

"I send you seven thousand dollars of my own private funds, which is to be dedicated to the rebuilding of the House of Charity, the ruinous state of which made me feel sad yesterday: so that the unfortunate ones may return to inhabit it who found themselves deprived of shelter.

"Señor Prefect, assure my compatriots of Puebla that they possess, and will always possess, my affections.

"CARLOTA.

"PUEBLA, 7th June, 1864."

Her acts of charity were unbounded. It was the greatest pleasure of her life to relieve suffering humanity. In this respect she was remarkable.

The *Paseo*, or pleasure-walk of the city of Mexico, with its shrubbery and flowers, is another illustration of her generosity, her taste, and her desire to please her subjects. Before she arrived in that city, not a flower nor bush, save the large trees, graced that pleasure-ground, nor the grand square, in front of the palace. She scattered there her own funds; from which have sprung up sweet-scented flowers and green bushes, that delight and attract the multitude, after the weary hours of labor are ended. One can now scarcely visit those pleasure-grounds, who saw them a few years ago, without bringing to mind the good heart that beautified them.

I once heard a very intelligent gentleman say, in the city of Mexico, that if that country had ever had a President with half the ambition, energy, and honesty of the Empress, it would be in a far more prosperous condition than it is, or ever had been.

Her intellectual capacity was certainly great, and her

administrative abilities of no mean order, added to a remarkable political sagacity. She was not surpassed by any living woman, in those qualities. Had she been a man at the head of a powerful government, she would have been considered the leading sovereign of the age. With all these qualities, usually sought for, and more generally expected to be found in the other sex, she did not fail to possess that grace and refinement of manner, at all times and under all circumstances, which are the peculiar attributes of an accomplished lady.

The brightest jewel she possessed nature gave her. It was CHARITY. Wherever she went, the squalid face of poverty received an illuminating smile of happiness from the reflection of that ornament. A view of her beaming face always produced a pleasant thought. The influence of her presence was like that of the rising sun, as it comes rolling up, spreading its soft genial rays all around, dispelling the bitter coolness of the morn.

The Empress was by no means possessed of idle habits. She was usually up at half-past six, and at seven in the saddle, taking her exercise, accompanied by her lady of honor and an officer. For many days she would ride every morning; and then, for a period, only every other day. Between eight and nine in the morning was the time for prayer; then came breakfast, which she usually ate alone—sometimes with one of her ladies' of honor. After which, accompanied by one of those ladies, she visited in her carriage the schools, hospitals, and the poor people that were in want, at their respective homes; or attended to some business affair pertaining to the Society of Charity, of which she was president. At two o'clock she went out to the palace of Chepultepec, where she usually resided, or at least spent the most of her time. At half-past three she dined in company with the Emperor, and frequently with friends invited by His Majesty. After dinner she promenaded in the grove around the palace; then returning to the palace, would read awhile, or use the pencil or brush, for which she had a fondness. Her general hour for retiring was nine.

She carefully read the newspapers, and scanned closely whatever was written upon the subject of Mexico and its sovereign. She marked with a pencil every article or paragraph which she considered of any importance, for the perusal of His Majesty: as he was busy, it was a saving of time to have the matter, which was worthy of consideration, brought immediately to his attention. She was either engaged in some of the foregoing occupations, or improving the flower-gardens. She was apparently never idle.

She was accustomed to wear, in the summer, dresses of cambric muslin; and in the winter, those of wool or silk, but not of a costly character. In fact, they were extremely plain, but made and fitted with remarkably good taste.

In the winter season she gave *soirées* every Monday. She never wore the same dress twice on those occasions. She danced four quadrilles during the evening, which was the extent of that kind of exercise with her.

When grand receptions were given at court, she wore a rich white satin dress, with low neck, trimmed with gold and brilliants; a purple velvet mantle, bordered with gold; a diadem of brilliants; jewelry of great value; the Grand Cross of San Carlos, the Grand Starred Cross of Austria, and that of Brazil.

Through all that imperial splendor, shone with a far brighter lustre her smiling face, the index of a gentle and affectionate heart.

The breath of scandal never discolored the fair name of the Empress. She was above suspicion. Such perfect disinterestedness manifest in all her acts of charity —such superiority to all selfish considerations—such zeal for good, and such sanctity of life, were virtues which shone so eminently conspicuous in all her behavior, that the unprejudiced who have been inimical to her form of government, and to the reign of their Majesties in Mexico, have been free to credit her with the perfections ascribed to her by her friends.

She had two ladies of the palace, who received each a salary of four thousand dollars per annum. One was Miss Josefa Varela, and the other Mrs. Concepcion P. Pacheco. The former is about the age of twenty-two, of dark Mexican complexion, from Texcoco, which is about twenty miles from the capital. She is a descendant of Moctezuma, and for that reason was selected for the position. She said to me that the genealogy of her family had been given to the Emperor. She is a pleasant young lady, not at all diffident in the presence of strangers, and shows a knowledge of society. She had received beneficial lessons from the Empress, with whom she was a favorite.

There were numerous ladies of honor attached to the Empress, who did not remain in the palace, and who received no compensation. They resided in their respective homes, and went to the palace on reception-days, and whenever the Empress desired their company in visiting the hospitals or other places of charity.

In 1865, it was considered necessary that a tour of inspection should be made through Yucatan. His Majesty could not well go, on account of business requiring his presence at the capital. It was therefore decided that the Empress should proceed to make the tour. And on the 6th of November of that year, she, with her lady of honor, Miss Josefa Varela, started, escorted by numerous officers, among whom was General José Lopez Uraga, commander of the escort; Señor Ramirez, Minister of Relations; the Belgian and Spanish Ministers, and several others, numbering twenty-four. She was received at Vera Cruz with great demonstrations of joy;

and still more, and greater enthusiasm at Yucatan, considering the number of the population.

On her arrival at Merida, in Yucatan, she was elegantly yet plainly attired. She wore a white dress with blue trimmings, and a graceful hat, likewise decked with blue. Her person was unadorned with jewelry. She was received by a large concourse of people—women and children surrounding her, with their offerings of sweet-scented bouquets; the military in their full-dress uniform: and in short, the whole community were out to gaze on her with perfect admiration.

Her Majesty was received at the entrance of the cathedral by the Rev. Dr. Lerado Rodriguez de la Sala; and as a religious ceremony was performed therein, that temple was crowded to its utmost.

She was addressed by the political Prefect. And while in her apartments, on the 23d of November, the multitude, anxious to gaze on her, and to hear some pleasant word from her, called loudly for her; and for their gratification she presented herself upon the balcony, and spoke as follows:

"We have long wished to visit you, in order to study your necessities and learn your desires. The Emperor being prevented from effecting this important object, has sent me to you to present you his cordial greetings. I assure you from my heart that he deeply regrets that he cannot be here with me, to tell you how great is his affection toward you. He will regret it still more when I inform him of the enthusiastic reception you have given me. He desires, and by all means will endeavor, to secure the prosperity and happiness of the people of Yucatan."

She visited the hospitals, prisons, houses of the needy, and made donations for them. She donated the sum of two thousand and five hundred dollars for the establishment of a free-school for girls; three thousand dollars to the general hospital; three thousand dollars to be distributed among the poor; one thousand dollars to complete the cathedral; besides many smaller presents to persons in the house where she remained during her stay there.

The following language from the "Yucatanos," addressed to the Empress, is illustrative of their good feeling toward her:

"The daughter of a King, the wife of a Monarch! Beautiful and affectionate Carlota! As the ship which brought you to our shores appeared in our horizon, we saluted you as the aurora of our happiest day; as you touched the sand of our port, we received you as the sovereign benefactor who filled us with hope; on hearing your sweet and consoling words which you addressed us at the foot of the throne, we listened to you as the cherub of benevolence; and to-day, Madam, as you give us new proof of your goodness, saving us from a great affliction, we contemplate you as the white and pure dove of the ark, the bearer of peace, and of reconciliation between God and man. Blessed be thou, Imperial dove! Blessed be thou, beneficent Empress! Were it possible for us to cover your road with pearls and diamonds we would do it with pleasure, in order that your feeling might palpitate the demonstration of our gratitude; but since that cannot be, you will comprehend, just and elevated spirit, the gratitude of our hearts. The mothers, the wives, and the sons of the poor, salute you as their redeemer.

"Accept, Madam, our wishes.

"MERIDA, November 26th, 1865."

Her Majesty left Merida on the 4th of December, in the morning, for the city of Campeachy, passing through Uxmal. A large number of young men, resident at

Merida, voluntarily, as a guard of honor, escorted her to the limits of that department. She made a short visit at Uxmal, where she also visited the hospital, the schools, and gave money to the poor. She ordered copies of the things which she saw there that were noteworthy. .She was particularly pleased with the palace of the monks, and the house called the *Tortugas*, of which she had drawings taken.

While returning, on the road from Vera Cruz, where she stopped a short time, a poor woman offered her the breakfast which she had spread for her own family. The Empress, to please her, sat down and ate. While thus eating, the poor Indian woman said, with a great deal of simplicity, "I like Your Majesty very much, because you are very good, and because you have an Indian lady of honor, which proves that Your Majesty does not dislike, but rather loves the Indians." When Her Majesty left, she gave twenty dollars to the woman. There is no doubt of one fact, that the Indians became much pleased with her and the Emperor, on acquaintance with them. Their Majesties, on all occasions, were particular to see that that class of people were properly treated.

In the city of Puebla, she extended her visit to the hospitals; decorated some soldiers who had distinguished themselves for bravery; also some ladies who had given their services to the care of the sick and wounded soldiers, and several civil officers who had shown a great zeal in the advancement of the welfare of the country.

She requested to see the Americans that were living near and around Orizaba and Cordova; some of whom were engaged in the service of the railroad company. Many of them had but a small amount of means, which they had use for otherwise than expending for fine wearing apparel, and did not consider that they were suitably arrayed to enter the presence of Her Majesty. When she was informed of that fact, she said, "Tell them to come without fine clothes." She had the faculty of pleasing every one.

She reached the capital, on her return, about the first of the following year. Soon after that, the sad intelligence of her father's death was communicated to her. It was a heavy blow to her, and it affected her long and seriously. Having lost her mother at an early age, she cherished more than ordinary love and affection for that remaining parent.

She founded the House of Maternity; and watched like a nursing-mother over those that needed assistance from the hand of charity.

As President of the General Council of Charity, she made a written report to His Majesty, on the 14th of April, 1866, setting forth briefly what had been done, and the condition of the society; saying therein, "I have presided at the various meetings which occurred in 1865, up to the time of my departure for Yucatan." Thereby showing that she never failed to be present, doing duty in the regular works of assistance to the needy.

Her energy was unbounded; she was ever ready to promote the happiness of the people, improve the condition of the country, and develop its resources. It became necessary for His Majesty to have a confidential representative in Europe, and to make some explanations and requests of Napoleon. She was prepared and willing to undertake the task. With that view she left the palace of Chapultepec at three o'clock on the morning of the 8th of July, 1866, for the church of Guadalupe, in the village of the same name, about a league to the north of the capital. She there attended Mass. At the conclusion of that ceremony she took her departure for Vera Cruz. His Majesty accompanied her as far as Rio Frio, and there saw her for the last time—Ay, a parting forever! Little was such his thought then. She sailed from Vera Cruz on the 13th of the month, in company with the Minister of State, Castillo; Count de Valle, the Grand Chamberlain; Felip U. del Barrio, Chamberlain; Mrs. Gutierrez Estrada y Barrio, Lady of Honor; and Doctor Bowslaveck. At Orizaba, she asked for the prayers of her friends, saying, "I shall need them." From Havana she wrote to the Emperor, and also to her lady of honor, Miss Josefa Varela—the pet name of "Josefa" being *Pepita*. The letter to the latter was in the following words:

"My Dear Pepita:

"Only a few words, before the steamer leaves. I am quite well, and ever thinking of you all. I had only one day of sickness. The heat is intense, and the voyage a long one. It is only out of pure patriotism that one undertakes these things with feelings of pleasure. From this to St. Thomas will be the last sojourn over American seas! All the Spanish authorities have treated me with the utmost deference; although I did not land, as the Emperor did not wish me to do so. The bay is very beautiful, and I should also say the town, where there exist fortunes of twenty-five millions and upwards. I have received visits from the principal personages. Many of the dignitaries had walking-sticks, which reminded me of Mexico, and pleased me. The Bishop was very polite. There also seems to exist here a great reverence for the temporal authorities. I have also seen the President of the "Royal Audience:" he reminded me of the ancient history of our country. He also sports a tortoise-shell walking-stick, which from its exquisite loveliness must be from Yucatan. Talking of this peninsula, I must tell you that I have seen Arthur

Peon, who was overjoyed to see me. He seems satisfied with the state of things at home. The gratitude of the Yucatecos to me has given me great pleasure. One of the chamberlains from Campeche, Señor Lavalle, is to come on board to-day, on his voyage to France. You can form no idea of the state of the road; from Cordova all the carriages of my gentlemen were upset. My coachman assured me that it was only through the help of the Virgin that I was not upset. I suppose he meant the Guadalupe one.

"Good-bye, my dear Pepita; my heart remains in Mexico. Write to me, and believe in the affection of

"CARLOTA."

After her arrival in Europe, she had several interviews with Napoleon, accompanied by her minister, Castillo, relative to important business concerning the Empire of Mexico. The object of her voyage was generally understood to be for the purpose of prevailing upon Napoleon to furnish Maximilian with more funds, and also to induce him to prolong the period of the stay of the French troops in Mexico. She left her adopted home with a great deal of solicitude.

She saw near at hand a powerful republic, having no reverence for monarchical institutions, and whose diplomatic correspondence was in the highest degree threatening to the tranquillity of her home. The situation of Maximilian was critical, requiring immediate succor. The reflection that, although the distant auxiliaries which she hoped for might possibly be obtained, and yet that their possession might not be a positive guarantee to the stability of the Empire, was productive of the most serious consequences.

It was said that such thoughts, added to her ill-success, were more than her agitated brain could support; and that in consequence thereof, despondency and dejection became so oppressive, that her mental faculties completely succumbed to the weight. It has since been doubted that the foregoing excitement was the cause of the loss of her mind. Of that, more will be said hereafter.

Her Majesty reached Miramar on the 15th day of August. Orders were given at Vienna to the officers of the navy, to receive her in a manner becoming to her rank. The morning of that day was serene; but by the time Her Majesty neared the surrounding waters that laved the walls of Miramar, where the Austrian squadron were stationed, the angry clouds had gathered, the whistling wind became furious, and the boisterous storm nearly drowned the roar of the loud-mouthed cannon.

On the 16th of September, the anniversary of the independence of Mexico, the Empress gave a grand celebration in honor of the day, at Miramar. Mass was said at the chapel, in the morning; and in the afternoon a banquet was given, where were assembled the Mexicans who were there temporarily, the Mexican Consul at Trieste, the Mexican Minister near Austriá, the Prefect of Trieste, and several others. The Mexican colors were waving over the castle, and salvos of artillery were echoed and re-echoed over sea and land.

On the 18th of September, the Empress and suite, which was composed of the same parties who left Vera Cruz in her company, and D. José Blasio, two *valets de chambre*, four Mexican and two Italian servants, started for Rome. As there were several cases of cholera at Trieste, the vessels sailing from that port to Ancona were required to remain in quarantine a few days in the latter port; in consequence thereof, Her Majesty preferred to make the trip by land. They travelled in post-carriages through Tyrol, where there was no railroad, stopping at Bingston, Botzen, Verona, Mantua—

crossed the Po, and passed through Reggia to Bologna, where they took a special train of cars to Ancona.

The first symptom of derangement was observed at Botzen, in the room where she stopped. She remarked to Mrs. Estrada y Barrio, "I do not wish to go to Rome, because I am afraid they will poison me. I wish to go back to Miramar." The Minister Castillo observed that he thought it a strange remark; but that he did not think her mind was affected. At Ancona was a deputation in waiting to receive Her Majesty, composed of Mr. Valasquez de Leon, the Mexican Minister near the Papal See; Bishop Ramirez; Don Maria Degollado, and many others; all of whom were transported by the cars through the Apennines, to Rome. In all the towns through which her Majesty passed, she was received by civic and military bodies, with great honors, amid cheering, cannonading, and musical demonstrations.

At Rome, the diplomatic corps and other distinguished persons presented themselves, and paid her marked attention. She was thus far, with the exception mentioned, to all appearances well, giving not the slightest evidence of insanity. She addressed the visitors in their respective languages, which, to them, was highly pleasing. On her fourth day in Rome there was a sudden change in her actions. She spoke of a desire on the part of some of her party to poison her. She said that Mrs. Kuhachevich, Count de Valle, and Dr. Bowslaveck, had been hired by Napoleon to poison her. As she said this, she addressed herself to Mrs. Kuhachevich. She then requested the Mexican minister near Rome, and Cardinal Antonelli, to have the three suspected persons arrested. After that, those three kept from her sight. About three days afterward she called at the Vatican, to see the Pope. She said to him that she did not wish to leave his residence, as it was the only safe place where she could remain without being poisoned. She remained there all night, sitting on the sofa, accompanied by Mrs. Estrada y Barrio, the Minister of State, Castillo, and Mr. Barrio, the Chamberlain.

On the following morning, they all returned to the hotel where Her Majesty's apartments were, known as the "Albergo di Roma." She was afraid to eat or drink anything given her from the hotel. She rode out every day, in her carriage, with Mrs. Estrada y Barrio, taking a jar to the public fountain, and filling it with water, which she carried to her room to drink. She also purchased chestnuts in the streets, which she took to her apartments to eat. They are a common article of food in Italy, and very excellent. She selected one of her servants in whom she had confidence, and whom she daily sent for meat, vegetables, eggs, etc., which were brought to her room, and cooked in her presence. These articles thus prepared she ate without fear.

She remained in Rome about twenty days; when her brother, the Duke of Flanders, arrived there, and after one day's preparation, embarked with her at Ancona for Trieste. He took her to the castle of Miramar, and provided her with the best physicians that could be procured.

At the request of the King of Belgium, Dr. Bulkens, Director of the House of the Insane, at Gheel, proceeded to the castle of Miramar, to take charge of the Empress. He returned to Belgium with her, on the 31st of July last, when she was placed in apartments prepared for her at the palace of Tervueren. She was accompanied, also, on her return, by the Queen of Belgium. King Leopold, and the Prince of Wales went out to the frontier to meet them. Orders were given that no noise should be made at the stations on the line of railroads. The court carriage drove so close to the car at the station of Groenendal, that the Empress passed into it unnoticed. That station is near the line of Luxemburg, and about three miles from the said palace, and situate in an open space in the woods of Soignes.

The palace of Tervueren and its surroundings present one of the most picturesque views in the neighborhood of Brussels. It belongs to the national domain; but, by a law, it was placed at the disposition of the royal family. During certain seasons of the year the princes of the family of Orange occupied it, prior to the revolution of 1830. It has been preserved in the same condition, with scarcely a change, as it was then seen. The traveller, until recently, has been denied the privilege of gazing at its gorgeously glittering ballroom, and the elegant apartments where the Princess of Orange nestled in her splendor.

It has been said that it was erected for the accommodation of the mighty hunters of royal privileges. Around that mass of adornment extends a large and beautiful park, protected by a wall; and over its grassy lawns leap the bounding game, in variety innumerable, and pass their hours of slumber in greater quietude, perhaps, than their royal owner, and frisk in greater merriment, save when the rifle's crack carries them to that owner's banquet.

The Empress seemed to be aware of the death of her husband, but believed that it was caused by sickness. At times she suffered from violent fits of raving, and became quite prostrated, and almost inconsolable on account of the absence of the Emperor. But in moments of calmness she seemed reconciled to her misfortunes.

Her physicians have lately attributed her insanity to the effect of poison. They are of opinion that her physical condition evidenced that fact. Dr. Bulkens has said that there were great hopes of her being restored to her natural mind.

There are rumors afloat in Mexico, and have been for many months, in support of the opinion of the European physicians, as to the cause of her derangement. In the fall of 1866, His Majesty Maximilian received an anonymous letter, stating that the Empress had been poisoned in Cuernavaca. The lady who wrote that letter communicated the fact of her writing and sending it to an acquaintance of mine. She had heard statements which appeared to her quite satisfactory that poison had been administered to the Empress. Her insanity, as eminating from such a source, had been talked about in Mexico, before the news of its actual occurrence could have been conveyed from Europe to that country. It was the opinion in Mexico that she had eaten fruit in which had been placed some of the juice of a tree known by the name of *palo de leche*—the milk-tree.

The Mexican journals have recently denied that she was poisoned in their country, by their people. They allege that they do not conquer a foe in that way; but they are of opinion that Napoleon or Bazaine performed the barbarous work,—believing that either of them would pursue such a course to carry out their political plans. They seem to harbor no doubt that Bazaine would do it, and really think he did. They ask, what would not a general do, who would offer to sell out the Emperor Maximilian, under whom he was acting, to the Liberal general, Porfirio Diaz?

The world, outside of Mexico, will hardly credit any story that charges Napoleon or even Bazaine with such barbarous cruelty as that; although the character of the latter, in Mexico, is not enviable.

The death of the Emperor is a heavy weight on the crazed brain of the Empress. His image is permanently mirrored thereon, whether in the brief moments of tranquillity, or during the raging storm of her intellect. Will she forget him?

"No—of the one, one only object traced
In her heart's core too deep to be effaced;
The one whose memory, fresh as life, is twined
With every broken link of her lost mind;
Whose image lives, though Reason's self be wrecked,
Safe 'mid the ruins of her intellect!"

Let us hope that she who dealt so lavishly unto the needy, may receive from the Giver of all perfect gifts, that aid which will enable her soon to show forth her mind in all its former lustre.

CHAPTER IV.

MIRAMAR.

THE castle of Miramar, the palatial residence of Ferdinand Maximilian, before he ascended the throne of Mexico, is situated a league distant from the city of Trieste, on a rocky promontory, the base of which the Adriatic Sea laves with its foamy waves, holding photographed beneath its sheeny surface, in the quietude of its calm, the turreted castle and wavy sky.

Through all the spacious halls of that architectural pile, in the silent hours, the whisperings of the ever-murmuring sea fall upon the ear. And as its owner's chain of slumber now and then lost a link by the pilfering hand of wakefulness, he would half forget whether he was balancing on the oaken beams of the Austrian fleet, o'er the heaving sea, or quietly nestling within those castellated walls, supported by a terrestrial base. And as the blue deep was his accustomed element, it was a pleasure to him, while resting from professional labors, at home among the flower-beds, to gaze at the mysterious sea, and listen to its variant notes as they changed from gentle murmurs to the sullen roar of the storm.

Scarcely a dozen years have been recorded in the past, since the grounds of Miramar were observed untouched by the decorative hand of Art; and the drapery of Nature was then, by no means, gorgeous.

The castle is built of stone, is cream-colored, and stands facing the west, sixty feet high, with a front about eighty-four feet wide, flanked by a tower that rises nearly one hundred and forty feet above the water's edge, and is not far from twenty-four feet square. The castle and tower are surmounted with a perforated parapet, with turreted corners and ornamental pendants on the cornice. It is only half the size of the original plan, the intention having been to extend it on the east.

On the front of the edifice is inscribed, in large gilt letters, the day and hour when Maximilian accepted the crown of Mexico.

On the first floor, in the tower, is a small drawing-room, which was much occupied by Carlota, and which opens into a saloon in the main building. The room adjoining the latter on the north was her sleeping-apartment, and the next one her dressing-room, which joined that of her servant.

In the second story, and in the rear of the latter room, was the wardrobe of Her Majesty. The northern part of the front building is divided into three stories—the southern part into two;—the grand saloon being in the latter division, extends to the cornice, a height of nearly forty feet, is forty-five feet by twenty-six, and is decorated with fine paintings and elegant furniture.

A closed balcony, about nine by twelve feet in dimensions, supported by four stone columns, embellishes the front of the castle. It has three windows looking out upon the sea, and two on either side.

The centre building contains, on the first floor, the library and dining-room, each being twenty-five by fifty feet. Over the dining-room is an unfinished saloon. The chapel and sleeping apartment of Carlota open into the dining-room. The private room of Maximilian was east of and adjoining the library. He accepted the crown of Mexico in the sleeping-apartment of Carlota, the same having been first arranged and decorated for the occasion.

The library contains a large collection of books written in the various ancient and modern European languages, among which are the works of Munguia and other Mexican authors: also quite an extensive museum of natural curiosities,—stuffed birds, reptiles, and other animals, many of which came from Mexico.

The artistic skill of the Grecians and Romans also contributes to swell the list of ornaments.

The Mexican coat-of-arms, woven in rich brocade, adorns the walls of several apartments.

The paintings from the hands of the Italian masters attest the elegant taste of the owner of that mansion, which is so richly embellished with them.

A carriage-road about twenty feet wide encircles the castle, and is skirted with rose-bushes on the south side of the edifice. In the rear of the buildings is a circular parterre, nearly fifty yards in diameter, girted with flower-beds; in the centre of which is a fountain throwing its silvery dews on the surrounding shrubbery and Flora's richly painted hues.

Near the stairway on the north side, which leads down to the sea, may be seen a beautiful marble statue resting in a niche. Near by the stairway is a small parterre measuring some thirty by fifteen yards, oval in form, and containing exquisite flowers that perfume the salt sea air, and flavor your breath momentarily as your bark glides from the rocky base out into the deep blue.

From the larger parterre, in the rear of the castle, extends a bower of roses to the summer-house, which is also arched with the same bush and flower.

South of the castle, several hundred yards distant, are large stables built of stone and brick, situated near the road that circles around the sea to Trieste.

A serpentine road leads to the garden, which is back a short distance, on rising ground. It possesses many plants from the tropical climes. The maguey, the oleander, and the cactus remind one of Mexico, although the maguey was brought by Maximilian from Dalmatia. The premises contain a few fruit-trees only. Several oaks and pines shade the ground here and there. A marble statue of Napoleon I. stands back some distance from the castle, looking as if it had command of the surrounding hills. Numerous pieces of Egyptian and Grecian sculpture are scattered over the ground, appearing as though they had rested there for ages, but which Maximilian had gathered in his different voyages to the lands of the ancient artists.

Half a mile or more from the sea stands a beautiful cottage, occupied by Maximilian while the castle was building. He was there watching and directing the erection of that elegant edifice, exhibiting a high degree of architectural taste and judgment. He had no particular fondness for the Gothic style. A mile from the castle, near the garden grounds, is a private railway station, for the accommodation of the premises; also a telegraph-office.

It has not been the intention of the author to give herein a minute or professional description of the architectural splendor represented in the engraving, but only to portray in general terms some of the main features thereof, couched in plain language, unmingled with technical expressions.

CHAPTER V.

Cause of intervention—Assembly of Notables and their acts—Monarchy adopted—Mexican deputation visit Maximilian—Their address to him—His reply—Second deputation sent—Preparations of Maximilian with his family.

BEFORE recording the history of Maximilian, as it pertains to Mexico, it will be necessary to take a cursory view of the late political condition of that country. If we pass in review that nation's record for the last fifty years, our illustration of its real condition would not be erroneous should we allege that the sea has been its emblem. The alternate storms and calms have scarcely been more frequent of the one than of the other. If the one has been considered the depository of great riches, so has the other. The treasury of both lies buried. If the toilers in search of wealth in the elements of the one, have been wrecked, the same has likewise been the fate of those who have battled with the elements in the other. The diggers in the one, and the divers in the other, have felt the effect of the storms.

The Liberal party built a Ship of State, on which they placed in large gilt letters, "CONSTITUTION." That party insisted that the Church party should board her, and it was contended that the latter would be safe on her quarter-deck. The Church party did not have as much faith in these allurements as it did in the ten commandments. The chiefs thereof were afraid to step aboard with their funds. They were aware that the ship was heavily laden with a bottomry bond; and that her officers were in pursuit of Church funds to discharge her. And, besides, they had no confidence that the vessel would be navigated according to the rules laid down in the "CONSTITUTION." Hence the disagreement. Dismissing the figure of speech, it is quite apparent that disorder has been the prevalent condition of the country.

It is well understood that Comonfort renounced the presidency in January, 1858; and thereupon the Church party seized the capital of the nation. Whatever might have been the intention of the Church party at that time—whether to support the Constitution or not—they certainly were not in harmony with the Liberals. It has been observed that the Church party was not desirous of overthrowing the constitutional government. Juarez, at the head of the Liberals, was still declaring to the people that he stood upon the Constitution, and that his organization was the only legally constituted one. Which was the government *de facto* it is here unnecessary to decide. At that time the decision was made by foreign governments in favor of the Church party. The diplomatic corps in Mexico officially acknowledged no other.

The treatment towards foreigners resident became such, in their opinion, that the respective governments to which they belonged deemed it necessary to interfere in behalf of their subjects. Thus, in 1861, England, France, and Spain united with a view of demanding from Mexico payment for their respective claims, and just reparation for repeated injuries. England required satisfaction on account of what she termed the illegal taking of funds by Miramon, who, on the 16th day of November, 1860, had laid his hands on one hundred and fifty-two thousand pounds sterling, which was the property of Englishmen. England was aware that highwaymen were not a small class of individuals in Mexico, but she had never learned that writers upon international law had laid it down that an army had a legal right to rob the house of the British Legation, and that the flag was no protection. The money so taken was in the house of that Legation.

The Mon-Almonte treaty, made at Paris in September, 1859, between Spain and the Church party, provided for the payment of Spanish claims. The downfall of that party had the effect to annul that treaty, in the judgment of the reigning power, as they refused to recognize it. Mexico had assumed the position that the home debt due to her citizens should be paid in preference to foreign claims. Spain, therefore, refused to submit to what she termed a denial of justice.

A Swiss banker, named Jecker, who came to Mexico some years ago, had amassed a fortune that was numbered by millions. Such a man, with such a fortune, was not an undesirable friend for any one wishing to carry on bold and expensive undertakings. Miramon considered the friendship of that man of value, and the heads of the two were brought together. Between the financial abilities of the two, a scheme was planned for enriching the Church party—at least for the benefit of Jecker and Miramon. A decree was issued on the 29th day of October, 1859, at the instigation of Miramon, that three million pounds sterling should be circulated in bonds. The decree provided that the bonds should be taken for taxes and import duties, and that they should bear interest at six per cent. per annum; it also provided that the house of Jecker would pay one-half of the interest for five years. Certain regulations provided that the holders of these bonds could transfer them, and receive in their stead Jecker bonds; this was to be done by paying a certain percentage. Jecker was the person to issue the said amount of bonds. He was to be paid five per cent. on the issue. It appears that the arrangement entered into was not executed, on the part of Jecker, as the provisions of the decree required. At the suggestion of Jecker, the contract was modified.

And the final result of their making and unmaking of contracts, was to leave the Church party liable for the sum of three millions seven hundred and twenty thousand pounds sterling, and Jecker in such condition as to be unable to comply with his agreement. In fact, his house, in May, 1860, suspended payment. The bonds went into the possession of his creditors. The Liberal party coming into power, refused to acknowledge any debt based upon the foregoing transactions. France considered it a legitimate claim against the Mexican Government, regardless of the name of the reigning party, and that it ought to be paid. France had other claims against Mexico, amounting to twelve millions of dollars. The foregoing claims, added to the complaints for maltreatment of the subjects of the three powers, formed the basis of the allied intervention.

The Mexican Government assumed the position that it never had refused to enter into an equitable and just arrangement with Mr. Jecker; that is to say, to pay him the amount of money actually advanced to the Government by him, with interest, or some compensation for its use. That Government further contended that Jecker, instead of applying to the finance department for an arrangement, or to the court of justice, to sue the Government, resorted to the Legation. France proposed to take a certain sum, about ten millions of dollars, payable out of the proceeds of the custom-house; and if the proposition was not accepted, her intimation was, war to destruction.

Mexico was firmly of opinion that the claims demanded were exorbitant, and far more than justice would dictate.

I have not herein set forth the particulars of the respective claims of the allied powers; such a statement is not requisite for the purposes of this work. Neither is it my province to weigh said claims in the scales of justice. The general nature of the claims has been given which formed the ground-work of that intervention which was introductory to the establishment of the empire over which the unfortunate Maximilian reigned.

The three complaining powers already mentioned agreed, in convention at London, October, 1861, that each of them should send to Mexico an equal naval force; and as to the number of troops to be furnished by each, that that should be regulated according to the number of subjects which the respective powers had in Mexico. It was understood by said powers that the intervention was only for the purpose of enforcing payment of their respective claims. England did not appear satisfied with the justness of the whole of the French demand. Spain coincided with England upon that point. Notwithstanding that, the allied powers sent a joint fleet to Vera Cruz, which, on the 6th of January, 1862, reached the port of its destination. On the following day they disembarked the following number of troops: six thousand three hundred Spanish, two thousand eight hundred French, and eight hundred English. By virtue of a treaty signed at Soledad, February 19th, 1862, the allied forces were permitted to leave the unhealthy coast, and to take up their quarters near Orizaba, where they might inhale the pure mountain air. The leaders of the respective armies did not agree in all matters of discussion in their conference. The English and Spanish officers did not differ on another proposition; and that was, that they would leave the French forces alone in their glory. The chiefs of the forces of the two former powers decided to right-about face, and steer homeward, which they did in the following April.

On the 17th of May, 1863, the city of Puebla, after a siege of sixty-two days, surrendered to the French army, which entered the city two days later, by order of General Forey, commander-in-chief thereof. Soon thereafter, that army, in conjunction with certain Mexican forces under General Marquez, took up their line of march for the city of Mexico. On the 31st of May, the Juarez party fell back from that city; and on the 10th of June following, the allied forces entered the city without resistance. On the 16th, the French General issued a decree that a provisional government should be formed; and that the citizens to be invested with governmental powers should be elected by a Superior Junta of government, composed of thirty-five persons, in accordance with another decree which was issued on the 18th. The Junta elected for its President Señor D. Teodosio Lares, and for its Secretary, Sres. D. José Maria Andrade and D. Alejandro Arango y Escandon. On the 22d, the Superior Junta of government invested the Provisional Executive Power in General D. Juan N. Almonte, Archbishop D. Palagio Antonio de Labastida, and General D. José Mariano Salas; and as *suplentes* (supernumeraries), Dr. D. Juan B. Omaechea, Bishop of Tulancingo, and D. Ignacio Pavon, a lawyer.

This new government assembled with great solemnity on the 25th of June. On the 2d of July they published an edict containing a list of two hundred and fifteen persons, who, jointly with the Superior Junta, were thereby declared to constitute the Assembly of Notables, intrusted with the duty of providing a plan for a permanent government. This Assembly chose for its president and secretaries, respectively, the same persons that held those positions in the Superior Junta. They were solemnly installed on the 8th of July, in presence of the Executive, the French commander-in-chief, and Count Dubois de Saligny, Minister Plenipotentiary of France. A committee was appointed by the Assembly to draft a form of government. On the 10th, the committee submitted their plan to the Assembly, which was unanimously adopted. There were present two hundred and thirty members. Ten had resigned, and the remaining ten, through sickness and pressing business of their own, failed to attend. In accordance with the plan, the Assembly issued a decree, which was published on the 11th of July, containing the following:

"Manuel G. Aguirre, Political Prefect of the District of Mexico, to its inhabitants. Know ye:

"That by the Secretary of State and of the Office of Foreign Relations, has been communicated to me the following decree:

PALACE OF THE SUPREME EXECUTIVE POWER,
MEXICO, July 11th, 1863.

'The Supreme Provisional Executive Power has been pleased to transmit me the decree which follows:

'The Supreme Provisional Executive Power of the Nation, to the inhabitants thereof. Know ye:

'That the Assembly of Notables, by virtue of the decree of the 16th, last passed, for the purpose of making known the form of government most agreeable to the nation, in the exercise of the full power which the nation has, to establish itself, and as the organ and interpreter of the nation, declares with absolute independence and liberty, the following:

'1st. The Mexican Nation adopts for its form of government, a limited, hereditary monarchy, with a Catholic prince.

'2d. The Sovereign will take the title of Emperor of Mexico.

'3d. The Imperial Crown of Mexico is offered to His Imperial Highness, Prince Ferdinand Maximilian, Archduke of Austria, for him and his descendants.

'4th. In case of any circumstances, impossible to foresee, the Archduke Ferdinand Maximilian should not take possession of the throne which is offered him, the Mexican nation submits to the benevolence of Napoleon III., Emperor of the French, to indicate to her another Catholic prince.

'Given in the Hall of Sessions of the Assembly, on the 10th day of July, 1863.

'TEODOSIO LARES, President.

'ALEJANDRO ARANGO Y ESCANDON, Secretary.

'JOSÉ MARIA ANDRADE, Secretary."

'Therefore, it is ordered that the same be printed, published by a national edict, circulated, and that due compliance be therewith given.

'Given in the Palace of the Supreme Executive Power, in Mexico, on the 11th of July, 1863.

'JUAN N. ALMONTE,
'JOSÉ MARIA SALAS,
'JUAN B. OMAECHEA.'

'To the Sub-secretary of State and of the Office of Foreign Relations.'

'And I communicate it to you for your information and the consequent terminations.

J. MIGUEL ARROZO,
Sub-secretary of State and of
the Office of Foreign Relations

'Señor Political Prefect of Mexico.'

"And in order that notice of it may reach every one, I order that it be printed, published, and circulated by the persons charged with the same.

"MANUEL G. AGUIRRE,
"Political Prefect.

"MEXICO, July 13th, 1863.

"To José M. de Garay, Secretary General of the Prefecture."

By a decree of the 11th of July, the Assembly of Notables abolished the name of "Provisional Executive

Power," and adopted that of "Regency of the Empire," in its stead.

Soon after that the Regency appointed a commission to carry to the Archduke Maximilian of Austria the decree of the Assembly, and offer him the crown of Mexico. This commission was composed of Señores D. José M. Gutierrez Estrado, D. José Hidalgo, D. Antonio Escandon, D. Tomas Murphy, General D. Adrian Woll, D. Ignacio Aguilar, D. Joaquin Velasquez de Leon, D. Francisco Javier Miranda, a priest, and D. Angel Iglesias as Secretary. The four first were at that time in Europe; the others embarked at Vera Cruz for San Nazario about the 15th of August.

On the 3d of October, 1863, the deputation was officially received by the Archduke Maximilian, in the Palace of Miramar, his usual residence, near Trieste.

The president of the deputation, Señor Gutierrez de Estrada, delivered to the Archduke the following discourse:

"PRINCE:

"The Mexican nation, scarcely restored to its liberty by the beneficial influence of a powerful and magnanimous monarch, sends us to present ourselves to Your Imperial Highness, the object and centre, to-day, of its purest wishes and most flattering hopes.

"We will not speak, Prince, of our tribulations and our misfortunes, known by every one, and which have been extended so far that the name of Mexico has become synonymous with desolation and ruin.

"Struggling a long time ago to extricate ourselves from so painful a situation, and which, if possible, is even bitterer, on account of the sad future placed before our eyes, than the present evils; there has been no arbitrator to whom this unhappy nation could have been submitted; a trial which could not have been made in the fatal circle in which it was placed,—having unskilfully adopted and confided in republican institutions, so contrary to our natural constitution, our natural customs and traditions, and which, while increasing the greatness and pride of a neighboring people, have been for us but an incessant source of the most cruel misfortunes.

"Our country has passed nearly half a century in that sad existence, full of unprofitable suffering and intolerable shame. But, all the spirit of life and all faith in the future were not extinguished in us. Our firm confidence being placed in the Sovereign Regulator and Arbitrator of nations, we did not cease hoping and soliciting with eagerness the desired remedy for its ever-increasing torments.

"And our hopes were not in vain. The mysterious ways are visible through which Divine Providence has led us to that fortunate situation in which we now find ourselves, and which the highest intelligence scarcely conceived possible.

"Mexico, then, again master of her destinies, and taught by the experience of past errors, now makes a supreme effort to regain herself.

"To other political institutions she recurs anxiously and hopingly, promising herself that she will be even more prosperous than when she was a monarchical colony of Europe; and still more if she should succeed in having at her head a Catholic Prince, who, with his eminent and acknowledged merit, unites also that nobleness of sentiment, that force of will, and that rare abnegation which is the privilege of men predestined to govern, to regenerate, and to save misled and unhappy nations at the decisive hour of their acknowledged error and danger.

"Mexico promises herself much, Prince, from the institutions which governed her for the space of three centuries, and which left us, when they disappeared, a splendid

ENDICOTT & CO. LITH. N.Y.

MIRAMAR.

legacy, that we did not know how to preserve under the Republic.

"But if that faith in monarchical institutions is great and profound, it cannot be complete if these institutions are not personified in a Prince endowed with the high gifts which Heaven has dealt out to you with a prodigal hand.

"A monarch can, without great gifts of intelligence or character, increase the fortunes of his people, when that monarch is but the successor to an ancient monarchy, in a country of ancient monarchies; but a Prince requires exceptional qualities when he has to be the first of a series of kings—in short, the founder of a dynasty and the heir of a Republic.

"Without Your Imperial Highness—believe these lips, that have never been stained with flattery—it would be inefficacious and ephemeral, whatever might be the attempt, to raise our country from the abyss in which it lies; and besides, the generous views of the powerful monarch whose sword has redeemed us, and whose strong arm now sustains us, would be frustrated.

"With Your Highness, so versed in the difficult science of government, the institutions will be what they ought to be, to secure the prosperity and independence of their new country, which has for its basis that true and progressive Liberty, the sister of Justice, which is its first condition, and not that false liberty, unknown among us except by its excesses and ravages.

"Those institutions, with the modifications which prudence dictates and the necessity of the times requires, will serve as an insurmountable defence to our national independence.

"These convictions and these sentiments, of which long ago many Mexicans were possessed, are found, to-day, Prince, in the consciences of all, and spring from every heart. In Europe, even, whatever may be the sympathies or opposition, there is only one voice in regard to Your Imperial Highness and your august spouse, so distinguished for her high qualities and exemplary virtues, who soon will share your throne and our hearts, and will be loved, exalted, and blessed by every Mexican.

"We, who are but feeble interpreters of that general applause of love, of the hopes and prayers of a whole nation, come to present in that nation's name, to Your Imperial Highness, the crown of the Mexican Empire, which the people offer you, Prince, freely and spontaneously, by a solemn decree of the Notables, already ratified by many provinces, and which soon will be, as every one says, by the entire nation.

"We cannot forget, Prince, that this act meets with a happy coincidence—that of the country celebrating the anniversary of the day when the national army triumphantly planted, in the capital of Mexico, the standard of independence and of monarchy, calling to the throne an Archduke of Austria, in default of an Infante of Spain.

"Accept, Prince, favorably, the wishes of a people who invoke your assistance, and who fervently pray Heaven to crown the glorious work of Your Highness; and who ask God also that power may be granted unto them to worthily respond to the persevering efforts of Your Imperial Highness.

"Lastly, Prince, may the aurora of happier times shine forth for Mexico, after so much suffering, and may we have the incomparable happiness of being able to announce to the Mexicans the good news which they are so anxiously desiring;—good news not only for us, but also for France, whose name to-day is as inseparable from our history as it will be from our gratitude; good news for England and Spain, who commenced this great work at the convention in London, after having been the first to recognize its justice, and to proclaim its imperative necessity; and finally, for the renowned dynasty of Hapsburg, that crowns this great work with Your Imperial and Royal Highness.

"We are not ignorant, Prince, I repeat it, of the abnegation which Your Imperial Highness requires, and which alone can make agreeable the thoughts of your duties so pleasing to Divine Providence (who does not create princes and give them great qualities in vain), since Your Imperial Highness has been disposed to accept, with all its consequences, a mission so difficult and arduous, at such a distance from your country, and from the illustrious and powerful throne, on the first step to which is found Your Imperial Highness; and so far from this Europe which is the centre and emporium of the civilization of the world.

"Yes, Prince, the crown is very heavy which our admiration and love offers you to-day; but the day will come, we hope, when its possession will be enviable (thanks to your efforts, which Heaven will know how to recompense), with our co-operation and unalterable gratitude and loyalty.

"Great have been our errors, alarming is our fall; but we are the sons of those, Prince, who, at the cry of *Religion*, *Country*, and *King* (three great things which so well unite with liberty), that there has been no undertaking, however great, that we would not have attempted—no sacrifice that we would not have known how to encounter, firmly and boldly.

"Such are the sentiments of Mexico, on its regeneration, such the aspirations with which we have received the honorable charge of presenting faithfully and respectfully to Your Imperial and Royal Highness, the worthy scion of the illustrious dynasty which counts among its glories that of having carried Christian civilization to our own soil on which we live, Prince, and by which you establish, in this nineteenth century, by so memorable titles, order and true liberty—the happy fruits of that same civilization.

"The task is great, but our confidence in Providence is greater; and that our confidence ought to be so, Mexico as it now is, and Miramar, of this glorious day, thus tell us."

Archduke Maximilian responded to the foregoing address in the following manner:

"GENTLEMEN:

"I am profoundly grateful for the wishes expressed by the Assembly of Notables, in Mexico, in their session, on the 10th of July, and that you are charged to communicate the same to me.

"It is flattering to our house that the eyes of your compatriots were turned towards the family of Charles V., as soon as the word monarchy was pronounced.

"However noble the task may be of securing the independence and prosperity of Mexico, under the exit of institutions equally stable and free, I do not fail to agree with His Majesty the Emperor of the French, whose glorious initiative has made possible the regeneration of your beautiful country, that the monarchy could not be re-established there, on a perfectly legitimate and solid basis, unless the whole nation, expressing freely its will, would wish to ratify the wishes of the capital. So, then, upon the result of the generality of the votes of the country, I must make depend, in the first place, the acceptance of the throne which is offered me.

"On the other hand, comprehending the sacred duties of a Sovereign, it is necessary that I should demand in favor of the Empire, which is under consideration, the indispensable guarantees in order to place it under protection from the dangers which might threaten its integrity and independence. In case those pledges for future security should be obtained, and the election of the noble Mexican people, taken as a whole, should fall upon me, I shall be ready, with the consent of the august chief of my family, and confiding in the support of the Almighty, to accept the crown.

"If Providence should call me to the high civilizing mission which is attached to that crown, I declare to you, henceforth, Gentlemen, my firm resolution of following the salutary example of the Emperor my brother, by opening to the country the wide road of progress, by means of a constitutional *régime*, based on order and morality; and to seal with my oath, as soon as that vast territory may be pacified, the fundamental pact with the nation. It is only in this manner that a new and truly national policy can be inaugurated, in which all parties, forgetting their quarrels, will work together to give Mexico the eminent place which appears to be destined for her among nations, under a government which has for its principle equity in justice.

"Remember, Gentlemen, to communicate to your countrymen the determinations which I have just announced to you frankly, and to take the necessary measures to consult with the nation as to the form of government they intend to adopt."

Turning back again to the territory of Mexico, it was very apparent that, as the French and Mexican allies advanced into the interior, the cities, towns, and villas gave strong evidence of a willing adherence to the Empire. Many chiefs of the Liberal party came under the Imperial banner, while the President and a very few others took refuge in the northern part of the Mexican territory. And the Regency having seen what they considered an expression of a majority of the people in behalf of the Empire, believed the time had arrived when they ought to present to the Archduke Maximilian that fact, and solicit him to comply with his promise previously made to the Mexican deputation.

In accordance with these views, the Regency appointed a Mexican deputation composed of the following gentlemen: Señores D. José N. Gutierrez Estrada, D. Ignacio Aguilar, D. José Hidalgo, General D. Adrian Woll, D. Antonio Escandon, D. José M. de Landa; and D. Angel Iglesias, as Secretary.

This deputation met in the city of Trieste, prepared to execute the duties assigned them, as will be hereinafter seen.

In the month of March, 1864, Archduke Maximilian and the Archduchess Carlota, having been informed of the late acts of the Mexican people, and the intention of the deputation, visited Paris, London, Vienna, and Brussels, to say farewell to family relatives; and to treat with Napoleon III., in regard to the affairs of the contemplated new Empire. After that was accomplished, it became necessary to transact family business, pertaining to Austria. The most important was that of renouncing his, Maximilian's, right to the crown of Austria, in accordance with the laws of that dynasty and empire. After a few days' consultation the affairs were settled, and the family agreement was signed April 9th.

CHAPTER VI.

Mexican deputation at Trieste and Miramar—Ceremonies of offering and accepting the Crown—Decrees—Address of deputation to Maximilian—His answer—Reply of deputation to his answer—Oath as Emperor.

IN the Hotel de Ville, at Trieste, the Mexican Deputation occupied apartments elegantly furnished by Archduke Maximilian. They had been notified that it would be expected that at the appointed hour they would be in readiness there, properly attired, to leave, in order to present themselves, on the tenth day of April, at the palace of Miramar, when and where they would be received by the Archduke, according to the programme already provided.

The tenth day of that month was Sunday—the day of the week on which the poor, having ceased their week's labor, may feast their eyes on that stately palace, the green lawns, the mosaic flower-beds, the gracefully bending leafy boughs, all pervaded by sweet-scented air, so that one's fancy suggests that nature had just perfumed herself for a banquet with the gods.

The inhabitants of Trieste and its suburbs were all agog that morning. The double attraction of seeing Nature decked in her gorgeous apparel, breathing forth intoxicating air, and decorated nobility in shining lustre, richly caparisoned steeds, carriages rolling in splendor—brought forth an unusual number of people, gliding like a living avalanche, on foot, and horse, and in brightly gilded and varnished vehicles.

At ten o'clock in the morning, the gentlemen of the service, Count Hadick, an old Grand Master of His Highness, and Vice-Admiral of the Austrian navy, proceeded to the city for the Mexican deputation; and in fifteen minutes, clad in their elegant dress for the occasion, they were rolling in four shining carriages having the livery of His Highness the Archduke, and drawn by splendid prancing steeds, preceded by a mounted escort. Those carriages were followed by others containing persons of distinction, composed of Mexicans, Austrians, diplomats, generals, colonels, in full dress, with their decorations on their breasts; also officers of the house of the Archduke.

They were soon before the entrance of the palace of Miramar. There they were received by Marquis Corio, Grand Master of Ceremonies; and soon thereafter, preceded by the same officer, they entered the apartments provided for foreigners, where they were received by the Grand Master of the house of the Archduke, Count Zichy.

At twelve o'clock, M., the Grand Master, preceded by the Grand Master of Ceremonies, conducted the deputation through the waiting saloon, the library, and the blue-room, to the hall of reception, where the Archduke was in readiness to receive them.

His Highness stood in front of a table covered with magnificent tapestry, upon which were seen innumerable acts of adhesion to the new empire which had been created in Mexico. He was dressed in the uniform of a Vice-Admiral of the Austrian navy, on which was placed the Order of the Golden Fleece, and the Grand Cross of Saint Stephen. Standing on his left was his august spouse, the Archduchess Carlota. She was richly attired in an elegant rose-colored silk, adorned with the finest Brussels lace, a diadem, necklace, and earrings of diamonds, and the Black Cord of the Order of Malta. She particularly attracted the attention of the whole audience. Her commanding form, her exquisite beauty, her beaming countenance, and her superb apparel, all united to make her appear like an enchantress—a being of poetical imagination.

Their Imperial Highnesses occupied one angle of the room, accompanied by General Frassart, Adjutant of the Field of Napoleon III., and the Imperial delegate, Señor Hurbet. The Grand Master stood at one side, in the rear of their Highnesses, while the Grand Master of Ceremonies occupied a position in front of the door.

In another angle of the room were the ladies of honor, the Princess of Metternich and the Marchioness de Ville, Countesses Zichy and Kollonitz, the Belgian Minister near Austria, Mon. Monier, commander of the French frigate *Thémis*, and other distinguished personages.

The Mexican deputation took their position in the form of a semicircle, in front of the Archduke and Archduchess; Señor Gutierrez Estrada, the President of the deputation, stood in the centre of the outer points of the semicircle. In the rear stood other Mexicans, who were as follows: Don Francisco de P. Arrangoiz y Berzabal, E. Tomas Murphy, Colonel D. Francisco Facio, D. Andres Negrete, D. Isidoro Diaz, D. Pedro Escandon, Colonel D. José Armero y Ruiz, D. Ignacio Montesdeoca (a priest), Dr. D. Pablo Martinez del Rio, D. Fernando Gutierrez Estrada (son of the President of the deputation), D. Ignacio Arnor, D. Pedro Ontiveras, and D. Joaquin Manuel Rodriguez. The two latter were prisoners at Puebla, but having recognized the Empire, were called into the service of His Highness; making the number of twenty-one Mexicans present at the august ceremonies.

For a short time a profound silence reigned, and that emotion which usually precedes great events. At last, Señor Gutierrez Estrada read with a firm voice, although occasionally a little tremulous, the address which will be hereinafter seen, and which the Archduke answered, accepting definitely the crown of Mexico.

The Archduke had scarcely finished speaking, when a salvo of artillery from the bulwarks of the castle announced the great event which had just been concluded, and that salvo was answered from the ships in the port, and from the forts of the city.

At the conclusion of His Highness' speech, Señor Gutierrez Estrada knelt down and kissed the hand of the newly-made Emperor, in sign of homage, according to the Spanish custom, saying, "God save His Majesty, Maximilian I., Emperor of Mexico!" to which announcement all the Mexicans present responded by one united voice.

The same demonstration of homage was made to the Empress. After that, the Abbot of Lacroma presented himself with mitre and staff, assisted by Fr. Tomas Gomez, a Spaniard of the Order of San Francisco, and by Dr. D. Ignacio Montesdeoca, a Mexican priest. Everything then being ready, the Emperor took the oath, which will be seen herein, placing his hand at the same time on the Book of the Evangelists, held by Señor Montesdeoca.

The Mexican flag was then raised upon the castle, and the frigate Bellona, of the Austrian navy, gave a salute of twenty-one guns, which was responded to by the frigate *Thémis*, and the artillery of the forts.

Soon thereafter the deputation passed into the library, preceded by the grand master of ceremonies, and there waited until the Te Deum was announced; at which time they were escorted to the seats reserved for them in the chapel of the palace. Their Majesties then proceeded to the chapel, followed by the ladies of the court, and Count Hadick. The Abbot of Lacroma received them at the door. Their Majesties were in front of the audience. At the conclusion of the solemn Te Deum, Their Majesties withdrew. In a few moments thereafter, the grand master conducted into the presence of the

Emperor Señor Velazquez de Leon, Minister of State, General Woll, Adjutant of the Field, and Señor Iglesias, Secretary of the Cabinet; all of whom took the oath before His Majesty to faithfully comply with the duties of their respective offices; and immediately entered upon the discharge of them.

Thus ended the grand and imposing ceremony that surrounded the introduction of the reign of Maximilian I. of Mexico. The solemn proceeding produced many a tear from Mexican eyes. They viewed it as a good omen, foreshadowing happy days to them and their country.

The day before the ceremony the Emperor of Austria, and the Archdukes, his brothers, arrived. They remained until certain family affairs were arranged, when they returned to Vienna. The parting of the two imperial brothers was most affectionate. They embraced each other several times, and for a moment remained clasped, while tears trickled down their cheeks. The thought which occupied their minds then, alas! has been too truly realized. It was, that that embrace might be the last.

On the 10th, the day of that ceremony, the Emperor issued a decree commissioning D. Juan N. Almonte, his Lieutenant-General, to act at the head of affairs, until he, the Emperor, should arrive in Mexico; also that the functions of the Regency should cease on the arrival of his Lieutenant-General. Also, by another decree, Señor D. Joaquin Velazquez de Leon was appointed Minister of State.

On that day was signed the treaty of Miramar, between Maximilian and Napoleon.

His Majesty appointed ministers plenipotentiary to notify his advent to the Courts of the Tuileries, St. James, the Holy See, and at Madrid and Brussels.

He also re-established, by a decree, the Order of Guadalupe, which was created by a decree of the Regency, on the 29th day of September, 1863: also providing that there should be five different classes of gentlemen— 1st, Order of the Grand Cross; 2d, of the Grand Officials; 3d, of the Commentators; 4th, of Officers; and 5th, of Gentlemen.

On the same day he decorated with the Order of Grand Cross, Señor D. José M. Gutierrez Estrada, and Generals D. Leonardo Marquez and Tomas Mejia; with the Order of Grand Officials, D. Francisco Arrangoiz y Berzabal, Tomas Murphy, D. Ignacio Aguilar y Marocho, D. Joaquin Velazquez de Leon, General D. Adrian Woll, and D. José Hidalgo; with the Order of Commentators, D. Antonio Escandon, D. José M. de Landa, D. Francisco Facio, D. Andres Negrete, and D. Pablo Martinez del Rio; with the Order of Officers, D. Angel Iglesias Dominguez, D. Fernando Gutierrez Estrada, D. José J. Rus, and D. Manuel Mora y Ozta.

The following is a copy of the decree appointing Señor Velazquez de Leon Minister of State:

"MY DEAR VELAZQUEZ DE LEON:

"I have just appointed you my Minister, *sin catera* (without full power), and charge you, until the formation of my Cabinet, with the office of the affairs of State, committing to your care the corresponding seal.

"You will remain in charge of these functions, under the instructions which will be given you hereafter on my part.

"Given in the Castle of Miramar, the 10th of April, 1864.

"MAXIMILIAN."

The Emperor, considering all the possibilities of the future, and desiring that in no case the government should be without a head, issued the following decree:

" Considering that nothing is so important as the providing for the stability of the legitimate government of the nation that has chosen us Sovereign; and, to guard against all casualties that may happen, I have just decreed: That in case of death or any other contingency that may place us without the possibility of continuing to govern, the Empress, our august spouse, is the one who will be charged with the Regency of the Empire.

"My present Minister of State, or, in case of his inability, the respective Minister, will be charged with the execution of this decree.

" Given in the Castle of Miramar, the tenth day of April, one thousand eight hundred and sixty-four.

"MAXIMILIAN.

"To my Minister of State,
D. Joaquin Velazquez de Leon.

"By order of His Imperial Majesty,

"JOAQUIN VELAZQUEZ DE LEON."

As was observed hereinbefore, the President of the Mexican deputation delivered an address to Maximilian as Archduke, before his final confirmation as Emperor, which was in the following language:

"PRINCE:

"The Mexican deputation has the pleasure of finding themselves again in your august presence; and they experience an unspeakable joy in considering the motives which brought them here. In fact, Prince, our happiness is complete, in informing you, in the name of the Regency of the Empire, that the vote of the Notables, by which you have been designated for the crown of Mexico, is now ratified by the enthusiastic adhesion of an immense majority of the country, by the municipal authorities and by the town corporations; and thus consecrated, that unanimous proclamation has become, by its moral importance and by its numerical strength, truly a national vote.

"By this glorious title, and supported by the promise of the third of October, one thousand eight hundred and sixty-three, which created in the country such strong hopes, we present ourselves now to solicit of Your Imperial Highness the full and definite acceptation of the throne of Mexico; which act will become the commencement of a union and a source of prosperity for the people, who have been subject, for so many years, to very severe and sad experiences. Those experiences have been such, that the people would have unquestionably succumbed under the weight of their misfortunes, without the help of one of the greatest empires of Europe, without the eminent qualities and the admirable self-denial of Your Imperial Highness, and lastly, without the freedom of action, for which you are indebted to the noble sentiments of the Emperor, your august brother—a worthy chief, by a thousand titles, of the illustrious House of Austria.

"Honor and gratitude to those two Princes! Honor and gratitude also to the glorious nation which, at the call of its Sovereign, has not vacillated in spilling its blood for our political redemption; and creating in this manner, between the two continents, a new faternity in history, when history has exhibited us in Europe, until now, as tyrannical. Honor and gratitude to that Emperor, as great as he is generous, who, in making the French interest the whole interest of the world, within a few years, and in spite of passing objects, has had the glory and the fortune of raising the flag of France (always feared, but always sympathetical), in the distant confines of the Chinese Empire, and in the remote limits of the divided Empire of Mexico. Honor and gratitude to such a people and to such Princes, is the cry of every true Mexican.

"In conquering the love of nations, you have learned the art of governing them. Thus it is, that after so many struggles, our country, which experiences the imperious necessity of a union, will owe to you some day the inestimable favor of having reconciled the hearts of the Mexicans, whom public misfortunes and the blindness of passion have divided, but who are only waiting for your beneficial influence and the exercise of your paternal authority, to teach them to be animated by the same identical sentiments.

"A Princess, who is no less a queen by her graces than by her virtues and high intelligence, will know, without doubt, from the height of the throne, how to bring about a perfect union for the general respect of the country.

"In order to see these benefits realized, Mexico, with a filial confidence, places in your hands the sovereign and constituent power that must regulate its future destinies and secure its glorious future, promising you, in this moment of solemn alliance, a love without limits, and a fidelity unalterable.

"The people assure you, Prince, that being Catholic and monarchical by an uninterrupted secular tradition, they find in Your Imperial Highness, a worthy scion of the Emperor Charles V., and of the Empress Maria Theresa, the symbol and personification of those two great principles which are the bases of their primitive existence; and under the protection of which, with the institutions and the means which passing time has made necessary in the government of societies, they will be able to place themselves one day in the elevated rank which they are called to occupy among nations. *In hoc signo vinces.*

"To these two great principles, Catholic and monarchical, which were introduced into Mexico by the noble and generous people who made its discovery, and who rooted out therefrom the errors and the darkness of idolatry—to these principles, which created us for civilization, we shall be indebted this time also for our welfare, enlivened as they have been by our independence, and as they are to-day by the pleasing hopes which are perpetuated by the new-born Empire. On this day, which would not be one of happiness if it were not equally one of justice, our thoughts involuntarily turn to historic times, and to the series of glorious monarchs, among which are the illustrious ancestors of Your Imperial Highness, that excel in splendor.

"Nations, like individuals, ought in their hours of joy to speak with affectionate gratitude of their ancestors that no longer exist; and it is for us, Prince, a glorious honor to make that just acknowledgment apparent to the eyes of all, at the same moment when our unexpected fortune is attracting equally the eyes of the astonished world.

"On manifesting to you, Prince, our wish and our hopes, we do not say, we cannot say, that the task may not be difficult; for the founding of an empire always was and always will be so. The only thing which we can assure is, that the difficulties of to-day will be your glory to-morrow; and we will even add, that the work undertaken reveals in a patent form the hand of God. When the time shall arrive that our hopes will be satisfied, our predictions fulfilled; when Mexico shall appear prosperous and regenerated, then, when remembering that Europe sent, to save us, its valorous battalions to the top of the Anahuac, to the shores of the Pacific, in an epoch in which Europe itself was full of fears and dangers, neither Mexico nor Europe, nor the world, nor that other world which comes after us, nor that which is called history, can doubt that our salvation, which was obtained contrary to all human probabilities, will have been the work of Providence, and that Your Imperial Highness was the instrument selected to consummate it.

"And further, while thinking of the fortunate destiny of our country, we cannot forget, Prince, that in the hour of our rejoicing the most profound sadness reigns in other parts. We well understand that this Austrian country, and principally Trieste, your favorite abode, will be inconsolable on account of your absence, and we extend to them our sympathies; but the recollection of your good acts and the splendid reflection of your glory, will be a consolation to them.

"After having had the inestimable fortune to hear from the lips of Your Imperial Highness the words of hope, that your definite acceptation would be a reality, condescend, Prince, to concede to us the notable honor and unspeakable happiness of being the first among the Mexicans who reverently salute you, in the name of the country, as the Sovereign of Mexico, the Arbitrator of its destinies, and the depositary of its future. All the Mexican people that aspire with inexpressible impatience to possess you, will receive you in their favored land with a unanimous expression of gratitude and love.

"This brilliant spectacle, which for others would be the height of their desire, will only serve to give you new life, and increase your ambition.

"The recompense will providentially come, as the undertaking advances toward completion.

"There will be no premium more enviable than that which Your Highness will receive, in seeing, at no remote day, Mexico prosperous and respected; and in truth, you could not experience joy purer, nor pride more legitimate, than that of having founded, on the volcanic ground of the Moctezumas, a powerful empire, which would unite soon for its splendor and your glory, that favorable influence of that native wisdom with which Heaven has endowed our American land, to the most perfect of that which the justly praised European organization can offer.

"The ultimate conviction, Prince, that crowns us with such a happy presage is, that Mexico, which calls you beyond the seas, and the entire world that beholds you, will not be long in observing that Your Imperial Highness has not had in vain before your eyes from your infancy, on the triumphal arch of the Palace of his ancestors, that inscription so worthy of them, and which strikes the traveller with admiration: *Justitia regnorum fundamentum*—Justice is the foundation of Empires."

His Imperial Highness answered the foregoing address and request in the following terms:

"GENTLEMEN:

"A mature examination of the acts of adhesion which you have just presented me, gives me confidence that the vote of the Notables of Mexico, which brought you a short time ago, for the first time, to Miramar, has been ratified by an immense majority of your compatriots, and that I can consider myself henceforth, with good right, as the elect of the Mexican people. Thus, the first condition in my answer, which I gave on the 3d of October last, has been complied with.

"Another thing also I indicated to you then—namely, in relation to the securing of the necessary guarantees that the new-born Empire should calmly devote itself to the noble task of establishing on a solid basis its independence and prosperity. To-day, we can count upon those securities, thanks to His Majesty the Emperor of the French, who, in the course of the negotiations which have taken place upon this point, has shown himself constantly animated by a spirit of loyalty and of benevolence, the recollection of which I will always preserve in my memory.

"On the other hand, the august chief of my family has consented that I may take possession of the throne which is offered me.

"Now, then, I can comply with the conditional promise which I made you six months ago, and declare here, as solemnly I do declare, that, with the help of the Almighty, I accept from the hands of the Mexican nation the crown which it offers me. Mexico, following the traditions of that new continent, full of vigor and hopes for the future, has used the right which it possesses of choosing the form of government in conformity with its wishes and necessities, and has placed its hopes on a scion of the House of Hapsburg, which three centuries ago planted on its soil a Christian monarchy. I appreciate in its full value such a high proof of confidence, and I will try to sustain it. I accept the constituent power with which the nation whose organ you are, Gentlemen, has wished to invest me, but which I shall hold only so long as may be necessary to create regular order, and to establish institutions wisely liberal. So that, as I announced in my address of the 3d of October, I will hasten to place the monarchy under the authority of constitutional laws, as soon as the pacification of the country shall have been completely consummated. The power of a nation is secured, in my judgment, much more by the firmness than by the uncertainty of its limits; and I shall aspire to place those in official position, who, without the loss of their prestige, may be able to guarantee its stability.

"We shall prove, I hope, that liberty, correctly understood, is perfectly reconcilable with a well-governed empire. I shall know how to respect the first, and to cause to be respected the second.

"I shall not display less vigor in always maintaining, high elevated the standard of independence, that symbol of future greatness and prosperity.

"Great is the undertaking that is confided to me; but I do not doubt that I shall complete it, confiding, as I do, in Divine help, and in the co-operation of all good Mexicans.

"I will conclude, Gentlemen, assuring you again that my Government will never forget the obligation which it owes to the illustrious monarch whose friendly assistance has made the regeneration of our beautiful country possible.

"Lastly, Gentlemen, I ought to announce to you that, before departing for my new country, I shall be detained only by the time necessary to visit the Holy City, to receive from the Venerable Pontiff the blessings so precious for every Sovereign, but doubly important to me, who have been called to found a new empire."

The President of the deputation made the following reply to the acceptance of the crown by Maximilian:

"Being possessed of an unparalleled emotion, and overcome by an unspeakable joy, we receive, Sire, the solemn 'Yes' which Your Majesty has just pronounced. This acceptance, full and absolute, so ardently desired, and so earnestly hoped, is the happy prelude, and ought to be, with the help of God, the sure pledge for the salvation of Mexico, for its regeneration and future greatness. Then will our sons give thanks to Heaven for this truly extraordinary redemption.

"One duty still remains with us, Sire, to fulfil—that is the duty of placing at your feet the love of the Mexicans, their gratitude, and their homage of fidelity."

To complete the ceremony of making Maximilian Emperor, it became necessary for him to take the oath of office; and for that purpose the mitred Abbots of Miramar and Lacroma, Mr. George Racie with mitre and staff, assisted by Tomas Gomez, a friar of the Order of Francisco, and Dr. Ignacio Montesdeoca, presented themselves; and before them Maximilian took the oath in the following form: "I, Maximilian, Emperor of Mexico, swear to God by the Holy Evangelists, that I will try to promote, through all the means within my power, the welfare and prosperity of the nation, to defend its independence, and to preserve the whole of its territory."

This solemn act was subsequently greeted with shouts of "Long live the Emperor," and "Long live the Empress," by the whole audience, as with one united voice.

The audience then separated awhile, without any particular ceremony, waiting for the hour to arrive which had been appointed for the grand Te Deum, at which time all again assembled in the chapel. His Majesty appeared with the insignia of Grand Master of the Mexican Order of Guadalupe.

As the oath of office was completed, the flag of Imperial Mexico waved in the breeze over the tower of the castle. Guns from the frigate Bellona, of the Imperial navy of Austria, poured forth salutes in honor of the event, to the number of twenty-one. The castle of Trieste and the French frigate *Thémis* answered, with their gruff, rumbling notes, the salute from the Bellona, which echoed and re-echoed o'er the sea and the land.

A written act of this great event was executed, signed by the parties, in duplicate, and transmitted to the minister of foreign affairs and the archives of the Imperial House.

Thus ended one great act in the imperial drama of Maximilian's life—a step on that march which led him from the elegant pleasures of Miramar to a seat on a tottering throne, in the New World, in a volcanic region,—more dangerous from the surging of political waves than from the seething elements of its burning mountains.

CHAPTER VII.

Departure of Maximilian and Carlota from Miramar for Mexico—Ceremonies —Visit at Rome—Ceremonies there—Visits *en route*—Arrival at Vera Cruz.

The cannon's roar was heard afar,
Sweet music burst upon the air;
Good-bye, he said, to Miramar,
Farewell, brave men and women fair.

THE inhabitants of Trieste and the surrounding country will long remember the 14th day of April, A. D. 1864, as one of note in the calendar of remarkable events. In connection with it, the names of MAXIMILIAN and MIRAMAR will be most vivid. They will loom up in the heaven of their memory like the full-orbed moon, as she sweeps along amid the myriad of stars that are lost in the effulgence of her splendor.

The hum of business which Trieste usually presents was nearly silent on that day. It was a day of universal excitement, and the thoughts of money-making were buried. It was the day of the departure of His Majesty Maximilian and his august spouse for their new home, in a new empire across the far-resounding sea, to the land where lie entombed the remains of the famed Moctezuma.

The houses were emptied of their living inmates, and the out-door world was a heaving sea of humanity. The crowd was here and there; richly caparisoned steeds, with their loads of beauty and splendor, were prancing to the measure of well-timed music; rich and poor were dressed in their gala attire,—some on foot, some on horse, surging this way and that, like ocean waves,—all eager to catch the farewell glimpse of their true friend, their real benefactor, who was soon to be welcomed in a distant land, by a different race, and in a different tongue.

The morning of that eventful day was not one of calmness. The wind sharply whistled, and the roadstead of Trieste, in its angry ruffling motion, heaved upward and downward the little barks that were anchored on its bosom. But fortunately, near noon, the wind-spirit, as though suddenly bringing to its mind the importance of the occasion, quietly lulled itself away like a sleepy child, and the foamy white dissolved into the deep blue of the Adriatic. And the silent air, perforated by the genial rays of the mid-day sun, threw a radiant splendor on the glassy sea, on the grassy lawns, and the flower-decked land.

Not a cloud curtained the heavens; and far away above the distant horizon the Alps—those earthy mounds of nature—sat high up against the sky, like monarchs wrapped in imperial robes of white, all variegated with rainbow hues by the reflected light from their ornamental jewels of dazzling diamond icicles bathing in the sun-light.

Six steamers, belonging to the well-known Lloyd Company, were ploughing the Adriatic, to and fro, from the city of Trieste to the Archducal residence, the castle of Miramar. They conveyed the municipal officers of Trieste, the members of the Chamber of Commerce, the deputations from other cities, and also other invited guests. Three trains of cars were in continual motion, belting the air with their ribbons of smoke, freighting the living into the great storehouse of merriment and grandeur—the grounds of Miramar.

The castle, its surrounding heights, the walls, the gardens, the trees, and every prominent place, were all mantled with human beings. The sea-shore was all traced in footprints. The roads leading to the sea were filled with carriages, omnibuses, mounted men, all dovetailed in with footmen. Not an elevated place in sight could be descried that had not its eager gazer. One might have fancied that Nature's great human hive had just swarmed there.

Many of the enchanted multitude assembled there out of mere curiosity, to feast their strained eyes on the surrounding splendor and magnificence; but there was a mighty gathering of affectionate hearts, who hurried there in friendship's name, and in honor of a noble and generous prince, who had watched over their necessities with an anxious desire; who had never turned a deaf ear to begging poverty; whose friendship never turned cold; and who had built up and commanded their small but effective navy.

At two o'clock in the afternoon, the Empress, the beautiful Carlota, affectionately embraced the extended arm of the Emperor Maximilian within her own, and the two—*one* in heart and thought—departed from the palace, the cherished spot of His Majesty, winding their way across the terrace to the extreme end, where opened the stairway; and down, down the white marble steps they went to the sea. The deafening shouts of "farewell," the roaring cannon, the bugle-notes, the drum, all blending, drowned the murmuring song of the waves. The *advent* music, written for the occasion at Paris, by request of the Mexican deputation, was well executed by the band of the Trieste garrison; which music was carried to Mexico by Commander Rodriguez in the steamer San Nazario. Just before descending the steps, Their Majesties paused a moment, and returned the friendly salutations of the great multitude. A beautiful little boat, all canopied with purple and gold, lay waiting close to the bottom step, in which the Sovereigns seated themselves—then glided along to the steamer Novara, which was anchored to the cable of the castle.

The brother of Maximilian, Louis Victor, accompanied him as far as Rome; as also did General Woll, Chief of the Military House; Señor Velazquez de Leon, Minister of State; the ladies of honor of the Empress; the Countesses Zichy and Colonitz; Count Zichy, Grand Master; the Chamberlains, Count de Bombells and Marquis de Corio; Señor Iglesias, his Secretary; and Commander Ontiveras, Officer of Orders.

As they entered the little boat, the Novara, the *Thêmis*, and the stationary Austrian frigate, all raised their flags; and the different crews broke forth in wild shouts of joy; and the surrounding little crafts raised their oars in token of adieu, while the artillery from deck and castle spoke from their deep-toned throats. Soon after His Majesty had firmly placed his foot on the Novara, the Austrian colors were removed, and the flag of Mexico raised in its stead. A short period only elapsed thereafter, when the Novara weighed anchor and steamed away on her course, escorted by the French steamer, *Thêmis*, and an Austrian fleet of eleven steamers. The gallant yacht, Fantasia, which the Austrian government had usually placed at the disposition of the Archduke, during his residence at Miramar, led off the fleet. Then came the Novara, followed at some two cables' length by the *Thêmis*, which escorted the Sovereigns to Vera Cruz, commanded by Captain Morier; and behind all went the six Lloyd steamers.

The whole squadron defiled before the city of Trieste, among the ships anchored in the roadstead, bearing their respective colors. The coast batteries muttered their thunder-notes, and as the Novara passed, the firing was so rapid that it seemed like one continued sound. The fleet passed so near the shore that the cheering multitude could be distinctly heard. The Lloyd steamers were intended to escort the Sovereigns as far as Pisano, which is about an hour's sail distant; but some injury having happened to the machinery, prevented them from so doing. At Pisano was assembled a swarm of boats, and the fishermen were eager for an opportunity to salute the Sovereigns as they glided by. The little boats were so numerous that it put one in mind of the schools of fishes that follow beneath the surface.

That day and night the coasts of Italy and Dalmatia were visible; also the arsenals of Porenzo, Forigno, and Pola.

The Emperor had once concluded to visit for a few hours the Island of Lacroma, which is opposite Ragusa, and which is his private property. It is noted as the spot where Richard the Lion-Hearted touched on his return from Palestine. There were built a church and convent, the latter having been turned into a castle by Maximilian. It is an island of some note, as one of luxuriant vegetable productions, and of adaptability to the growth of tropical plants.

Maximilian changed his intention as to stopping there; and the Novara, leaving the eastern coast of the Adriatic, neared the coast of Italy. Everything went smoothly on, the accompanying vessels keeping true to their course, without requiring any signs of guidance from the Novara. On the 16th, they doubled the Cape of Otranto, near enough to see the city of the same name, beautifully situated on the picturesque coast of Italy.

About two hours later, having turned the heel of the Italian boot, they rounded the Cape of Santa Maria de Leuca, and entered into the Gulf of Tarento. Sunday morning, the 17th, about nine o'clock, they floated into the Strait of Messina. By noon they reached the foot of Stromboli, whose lofty crater was smoking away, like some tired giant resting from his labor. The next day, noon, they ruffled the waters of the roadstead of Civita Vecchia. Their contemplated arrival had been trumpeted ahead of them. Rome sent out smiling friends, among whom were General Montebello, commander-in-chief of the French army at Rome, with his staff; Baron Bach, Austrian Ambassador; Mr. de Carolus, Belgian

Minister; Señor D. Ignacio Aguilar, Minister Plenipotentiary of Mexico near the Holy See. The railroad station was magnificently decorated, exhibiting the coat of arms of His Majesty, with the initials of both Sovereigns, "M., C." The French and Pontifical troops formed a double line, and as Their Majesties disembarked, shouts went up from an immense concourse of people who had gathered on the wharf and shores to view the Imperial guests, and salvos of artillery from forts and ships announced with their sonorous voices the glad tidings of their arrival to the gazing multitude.

At six o'clock in the evening Their Majesties and suite reached the Eternal City, amid the roar of the guns that guard the ancient Castle of San Angelo. The Sovereigns stopped at the Marescotti palace, where Señor Gutierrez Estrada resided. This palace is one of the finest in the city. Its works of art are magnificent. Its frescoes were painted by Arpino; and its furniture is of a costly style, and in elegant taste. The rooms were gayly decorated for the occasion. A throne was erected in one of the saloons, and an immense quantity of red and white were exquisitely arranged so as to represent the Mexican flag.

The King of Naples paid his respects to Their Majesties; also Cardinal Antonelli, Prime Minister of His Holiness, presented himself.

At eight o'clock in the evening a grand banquet was served, at which were seated about thirty persons. The new Sovereigns and the Mexicans at Rome composed the company. After that a reception took place, at the conclusion of which Their Majesties wandered out to the Plaza of Saint Peter's, thence to gaze at the moonbeams as they silvered o'er the ancient ruins of the Coliseum,—a sight which the Empress had never before witnessed. There is something enchanting in the scene. He who beholds it at such an hour, departs reluctantly. He looks, and as he turns to leave it, he halts, and glances again and again. His mind is flooded with its ancient history; he forgets for a moment the age in which he lives.

On the morning of the 19th, the whole party visited the Holy Father at the Vatican; all were in their full uniform, ladies with elegant toilette, although in dark dresses, as is the custom in making such a visit. All along the street from the bridge of San Angelo were stationed mounted guards: in the avenues and court of the palace were placed sentinels on foot. The interior was guarded by the Swiss soldiers, with uniforms as neat as wax-work. Bishops, prelates, and officers of the house were presented to Their Majesties. Soon the Holy Father and the two new Sovereigns entered a small saloon, where they remained together and alone for over an hour. After that private audience the whole party had the opportunity of kissing the foot of His Holiness, which they did not fail to do.

His Majesty paid a short visit to His Eminence the Cardinal Secretary of State, during which time the Empress remained in the Vatican museum, amusing herself in examining the thousands of interesting and curious ancient and modern works of art, which have been gathered from all parts of the world.

After the Emperor had finished his visit, the whole party returned, surrounded by an immense throng of people, to the palace of Marescotti, and rested until after breakfast, after which His Majesty visited the King of Naples, and other princes, to whom he was united by strong ties of friendship. Having spent a few hours with them in social conversation upon the subject of Italy and his newly-adopted home, he returned to the palace. A richly-spread table was served, having the best that the market could afford, choice viands and wines, in a saloon exquisitely decorated. That repast having been concluded, a pleasant *soirée* followed, where the Court, the Roman nobility, and other distinguished personages, gathered in large numbers, filling the different saloons, which were most brilliantly lighted, showing to most superb advantage the rich and costly furniture, the glittering pendants, and the still brighter diamonds that adorned the beautiful and extravagantly-attired ladies. Every face wore a smile, every eye glittered like the surrounding brilliants. The scene presented a view of grandeur, of wealth, and of happiness.

On the day following, Their Majesties, accompanied by a part of the Mexican deputation, went to Mass, in a private chapel, where they received from the hands of His Holiness the communion. At the same time was delivered to them, by His Holiness, an eloquent, affectionate, and tender address, in the following words:

"Behold the Lamb of God which blots out the sins of the world. Through Him kings reign and govern; through Him kings do justice; and if He permits kings to be often afflicted, through Him, nevertheless, is exercised all power.

"I recommend to you, in His name, the happiness of the Catholic people, who have confided themselves to you. The rights of the people are great, and it is necessary to satisfy them; but greater and more sacred are the rights of the Church, the immaculate wife of Jesus Christ, who redeemed us with His blood—with this blood that is now going to redden your lips.

"Respect, then, the rights of your people and the rights of the Church; which means that you ought to procure, at the same time, the temporal and spiritual good of those people.

"And may our Lord Jesus Christ, through whom you are going to receive the communion, from the hands of his vicar, concede to you His grace in the abundance of

His mercy. *Misereatur vestri omnipotens Deus, et dimissis peccatis vestris perducat vos ad vitam æternam.* Amen."

At the conclusion of this Mass, another was said, in the presence of the whole party. Then a light collation, or what is termed in Mexico a *desayuno*, was taken, in the private library of the Holy Father. His Holiness, the two Sovereigns, and Cardinal Antonelli ate at one table,—the others eating at several small tables, in the same room, and within a short distance of the distinguished personages. Everything passed off pleasantly. without any stiffness. The audience was merry—the conversation at times being general; then again confined to their respective tables.

At the conclusion of this repast, Their Majesties bid "Good-morning" to His Holiness, and returned to Marescotti Palace. The remainder of the party left the Vatican at the same time. Not long after that, Señores Aguila and Velazquez took a walk of pleasure and profit —of pleasure to themselves, and of profit to the Church. They presented themselves at the house of the Minister of State, and in the name of the Mexican Empire, extended, as an oblation to the Holy Church, the sum of eight thousand dollars. It was most cordially received, and with a becoming grace. Was there ever a Church that would refuse such an offer?

A little past noon, the same day, the 20th, the Holy Father visited Their Majesties. The streets were thronged with people, and it was with difficulty that one could elbow his way along. Troops formed on either side of the street, through which His Holiness passed. The music of the brass bands mingled with that of the merry chiming bells, and the shouts of the living mass, as the gilded carriage rolled steadily along, drawn by six richly-caparisoned black horses, and escorted by the Guard Noble. His Holiness was indeed encircled with great splendor. When all that grandeur arrived at the palace, Their Majesties were in readiness at the entrance, to receive the Holy Father. As he approached quite near, the two Sovereigns, on bended knees, and the surrounding multitude in like position, received the benediction from His Holiness. His Majesty then arose, and giving his hand to the Holy Father, assisted him in descending from the carriage. Their Majesties and the Holy Father had a private interview; after which was given a public audience to all the friends that desired to be presented. A short time having been spent here, the Holy Father took an affectionate leave of Their Majesties, who escorted him to his carriage in becoming style.

Soon thereafter came breakfast; which being finished, the whole party was ordered to be in readiness at four o'clock, in the afternoon, with the carriages, for the depot. At the appointed time everything was ready. They all reached the station, surrounded by the gazing crowd as before. After a shaking of hands and a farewell-bidding to friends, Their Majesties, the ladies of honor, and Señor Velazquez, entered the same car.

Near the setting of the sun the train reached Civita Vecchia, when again the booming cannon was heard, music, and shouts, as on their first landing.

Between nine and ten o'clock, the Novara and *Thêmis* weighed anchor, and bore away on their course for Gibraltar. They coasted along the Islands of Baleares, and between five and six o'clock they saw the Island of Cabrera. Part of the time the wind blew pretty strongly, and the vessels plunged into the watery element, so that their guns nearly touched the water. The sky became cloudy; after which came a fog. But before reaching the Straits of Gibraltar, the weather became calm. The wind, while it blew, came astern, and sent the vessels along at the rate of twelve knots per hour.

They entered the bay at Gibraltar about the middle of the afternoon, saluted by the batteries of the citadel, and by an English vessel anchored in the port. Away in the distance was heard peal after peal, from the little Spanish town of Algeciras, saluting Their Majesties. The guns of the *Thémis* loudly responded.

Their Majesties were visited by the Governor of Gibraltar, General Count Codington, accompanied by his two adjutants, on board the Novara; who, by invitation, dined with the two Sovereigns. The consuls of Austria and Belgium, at Tangiers, crossed the water and paid the proper respects to Their Majesties.

On the 27th of April, the two steamers left Gibraltar, and steamed away for the American waters. Their passage was not unpleasant. They reached Martinique May 16th. On this island were many Mexicans, who were prisoners on account of their non-adherence to the party of the Intervention. His Majesty saw the prisoners. Being anxious to reach the land of his destination, he did not wish to remain there longer than necessary. There being a few spare births on the *Thémis*, His Majesty selected, on the night of his arrival, four Mexicans whom he liberated and sent to occupy those vacant births, that they might reach their homes. The impartiality of the Emperor was shown on this occasion. The authorities of the place had presented a list of four prisoners, whom they considered the most entitled to favor. But as His Majesty wished to have unbiased proof as to the character of the prisoners, he decided that he would not rely alone on the judgment of the officers under whose charge they were. He therefore said that the prisoners should vote among themselves as to which four were the most worthy of consideration. They did so, and the result was, that they elected the four already designated by the officers. These four expressed a strong desire to support the Empire. Eight more of the prisoners who had manifested a like adhesion, were furnished by the Emperor with funds to defray their expenses on the next vessel bound to Mexico. He also gave to those who were without funds the sum of two thousand francs; promising at the same time, on his arrival in Mexico, to give their claims all the consideration and attention to which they might be entitled. It would have been almost an impossibility for him to have passed them without extending to them some favor: such was the character of the man.

His acts of generosity being finished, the ships sailed on their way, arriving at Jamaica, May 21st. Remaining only one day, they steered directly for Vera Cruz, without visiting Havana, as many contemplated, and much to the regret of the Cubans.

They had not sailed far from the island of Jamaica, when the *Thēmis* took the lead, pressing on steam, in order to herald the glad tidings of the near approach of the coming Sovereigns, to the people of Vera Cruz. At about six o'clock of the morning of the 28th of May, the *Thēmis* dropped her anchor in the port of her destination. The news of the expected arrival of the new rulers spread with lightning speed all through the country.

While far away from the coast of Mexico, Their Majesties stood upon the quarter-deck of the Novara, straining their eyes to obtain a view of Orizaba peak, that mighty sentinel, that king of mountains, that pierces its hoary head high into the heavens, as though it were the supporting pier of the celestial canopy. But Nature, chary of the beauty of her architecture, threw a heavy mantle of clouds around the white drapery of snow, lest a summer's noonday sun should fringe it with rays.

A little after two o'clock in the afternoon, the Novara came steaming gallantly in, dropping anchor at a short distance to the south of the Castle of Uloa. The cannons thundered on sea and land, like the artillery of heaven; loud huzzas rent the air from the living mass that swarmed the wharf, sea-shore, and house-tops; rockets hissed through the heated air; musicians were blowing themselves into notice; hats, handkerchiefs, flags, and banners were waving, high and low; the crowd, looking as though their greatest expectations had been realized, could hardly believe what their eyes beheld. Never did the arrival of living man cause in Vera Cruz such a gala-day, such a shout of universal joy. The arrival of Cortez, more than three centuries ago, might have been more surprising, but not half so welcome.

CHAPTER VIII.

Maximilian's proclamation at Vera Cruz—Ceremonies there—En route to Cordova—Orizaba—Puebla—Guadalupe—At the Capital.

IN the afternoon of the 28th of May, soon after the arrival of the steamer Novara at Vera Cruz, the following proclamation was issued by Maximilian, and circulated through that city:

"MEXICANS:

"You have desired my presence! Your noble nation, by a voluntary majority, has chosen me to watch henceforth over your destinies! I gladly respond to this call.

"Painful as it has been for me to bid farewell forever to my own, my native country, I have done so, being convinced that the Almighty has pointed out to me, through you, the noble mission of devoting all my strength and heart to a people who, tired of war and disastrous contests, sincerely wish for peace and prosperity; to a people who, having gloriously obtained their independence, desire to reap the benefit of civilization and true progress.

"The confidence which animates you and me will be crowned by a brilliant success, if we always remain united to defend valiantly the great principles which are the only true and lasting bases of modern States—the principles of inviolable and immutable justice, equality before the law, an open road to every one to every career and social position, complete personal liberty well defined, having in it the protection of the individual and property, the improvement of national riches, the advancement of agriculture, of mining, and of industry, the establishment of ways of communication for an extensive commerce, and finally, the free development of intelligence in all that relates to the public interest.

"The blessings of Heaven, and with them progress and liberty, will not surely be wanting, if all parties, under the guidance of a strong and loyal government, unite to realize the objects I have just indicated, and if we always continue animated by the sentiment of religion, by which our country has been distinguished even in the most unfortunate times.

"The civilizing flag of France, raised to such a high position by her noble Emperor, to whom you owe the regeneration of order and peace, represents the same principles. This is what, some months ago, in sincere and disinterested language, the chief of her troops said to you, as the announcement of a new era of happiness.

"Every country which has desired to have a future, has succeeded in being great and strong by following this road. United, loyal, and firm, God will give us strength to reach the degree of prosperity which is the object of our ambition.

"Mexicans! the future of our beautiful country is in our hands. As to me, I offer you a sincere will, loyalty, and a firm intention to respect your laws, and to cause them to be respected with an invariable authority.

"God and your confidence constitute my strength: the flag of independence is my symbol: my motto you already know, 'Equity in Justice;' I will be faithful to it all my life. It is my duty to wield the sceptre conscientiously, and the sword of honor with firmness.

"The enviable task belongs to the Empress to consecrate to the country all the noble sentiments of Christian virtue, and the mildness of a tender mother.

"Let us unite to carry out a common object; let us

forget past sorrows; let us bury party hatred, and the Aurora of Peace and of deserved happiness will radiantly beam forth again over the new Empire.

"MAXIMILIAN.

"VERA CRUZ, May 28th, 1864."

Lieutenant-General Almonte being the highest officer in the Imperial service, was the proper one to receive the new Sovereigns. At five o'clock that morning he left Cordova for Vera Cruz, reaching there about five o'clock in the afternoon. Everybody was anxiously waiting his arrival. The fact was, the arrival of the distinguished personages was sooner than was anticipated; hence the delay in preparations.

A committee, composed of the city officers, assembled at the palace; and, on the arrival of General Almonte, escorted him to the wharf amid the roars of the cannon and the huzzas of the people. The General first had a private interview with the Emperor. Immediately after, the city officers, headed by the Prefect, D. Domingo Bureau, were presented by the Minister, Señor Velazquez de Leon.

His Majesty was in the saloon on the upper deck, dressed in a black frock-coat, white vest and pants, and black cravat. The committee were dressed in the same manner.

The presentation being completed, the Prefect addressed Their Majesties as follows:

"SIRE:

"Truly will the day be ever memorable on which Your Imperial Highness reached Mexico, as the desired savior to establish the Empire, which has been proclaimed under auspices so favorable, since no one having a good heart and a religious belief can fail to recognize the benign hand of Providence in the admirable events which have prepared the regeneration of this beautiful and desolated country, opening up an enviable future, under the illustrious and benign sceptre of Your Imperial Majesty.

"The new era which commences for the Mexicans is full of hope, founded on the wisdom and noble designs which inspire Your Imperial Majesty in raising this nation (now so low) to the height of a prosperous destiny.

"Your Imperial Majesty is welcome to your new country, with which, in doing it the honor of adopting it as your own, you have wished to identify your fate.

"May God bless the noble purpose which guides Your Imperial Majesty in favor of the Mexicans, and crown with the most complete success your grand, civilizing, and Christian undertaking.

"As Political Prefect of this District, and in the name of the authorities and inhabitants of the same, I have the honor and the satisfaction of congratulating Your Imperial Majesty, and Your Majesty the Empress, for your fortunate arrival on the soil of Mexico, and of presenting you our complete and sincere adhesion, as well as our most profound respect."

His Majesty made the following reply:

"I view with pleasure the arrival of the day when I can walk the soil of my new and beautiful country, and salute the people who have chosen me. May God grant that the good-will that led me toward you may be advantageous to you; and that all good Mexicans uniting to sustain me, there will be better days for the future. The important department and city of Vera Cruz, which have been so much distinguished for their patriotism, ought to be sure of my benevolence. This port being the principal entrance to the interior, my solicitude will be devoted to the opening and extending of its commerce.

"Gentlemen, I promise to return to see you in a more favorable season, and then to remain with you as long as it may be necessary."

His Majesty then entered the other saloon, and taking the Empress by the arm, walked to the centre of the saloon, in presence of the committee; then the Minister, Señor Velazquez de Leon, advanced and presented the committee to Her Majesty. The Prefect immediately complimented her in the following terms:

"MADAM:

"Your Majesty will please condescend to receive the most sincere congratulation and the most perfect homage from the authorities and inhabitants of this district. While I have the honor to present the committee to Your Majesty on your fortunate arrival, they are struck with admiration by the virtues and talents your noble character presents. Providence has offered Mexico the double benefit of an enlightened Sovereign, united in destiny with Your Majesty, an object of affection and respect with all good hearts, and Mexico recognizes in you a worthy spouse of our elected Emperor. The Mexicans, Madam, who expect so much from the good influence of Your Majesty in favor of all that is noble and great, of all that bears relation to the elevated sentiments of religion and of country, bless the moment in which Your Majesty reached the soil, and proclaim in one voice, 'Long live the Empress!'"

The Empress, very gracefully and briefly, in Spanish, responded.

Soon after this ceremony had taken place, Their Majesties retired, in company with General Almonte, and the committee of city officers returned on shore.

That day, on board the steamer, the Emperor appointed

General Almonte the Grand Marshal of the Court and Minister of the Imperial House.

He addressed the following note to the General:

"MY DEAR GENERAL ALMONTE:

"At the moment in which I receive from your hands the affairs of the Empire, I hasten to give you, in presence of the whole country, which owes you such great obligations, a public proof of my acknowledgment.

"I have decided to appoint you Grand Marshal of the Court and Minister of the Imperial House; remitting you, with your appointment, the regulations and instructions which will guide you in the fulfilment of such distinguished functions.

"Receive, General, the proof of my consideration and appreciation.

"MAXIMILIAN.

"ON BOARD THE 'NOVARA,' May 28th, 1864."

Their Majesties were quite anxious to remain a few days in Vera Cruz, to become better acquainted with the inhabitants, and to ascertain their wants. But on account of the hot season, a somewhat dangerous one for those not acclimated, and by some considerable solicitation on the part of their friends, they were persuaded to change their determination, and to hasten on to breathe the mountain air. It was therefore decided that they would disembark on the following morning, at an early hour. The committee of city officials presented themselves on board at a very early hour the next morning, and at five o'clock Mass was said in presence of Their Majesties and the committee. His Majesty then observed: "I wish, in the future, that there be no distinction made between those who are Indians and those who are not. All are Mexicans, and have equal right to my solicitude."

The small boats were ordered to be ready, and soon Their Majesties and retinue were gliding to the shore. On arriving upon the wharf, at the entrance of the city gate, the President of the Ayuntamiento, D. Salvador Carrau, accompanied by the Council and public officers, presented to His Majesty the key of the city, which was neatly wrought, and placed on a silver waiter; at the same time congratulating him on his arrival.

The Emperor made a very happy reply.

At the conclusion thereof, Their Majesties and General Almonte entered an open carriage and rode through the principal streets, followed by many other carriages, horse and footmen. Triumphal arches were raised at various points, richly and gayly decorated; windows were wreathed with flags and flowers, and verses in honor of the new Sovereigns were visible in every direction; while the loud huzzas almost drowned the music of the band.

A short time only was occupied in viewing the city. Their Majesties and suite were soon placed in a car, and the remainder of the escort in another. They reached Soledad at nine o'clock, where they breakfasted. The escort from Vera Cruz, composed of the municipal authorities, returned from Loma Alta—there bidding Their Majesties farewell. The party did not reach Cordova until two o'clock the following morning. Notwithstanding the lateness of the hour, the city was all alive—a blazing mass of illumination. The late arrival was caused by the breaking of one of the axletrees of the carriage in which Their Majesties rode; the night was dark and rainy; but the Sovereigns did not seem to be troubled by the accident in the least—they were so much delighted with the desire exhibited by their subjects to do all they could for them under the circumstances. Long before they reached Cordova, a number of Indians were sent out from that city with torches, which they carried in front of the carriage, and which enabled the driver to clearly see the road.

As they arrived at the *garita*, or entrance of the city limits, they were met by the President of the Ayuntamiento (or Town Council), and other city officers. The President then delivered to His Majesty the keys of the city of Cordova; at the same time addressing him in behalf of the city.

After their arrival in Cordova, that morning at ten o'clock there was a solemn *Te Deum* and Mass at the church. Soon after, the city authorities assembled at the palace, and were presented to Their Majesties. In response to the congratulations of those officers, the Emperor said:

"With true pleasure we see you, Gentlemen, near and around us, and we accept your good desires. May the day in which I find myself for the first time among you and in the heart of my new and beautiful country, be one of peace and sweet confidence. Being with all my heart a Mexican, it is my first and most ardent wish that all my compatriots may unite at my side, in order to be able, with zeal and perseverance, and upon free bases corresponding to our epoch, to work for the good of our noble country. In this simultaneous action will be found our strength and our future. You, Gentlemen, that are the representatives of this district and city, must, before all, give your fellow-citizens the example of union, of zeal, and of true patriotism."

His Majesty then addressed the Ayuntamiento thus:

"With sincere pleasure we salute you, Gentlemen. The sacred duties which the Mexican nation has imposed upon us, and those which we wish to enter upon with entire and loyal abnegation, call us forthwith to the

Capital of the Empire. We cannot then, I regret it, remain a long time in your beautiful and interesting city. Notwithstanding, say to your fellow-citizens, that the Empress and I propose, within a short time, to pass several days among you; and that then it will be for me an agreeable task and duty to study the wants and the desires of the city and its dependencies."

In the evening a fine dinner was given to the city authorities and other persons of note, numbering in all forty. Fireworks were blazing on every corner; while music was gladdening the hearts of the lookers-on.

The next morning, at eight o'clock, Their Majesties were again on the road to Orizaba, a distance of six leagues. Before reaching that place, they found a concourse of people assembled at Barranca de la Villegas, which they could not pass unnoticed. The Sovereigns and retinue halted awhile; and after receiving a complimentary speech, and making a short response, they moved on. Having arrived at the *Escarmela*, or entrance to the city limits of Orizaba, they found a deputation of city officials, and among them the Prefect, who saluted Their Majesties in the name of the city. The Emperor, resting one hand on a table, and having the Empress at his side, made a very affectionate reply.

There was a continual stream of people, banners, flowers, and music all along the road.

Subsequently, within the city of Orizaba, in answer to an address made by the Municipal Prefect, His Majesty said:

"With particular satisfaction, I and the Empress my wife receive your good wishes. The love with which our new country greets us, profoundly moves us, and we think it a happy sign of an agreeable future. If all unite with us with the sole end of promoting the lasting greatness and prosperity of our country, Providence then will crown our efforts; and as the Empire flourishes, the divers departments and cities will commence real progress. Orizaba, in particular, has a double interest in the completion of the railroad, which I propose not to lose sight of, and I believe the day will soon arrive when the Empress and I shall return to visit you by the new way open to steam."

He then spoke to the authorities of Orizaba in general, saying:

"In traversing the territory of my new and beautiful country, I receive with pleasure the demonstrations from the generous people who have called me to govern their destinies. May it please God to hear our prayers, and to give the Empire the era of peace which it so much requires to advance in greatness and prosperity.

"The benefit of really free institutions, an order of things regulated and lasting, united to the developed material which will offer you the means of easy communication, will assure you at last the complete exploration of the extraordinary riches with which Providence has favored your land above all the rest of the earth. My government will fix, particularly, its attention on your interest. You, Gentlemen, as their organs, I promise, will watch with zeal and patriotism the execution of my orders, and will take care of their punctual fulfilment."

On that day the Emperor wore white pants, a black frock coat, and a high-crown white hat, without any distinguishing mark of royalty. The Empress wore a dress and scarf of coffee-colored silk, and a hat of the same color.

Their Majesties were perfectly charmed with the country around Cordova and Orizaba. Its natural beauty and formation; its rich and luxuriant foliage; its valleys; the grandeur of the surrounding mountains,—all presented a magnificent panoramic view.

The remarkable beauty of the scenery which had been presented to them by books, by travellers, by the natives, began to be realized. They believed that their newly adopted country was equal to the sketch of their own bright fancies. As they cast their eyes upward and beheld the white mantle of winter's snow, while beneath and around them the rich plantations of coffee, sugar-cane, cotton, oranges, bananas, and all kinds of tropical fruit were spreading their beautiful, gently-hanging, green foliage, and scenting the balmy air with their honeyed breath; while the various feathered races, with their plumage dipped in the rainbow hues, were mingling their warbling notes with the soft-tuned guitar and the sweet accents of the fair daughters of Moctezuma; while they contemplated all this great picture-gallery of nature, with the productive soil beneath, and still deeper down a mighty body of mother earth all interlaced with arteries and veins of gold and silver, they were indeed enchanted. His Majesty exclaimed, "How beautiful our country is!"

As their Majesties were entering Orizaba, the people desired to take the mules from the carriage and draw it by hand; but His Majesty did not wish to accept such homage as that. After his positively refusing, they retired from the carriage with a perfect good-will, giving at the same time the wildest shouts of enthusiasm.

The following day, June 1st, about nine o'clock in the morning, the Empress received a committee of ladies from the district of Augustina, who, after congratulating her upon her arrival, presented her with a ring, which she placed upon her finger, saying that she would ever preserve it as a sweet recollection of her trip through Orizaba.

An hour later, Their Majesties attended Mass at the church. At the conclusion of the service they visited the schools and hospitals. The Emperor examined minutely the apartments occupied by the men; while the Empress gave a thorough look at the rooms and inmates in the female apartment. His Majesty then visited the prisons, asking each one therein how he was treated, and for what he was there.

Later in the day, at the palace, the curate of Naranjal (an Indian town) was presented to Their Majesties, together with the Alcalde and Rejidor of the town; also, two young Indian girls. The Alcalde made a speech to the Emperor in the Aztec language, which was as follows:

"No mahuistililoni tlactocatziné, nican tiquimopielia mo icno masehual conetzihua, ca san ye ohualacque o mitzmotlacpalhuiliztinoto, ihuan ica tiquimomachtis ca huel senca techyolpaqui mo hualialitzin impampa itech tiqueta aco se cosamalotl quixikintihuitz inon mexicolis mixtl nesi ye omochautiheaipan to thactocazotl. In senhulitini mitztitlania, ma ye huatzin mitzmochicahuili ica titechmaquixtis. Nis tiquinopielia inin maxochtzintl, quen se machiotl in tetlasotla litzin, mitzmo maquilia mo xocotitlan coneztzitzihua."

This speech was translated into Spanish, and in English reads thus:

"Our honorable Emperor, here you have these poor Indians, your children, who have come to salute you; and by that you know that your coming much pleases their hearts; because in it they see, as it were, a rainbow which dispels the clouds of discord that appear to have gathered in our kingdom. The Almighty sent you; it is He that gives you power to save us. Here is this flower; see in it the sign of our love. Your sons of Naranjal give it to you."

The flowers were woven with palm-leaves in the shape of a fan. They were peculiar to this country, called *siemprevivas* (ever-living). The colors were red and white, which, added to the green palm, constituted the colors of the Mexican flag.

The Emperor, in reply, addressed the Indians in the following words (which were spoken by him in Spanish, and interpreted to them):

"It is very pleasant to me, my dear children, to receive you as a commission from your town, because it is a proof of the confidence which you ought to place in me, in order to enjoy the peace and well-being which you have so long needed.

"You may count on the anxious care which I shall take to protect your interest, to favor your works and agricultural productions, and to improve in every manner your situation; and so you can tell it to the people of Naranjal."

The two Indian girls then presented the Empress with a little basket, a handkerchief, and a turtle-dove. Her Majesty thanked them very kindly, with a sweet smile on her face. This seemed to please the Indians highly. She then sent for a cage to put the dove in.

After visiting again the schools, examining the scholars in their different studies, and giving each a piece of gold money, Their Majesties returned to the palace to dine. A rich banquet was spread, at which the officers and some other prominent persons assisted. At eight and a half o'clock they retired from the table, to prepare for the ball, which took place at the residence of the French Consul, Señor Bernard. The house was most elegantly decorated for the occasion. The road to the house was lighted by torches, held by French soldiers. Their Majesties entered at ten o'clock, and were received by the municipal authorities and a committee of ladies and gentlemen at the entrance.

The first quadrille was formed as follows: The Emperor, with the lady of Gen. Almonte; the Empress, with Gen. Almonte; Señor Arrozo, with Madam Bernard; General Woll, with Madam Herrera; Gen. de Maussion, with Madam Adalid; Señor Suary Peredo, with Miss Swane.

The next quadrille His Majesty danced with Madam Herrera, and the Empress with General Maussion. Their Majesties retired at twelve o'clock, without partaking of the supper, remarking that it was not their custom to eat late at night. The ball went on till six in the morning.

The next morning at ten o'clock the Empress, plainly dressed, accompanied by two or three persons of her household, entered an ordinary carriage drawn by two mules, having a driver and lackey, and proceeded to visit the Carmelite Convent of Nuns. A collation had been prepared for Her Majesty, which was kindly accepted and eaten by her on a table before which, on two benches, the Nuns seated themselves. The Superior of the Convent requested the Nuns to take off their veils in honor of Her Majesty, and to remain uncovered until the eating was finished.

In the mean time the Emperor was occupied reading the newspapers, and receiving those who desired to meet him. Their Majesties contemplated a horseback ride at eleven o'clock, but on account of the weather they postponed it until four o'clock in the afternoon. As it rained at that hour of the afternoon slightly, they took a carriage and rode beyond the suburbs, as far as the cotton-factory called Cocolapam, about a mile distant; thence to the paper-mill; and thence to the Valley of Borrego. It soon ceased raining, then became clear, and the new rulers lingered awhile to contemplate the exquisite, the grand, the majestic beauty of the wild mountain-scenery. It would be difficult for the pen to over-color the appearance of nature around Orizaba. That section, and the Cordova Valley, are the gardens of Mexico.

That evening Their Majesties and the Grand Marshal ate together, exclusive of others. The people of Orizaba were very much surprised at the simplicity of their new Sovereigns. Their idea of royal personages was connected more with great dignity and pomp. And when they observed Their Majesties giving such attention to the poorest and most humble, it was beyond their expectation.

A small group of Republicans stood near where the Emperor was about to pass: of them it had been said that they did not intend to notice him when he neared them. His Majesty passed them, raising his hat very politely; and the group, by impulse as it were, immediately raised their hats. The gentleness of his manner overcame them, and they concluded that he was quite as democratic as they.

The Empress gave three hundred dollars to the Municipal Prefect for the benefit of the poor, and the sick of the hospitals.

At about eight o'clock the following morning Their Majesties were moving toward Puebla, escorted by mounted men, carriages, footmen, numbering thousands, amid the booming of artillery and the shooting of rockets. The air was freighted with music and perfumed by every kind of flower, like the ambrosial breeze of India; exquisitely-wreathed arches o'erhung the road,

6

while silvered apparel on horse and man glittered in the sun with diamond brightness; and fair gardens, ornamented with their golden fruit, burnished by the broad sunshine of the blushing moon, extended far and near. All, all this, drank in by the vision, with a mingled view of the wintry grandeur of Orizaba Peak, was enough for Fancy to call it the grand entrance to the golden bowers of Eden.

Their Majesties and retinue reached Acultzingo at half-past eleven, where they, for the first time, ate a Mexican breakfast of tortillas, chili (red peppers), and drank pulque, the fermented juice of the maguey plant. At this place they rested awhile, also taking another view of the country from a high hill. They could not refrain from seeking every prominent position to look at the scenery. They were enchanted. The road to Puebla was one continued bower of flowers, flags, banners, and poetical verses—it was a chain of ovations.

The Sovereigns entered the city of Puebla at ten o'clock on the morning of June 5th, surrounded by great splendor. Near the triumphal arch in the street of Alguacil, the ceremony of delivering the keys of the city to his Majesty by the Municipal Prefect took place, on which occasion the Emperor said:

"I accept, Gentlemen, with joy the keys of this city, because I see in this act that you place confidence in me, and understand my loyal intention; but being sure of your fidelity, I return them to you, asking only to possess your hearts."

After this the grand procession moved on into the city, and halted before the cathedral. Their Majesties stepped out of the carriage, and were received under a pall by the venerable Prelate and two Bishops; thence they passed into the temple, which was superbly adorned. A beautiful hymn was chanted, followed by other solemnities. At the conclusion, Their Majesties entered the Bishop's beautifully-decorated palace ; there the Political and Municipal Prefects each addressed them.

His Majesty responded first to the authorities of Puebla, thus :

" It is very flattering to us to see ourselves surrounded by the authorities of a department so important, and of a large and interesting city ; and with pleasure we receive your salutations. The noble Mexican people have placed in us their confidence. We shall consider it our duty to act accordingly, and to concentrate our efforts to procure for the nation the fulfilment of its just aspirations.

" Through the means of institutions really free, of exact justice, protection to persons and property, the Chief and his organs will be able to carry the country through the path of progress which leads to prosperity and true greatness.

" It belongs to Puebla, which is one of the largest central cities of the Empire, to shine forth as an example."

Then to the Ayuntamiento of Puebla he said :

" With a sentiment of pleasure mingled with grief, I see your city ;—with pleasure, I salute one of the largest, most beautiful, and important cities of the Empire ; with pain, I contemplate the unfortunate inhabitants agitated by the evils of political disruptions. The government to whose election you have contributed, will impose upon itself the task of healing your wounds as soon as possible, and of facilitating, through means of institutions which are in accordance with the age, the development of prosperity, so that the resources of this rich country may be cultivated in the highest degree. I hope the day is not far distant when the iron road will unite your valley with the ocean, and bring you such an abundant compensation that you will forget your past troubles. Then will this noble city be regenerated with new vigor and beauty."

On the 7th of June, the anniversary of the Empress's birthday, solemn Mass was said in the cathedral. Praises to the Almighty were sung by the Bishop, assisted by the choir and the whole audience. At seven o'clock in the evening a grand banquet was given at the palace, attended by about sixty persons.

At ten o'clock Their Majesties repaired to the Alhondiga, market building, where a grand ball was given in honor of Her Majesty's birthday. From the street to the foot of the stairway a carpet of flowers was strewn for Their Majesties to walk upon. In the angles of the court stood colossal pyramids, covered from their base up with crystal vases of variegated colors, which presented a group of rainbow hues, reflected from the brilliant evening lights.

Their Majesties entered, taking possession of the throne erected for the occasion. Presently a quadrille was called. His Majesty, accompanied by Señora Da Guadalupe Osio de Pardo, took his position; the Empress, with the Political Prefect, Señor D. Fernando Pardo, stood opposite: General Brincourt accompanied Señora Navarrete de Marion; and opposite them stood General D. Maussion, with Señora Da Dolores Quesada de Almonte: at the right of the Emperor was General Woll and Señora Da Emilia Cota de Tapia, and the Municipal Prefect, D. Juan E. de Uriarte, with Señora Da Guadalupe Pardo de Pardo; on the left, the Minister of State, D. J. M. de Arroyo, with Señora Da Guadalupe Almonte; and Colonel Jeanningras, with Señora Da Carmen Marron de Gonzales.

The Empress wore a plain but elegant white silk dress. On her head was a crown of diamonds and emeralds, with a red and a white rose—the Mexican colors. A superb necklace of diamonds brilliantly sparkled, and rich bracelets of precious stones dazzled in the evening light.

The Emperor with the Empress left the room at half past twelve. The next noonday they were again in the carriage, advancing toward Cholula, for the great Capital. Stopping occasionally to gratify the curiosity of their subjects, who showed unparalleled good-will, they reached Guadalupe on the eleventh of June, making their entry at two o'clock in the afternoon. They were with great solemnity received by the Archbishops of Mexico and Michoacan, under a pall, near the railroad station: they were also there met by the civil authorities of the town. They soon entered the renowned church of Guadalupe, and there occupied the throne in the presbytery. The illustrious Señor Labastida, accompanied by the other prelates present, intoned the *Domine Salvum fac Imperatorum.* After this solemn act, Their Majesties passed into the sacristy; thence into the chapter.

The authorities of the town being gathered into one of the halls, it was announced that Their Majesties would soon advance to the capital of the nation, one league distant from Guadalupe. Loud cheers rent the very air, and when silence prevailed, the Political Prefect of Mexico, Señor Villar y Bocanegra, remarked:

"At the foot of the prodigious hill of Tepeyac, and being separated only by a wall from the temple in which is venerated the protector and mother of the Mexicans, the Virgin Guadalupe—the Political Prefect of the first department of the Empire, the Municipal Prefect of the great Capital of Mexico, its Excellency the Ayuntamiento, the Illustrious Señor Archbishop, and other authorities, present themselves full of grateful pleasure, with their souls overflowing with joy, before their beloved Sovereigns, to congratulate them on their pleasant arrival at the gate of the city in which is erected the throne which has been raised by the Mexicans for them. Words fail me to manifest our gratitude; because you have, in compassion for our misfortunes, abandoned another throne, riches, country, parents, brothers, and friends, and condescended to come and try to make us happy and save us from the evils that were causing us to disappear from the catalogue of nations. Your Majesties only knew through statements and papers the will of the people who applauded you; and now, to-day, you see that you are not deceived; and that from the shores of Vera Cruz to the gate of the Capital, all applaud their Sovereigns with an unbounded enthusiasm. The Mexicans will so continue until the end; and I protest, Sire, in the name of the department within my charge, that all of us will obey and assist the Monarchs, whom by acclamation we have chosen."

Tremendous shouts followed this address. After which, His Majesty, with a great deal of emotion, answered in the following words:

"Profoundly moved, I say, by the universal enthusiasm which I have received in all the towns in my transit, my emotion and my gratitude acquire greater intensity as I find myself at the gate of the Capital, as I see gathered to salute me its principal authorities, in a place so much respected and loved by me and the Empress, and by all Mexicans.

"I happily receive your congratulations, and I salute

you with the effusion of one who loves you, and has identified his fate with yours."

As the grand procession moved stately on to the place called the Plain of Aragon, they halted in a double line. Their Majesties passing through to a place designated, were met by two deputations, one of ladies, the other of gentlemen; both of whom saluted the Sovereigns, and presented, in behalf of the inhabitants of the Capital of the Empire, congratulations; those to Maximilian were as follows, viz:

"SIRE:

"The undersigned, natives and foreigners, residents of the Capital of Mexico, all agreeing in their aspirations for peace and public order, without distinction of political opinions, and with the most profound respect, hasten to salute Your Imperial Majesty, voluntarily and sincerely, and also your august spouse, on your arrival at the Capital of the new-born Empire of Mexico.

"We well understand the magnitude of the arduous and glorious undertaking which is imposed on Your Imperial Majesty. We estimate the abnegation at its full value, also the faith and spirit which animate the illustrious founder of the Empire; and we foresee the good, for which the future of this unfortunate nation will be your debtor.

"We comply, therefore, with a sacred duty in offering before Your Imperial Majesty the effusion of our thanks, the testimony of our admiration, and the most solemn protest to co-operate with all our strength for the realization of the noble and generous mission which, by a decree of high Providence, has been committed to Your Imperial Majesty—that of redeeming and regenerating a people destroyed by civil discord.

"May it please Your Imperial Majesty to accept

favorably our wishes for the happiness of your person, and that of your august consort, and for the prosperity of your kingdom."

The deputation of ladies offered, in behalf of the ladies of the Capital, to Her Majesty the Empress, the following affectionate address:

"MADAM:

"The presence of Your Imperial Majesty in this part of the New World, as a companion of the magnanimous Prince destined by Heaven to govern it, has just realized the many honors which are reunited on the throne which is raised to-day upon the love of this people. Our happiness is complete, in representing before Your Imperial Majesty the families of the Empire, and of being the organ of these sentiments of affectionate adhesion and of purified fidelity with which Your Majesty is surrounded, in the midst of an applause and of a rejoicing which have no limits, and which would be the best title (if there could be any superior to your noble virtues) to the crown which encircles your brow, and which prepares for Mexico a worthy name from the glorious race which brought, with Christianity, to these distant regions, culture and civilization.

"Policy, Madam, will speak under a thousand different forms of the prosperous exchange which it realizes, and which excites such a lively and deep interest in Europe and America. It only belongs to us to contemplate your eminent qualities, with which divine Providence has endowed you, without doubt, with the design that there may shine in them all that is elevated in the majesty of the throne, all that is tender in the heart of princes, and all that is exemplary and modest in the bosom of private life. With Your Majesty and your august husband, who are the objects of public admiration, and the delight of this vast Empire, commences the dynasty which takes the name of your new country. It will be able to figure by the side of the country of Charles V. and Mary Theresa; by that of Louis Philippe and Napoleon III., and by that of the respected and beloved Sovereign the father of Your Imperial Majesty.

"We, Madam, shall never cease blessing you for the services you render Religion, the fountain of the greatness of Mexico, and of that generous character which is ennobled to-day by a model and by an example which cannot be less than admired. Your Imperial Majesty being a worthy heir of two great queens, your grandmother and your mother, religion can suffer nothing before your throne. And when Heaven, with a singular clemency, sent us a pledge of peace and union which may cause us to forget what has divided Mexicans, we cannot deceive ourselves by assuring Your Majesty that those wishes and that hope are going to be realized.

"Permit us, then, Your Majesty, to present you the profound homage of our respect and of our obedience, and the warm gratitude with which the families of the Capital are possessed, and who bless your name, and who will never cease asking Divine Providence for the happiness of the kingdom, and of your august husband, to whom He so visibly dispenses His bountiful protection. Your genius and your piety will assure your new country a worthy name in the world, and a prolonged peace."

The quarters reserved for Their Majesties were the Collegiate church. The Archbishop escorted them into it, and said to the Emperor, "This is the house provided for Your Majesty." He replied, "It is magnificent."

The Sovereigns remained over-night; and on that day and the following they received many people in their apartments.

The next day, Sunday, the 12th of June, after Mass

was said, Their Majesties entered the cars for the Capital. Arriving at the station in the city, they were surrounded by an immense throng, waiting to escort them to the cathedral and palace. Banners, flags, and flaunting streamers of all kinds were to be seen on every side. Triumphal arches festooned with orange-blossoms scented the balmy air; ribbons and roses, all tinselled, twisted, and curled, covered the earth, and were woven in wreaths at every window; portraits of the Sovereigns were smiling at you in every street; ladies were gayly attired, as for their wedding-day; polished carriages mirrored the passing objects; mounted men with their silver-corded broad-brimmed hats, were prancing their gallant steeds all mantled with saddles, bridles, and housings woven with silver and gold; uniformed soldiers all laced for review, with glittering lances and gold-burnished armory;—all, all, glittered like a bed of diamonds. And while all these were gleaming in the eye, artillerymen and musicians were tingling the ear with their variations, from the mellow breath of the flute and horn to the thunder-notes of the deep-toned cannon, mingled with shouts, the neigh of horses, and the chiming of bells; until it appeared as though the world was turned into a gorgeous show, where audience and actors were promiscuously mingled.

When Their Majesties, with their grand *cortège*, arrived at the stopping-place called *Parador de la Concepcion*, they halted, and received from the hands of the Municipal Prefect, D. Miguel Maria Azcárate, the keys of the city; at the delivery of which, the Prefect, in a short address, welcomed the new rulers in a most cordial manner. The Emperor, with a good deal of feeling, responded, as though he believed that the reverence paid him came from the depths of the Mexican heart.

The keys that were delivered to His Majesty were of gold, beautifully enamelled in places, and richly wrought by a Mexican artist. One had on its head an eagle; the other possessed the imperial diadem; and both were placed on a silver waiter of exquisite filigree-work.

The Sovereigns then entered their carriage again, and proceeded through the city, followed by the splendid procession, until they reached the ancient, the costly, and far-famed cathedral of the city of Mexico, adorned with massive silver and gold. Halting in front of that venerated temple, the imperial pair stepped down from their vehicle, and were received by the Archbishop, under a pall, a richly emblazoned canopy of metallic lustre, and entered the holy sanctuary. The main door of that immense, massive structure was decorated with an arch woven with red, white, and yellow flowers, surmounted with the imperial crown of the same material, made by the Indians of Xochimilco, and in which was interlaced this inscription, "Xochimilco to His Imperial Majesty Maximilian I." The arch was surmounted with a circular inscription, traced with flowers, as follows: "11th of June, 1864." At each door of the cathedral was an oil portrait of the Emperor. The interior was illuminated and decorated gorgeously. Velvet tapestry of bright cochineal hue, elegantly fringed with balls of gold pendent therefrom; streamers hanging from the arched dome, with trophies of national ensigns mingled therewith; Mexican, French, Austrian, and Belgian banners representing the friendly powers: and with all this magnificence, the mantle of solemnity was worn by all, in reverence for the place and occasion.

Their Majesties occupied the throne prepared for them. His Majesty was dressed in the uniform of a Mexican General, bearing upon his breast the insignia of Grand Master of the Order of Guadalupe. The Empress wore a blue-and-white silk dress, a blue scarf, and a hat adorned only with beautiful flowers, as fresh as her own fair cheek.

As the imperial pair took their position, the grand Te Deum commenced, intoned by the Most Reverend Señor Labastida, accompanied by the accomplished orchestra.

At the end of this solemn ceremony, Their Majesties, escorted by the Archbishop, Bishops, and clergy, proceeded on foot to the palace, over carpeted ground, beneath an elegant canopy, a distance of about six hundred feet. Having arrived in the palace, preparations were soon made to receive the officers of State and other distinguished persons.

The master of ceremonies, according to the rules of etiquette, called the authorities of the government in order, and presented them to Their Majesties. The first called were the acting Secretaries of State and General Bazaine. Soon after this, the Sovereigns rested awhile, and were ready to view the artificial lights at night, which are in Mexico, at times, presented in a superb style.

That night was illuminated beyond comparison; so that it seemed as if day had broken forth by mistake, from the disarrangement of the "orbed continent." Everything dazzled in the dancing lights, from house-tops down. Jets of fire whizzed here and there, like meteors in the heavens; stars were bursting in the sky, imitating the vault of the universe; wheels of rainbow-fire whirled on their axes as though turned by the wild lightning spirits that darted athwart the heavens with comet speed; and one might well have fancied that the great Pyrotechnist was that ancient war-god, Mexitli, who had been aroused from his five centuries of slumber by the announcement of that tumultuous demonstration of splendor, and, swelling forth a blast from his trump of battle, led on his mighty host in barbaric pomp, and flamed the heavens with his fiery elements of war.

With all that dazzling blaze ended the gay pomp of that gorgeously arrayed procession, that turned its back upon the sea, traced the heated sands, and, through richly enamelled vegetation, wound up the rugged steeps of picturesque grandeur. What a change! what a variety they passed through, as they left the murmurs of the loud-voiced ocean to view the glassy lakes around that fair city, where centuries ago the ancestors of Maximilian laid claim to its lands and waters, when the name of Moctezuma was synonymous with the god of earth.

If it be thought that this description is painted in too glowing colors, and considered but a sketch of fancy, let those speak who saw the glittering reality, and who will clearly testify that this is no web of fiction.

It would be no easy task to delineate in true shades the splendor and magnificence of the festivities in honor of that great event, the re-establishment of the Mexican Empire.

The smiling faces of the Mexican people at that time, among high and low, were the dial-plates of their hearts. Thus thought observing foreign residents.

It seems to me that it cannot well be denied that such an exhibition of magnificence may truly be considered as some evidence of the real affections of the people. That it could all be a disguise is not probable. Those who were close observers of all that show of pomp and merriment, are of opinion that it was a mirror which reflected the true sentiments of the citizens of Mexico.

CHAPTER IX.

National palace—Maximilian's course in Mexico—Personal character—Revenue as Emperor—Manner of living—Decrees—Palace of Chapultepec—Residence at Cuernavaca—Scenery on the road.

THE residence of the Emperor in the city of Mexico was the National Palace.

On the north side of the great square, or Plaza Mayor, stands the far-famed temple, the Cathedral. It has an exquisitely-wrought and costly façade, but its exterior is so dimmed by time that it carries your mind far back into the past. It reckons its age by centuries. As you turn your eyes from it, toward the rising east, you observe a long, very long and massive pile of stone and mortar, that stretches across the entire eastern side of that square, a distance of two hundred and forty-six varas, or Spanish yards. That is the National Palace. It has no architectural beauty, no polish of surface, but you are struck at the sight of its length with a little surprise, and you look again to see if you are not mistaken as to its being one building; then *immensity* is the word that your thoughts suggest.

The same ground supported the lordly palace of Moctezuma. This ancient city, called by the Aztecs Tenuchtitlan, was taken by the conquering soldiers of Cortez, August 13th, 1521, and then nearly destroyed. The Spaniards began its reconstruction in 1524. Then was laid a part of its present foundation. If the records be not incorrect, that palace belonged to the family of Cortez until 1562, when it was purchased by the king of Spain for the viceroy, for the sum of thirty-three thousand three hundred dollars. The royal officers took possession August 19th of the same year. The capacity of the building was, after many years' service, found inadequate for the purposes of governmental affairs, and, in 1693, it was rebuilt, at an expense of nearly a million of dollars.

Tradition has handed down a decree, written in the Book of Fate, which reads that no man can occupy that palace as a ruler over Mexico without coming to an unnatural death, or meeting with some sad misfortune,—that such a Sovereign should stoop from his pride of place, and answer to the call of the executioner, or misfortune's beck! As we look over the long list of chiefs, we see with what unerring judgment Fate has followed them. Arista among the dead, Juarez among the living, are the exceptions.

The palace covers a block of ground, and is square. The two front corners have each a tower. The floors are made of brick, with the exception of a few, which are wooden. It has three stories. There appears to be three general divisions. The southern part was occupied by the Emperor and Empress; the centre by officers of State; and the northern by soldiers and prisoners. The eastern half also was occupied by soldiers. There are three entrances into the façade. The centre one leads you into a court which is about one hundred and fifty feet square, surrounded by two corridors, one above the other, both of which are supported by ten arched stone columns on each side.

On the north side of this court is the apartment now occupied by the President, and formerly, under the Empire, by the Princess Iturbide. The southern entrance opens into a court about seventy-five feet by sixty, also surrounded by corridors. The northern door conducts into another court, without any corridor. There are several other courts in the eastern half, for the purposes of light, air, and convenience of communication.

The lower story was occupied by servants, and as store and carriage houses. The second story, with lower ceiling, was for offices.

The great reception-room, sometimes called the Iturbide Saloon, is in the front of the third story of the southern half of the palace, being about two hundred and fifty by thirty-six feet in dimensions. This is not a remarkably fine or costly room. The ceiling exhibits the cross-timbers, polished and varnished, with gilt edges. It has about a dozen candelabras pendent, and several supported by stands of large Chinese vases. The floor is of dark wood, neatly laid. This saloon contains many fine oil portraits — among which are those of General Washington, Emperor Iturbide, President Arista, Generals Guerro, Matamoras, and Mina; Curates Hidalgo and Morelas. That of the Emperor Maximilian has been taken down, leaving the frame in its position. They are all life-size, and in large gilt frames.

Adjoining, and running parallel on the east, is the Lion Saloon, so called because two marble lions lie as sentinels therein, which room is about sixty by twenty feet. It is adorned with portraits of Ferdinand and Isabella, in one frame; also those of Charles V. and his mother, likewise within one frame. These are ancient paintings. Passing out of the south end of the reception-room into a small room, then turn facing the east, you enter the audience-room, which is at a right angle with the reception-room, and is nearly forty by twenty feet in extent, having an oaken floor, neatly made like inlaid work. The walls are covered with crimson silk damask, in which there are woven at regular intervals the Mexican coat of arms, also the words, "*Equidad en Justia*" (Equity in Justice). An adjacent room, with like walls, and cedar floor, one hundred by twenty feet, is the picture-gallery, now unadorned by paintings.

The chapel is the room formerly used by the Senate, under the old Constitution, prior to 1857, when the legislative body had a Senate. It is seventy-five feet by twenty-five, with plastered walls, covered with silk for a space of twenty feet in length by fifteen in height on each side near the altar. The ceiling has a blue ground, spangled with stars. On each side of the aisle there is a row of nine pews, each capable of holding six persons. On the left, near the altar, were two seats for Their Majesties. The room is lighted by six semicircular windows near the ceiling. The altar was quite plain, having a cross with the Saviour, gilded, and six large candlesticks. There is also a gallery over the entrance.

Attached to the palace, and within the outer walls of the exterior, is a small garden, with not a large variety of flowers; but among them is one borne by a tree some twenty-feet high, which flower is in the shape of a bird's claw, flesh-color, called *manito* (small-hand), and blossoms in February. This is a rare tree, and it has been said to be the only one in Mexico. A fountain throws up its jets of water, that sparkle in the sun, and reflect prismatic hues. A small theatre was built therein for imperial recreation. Such is a partially delineated picture of that mansion where monarchs and presidents have held their courtly revels, nearly all of whom now dwell in mansions not coveted by man. Maximilian once observed that he always felt in that palace like a solitary nun in a convent.

As Maximilian became seated on his throne, and surveyed his new country, its people, their habits and customs, the condition of the exchequer, the friendly and inimical surrounding powers, it was quite apparent that there was a great scope for the exercise of administrative talent, as well as military.

It is true it was hoped that the contending struggle of the bordering Republic would so long continue that sufficient attention could not be given from that source to the new Empire, to endanger its permanency. And thus with the French elements—their bone and sinew, their munitions of war, for a few years, would give His Majesty time to have built a living wall out of the native material, that would be able to resist the disturbing factions within, which were mainly to be feared rather than any exterior attack. There was a contest against a great political principle, which is more hazardous than a mere struggle against man—Imperialism against Republicanism.

The great and continued enthusiasm which had been heaped upon him and the Empress, from the very moment they touched the shores of the Empire till they reached its capital, had brought the conviction to his mind that he was looked upon as their benefactor, and that the number of dissidents was far below the majority of the people. And yet he was not unmindful that, in an empire of such vast territorial extent, and in many parts so sparsely settled, diversified by mountain barriers, ready access to many important places, with adequate forces either defensive or offensive, was quite difficult. He saw the necessity, as it was plainly obvious, of having sufficient forces to keep down the spirit of civil discord fomented by the few malcontents. He was not ignorant of the fact that Mexico had always had at least two parties antagonistical to each other; and as it had thus been under a Republican form of government, the continuation of a disaffected party was in some degree to be expected; while, at the same time, it was by no means even *prima-facie* evidence that the latter was composed of anything near a majority of the citizens.

The Juarez party had fallen back from the heart of the country, until those that composed it found themselves away to the north, few in number, and without funds, while but a small part of the national territory acknowledged its sway.

The actual jurisdiction and possession of the Imperial forces had extended, like the rippling waves of the still waters from the drop of a pebble, until it embraced nearly all of the Mexican territory.

Whatever views the world, generally, may entertain as to the justness and correctness of the Emperor's conclusion in regard to the loyalty of the Mexicans, he was not alone in his judgment upon that point. There were but few foreign residents, if any, who had endeavored to observe affairs impartially, that did not coincide in that conclusion.

His Majesty began, immediately after his arrival, to busy himself in earnest with governmental operations. Many offices that were absolutely requisite for the just administration of affairs had been created and filled before his departure from Europe.

As he arrived on Sunday, the twelfth of June, at the Capital, one day was deemed necessary for rest and personal convenience. On the fourteenth he commenced business. Attention was forthwith given to the public debt, the repletion of the exchequer, the establishment of the national flag, the commissioning of the requisite officers, the appointing of ministers as representatives abroad, and of consuls, and the formation of courts of justice; all of which was illustrative of energy and ability.

It was a great principle with him, that all should be equal before the law; also, that whoever had cause of complaint should have a proper hearing, and before him in person, if they desired. In order that an opportunity should be given to address him personally, he decreed, in the latter part of June, 1864, that he would give a public audience at the National Palace at one o'clock on every Sunday, commencing on the first Sunday in the following July. Forty-eight hours' notice was required; also the registry of the name of the applicants in chronological order, not according to rank. Neither color nor poverty was a barrier to an interview with the Emperor, when any complaint was to be made or favor to be solicited.

On the 6th day of July, 1864, he issued a general amnesty to all political prisoners, which included those who had been sentenced.

The existing laws were speedily examined, in order that a just knowledge of the legislative wants of the people should be obtained. As rapidly as possible decrees were issued for the purpose of advancing immigration, education, commerce, mining and agricultural pursuits. Every stimulus was given to the business of developing the country, and increasing the modes of travelling and transportation, that could be, under the existing condition of affairs. Telegraphic and railroad enterprises were encouraged as much as possible.

The officials of the government were stimulated to the performance of their respective functions by medals of the different orders of merit, as His Majesty deemed them worthy.

The deportment of His Majesty toward all the officers in the various departments of government, from the highest to the lowest, was most affable and kind. He never exhibited the slightest haughtiness. Every act of the Emperor was as void of aristocratical rigor as the proceedings of any former sovereign who bore the name of "President." It was difficult for the greater mass of the Mexicans to distinguish any very remarkable difference between the forms of the government under the Empire from those of the Republic. The main distinction rested in the greater activity of all classes of business under the former, while in fact it savored quite as much of democracy. Under the Republic, the President issued decrees; under the Empire, the Emperor did likewise. The latter established laws equally liberal in every respect as the former; and his courts of justice were composed of the best class of men, the most learned in the science of jurisprudence. One of the Emperor's great leading maxims was justice. His motto, that met the eye in every public place, was, "Equity in Justice."

Sin, plated with gold, was no impenetrable armor to the sword of justice; and poverty clothed in rags received no greater infliction from the same weapon. There was a broad equality, which, if it had received the appellation of "republican," could hardly have appeared less oppressive to the mind or purse.

The great business community were of opinion that the nature of the institutions of the Empire were highly favorable to the advancement of commerce and the general interests of the country. The lower class perceived no objection to the reign of His Majesty, but were rather pleased with it. The Indians have been frequently observed drawing a piece of money from their pockets which had the form of His Majesty's head upon it, pointing to it, and saying, "That is the man who protects us." It is some proof, at least, that that class of the community were not impressed with the belief that oppression was allotted to them.

The Emperor and Empress both paid a great deal of attention to the education and support of the poor. Hospitals were established, visited, and cared for, by those sovereigns, as much as time would permit.

No ruler of the nation had a greater desire to develop the resources of the country, to advance its general prosperity, and to educate the people. Although a monarch, he did not believe that his empire would be better supported by the columns of ignorance. He was enthusiastically in favor of popular instruction. Solid, stable, as well as decorative knowledge, he thought should be widely diffused. He was equally enthusiastic in opposition to bigotry and intolerance. To have a few brilliant intellectual lights illuminating the general darkness, was for him insufficient; he wished every human being within his Empire to be a light of knowledge, whose brilliancy should be increased by the oil of perseverance and time. He was emphatically the friend of mankind. Probably no prince in Europe was more democratic in all his views than he.

His show of sympathy towards men was real; for he had in that no vanity, no pride, to be satisfied with the buzz of admiration. It was that satisfaction only which his conscience received from the performance of duty. He believed in his heart that it was his religious duty to enlighten his people. He viewed with admiration all moral advancement. He was a monarch by title—a republican in his actions.

One day, while in the city of Morelia, in the State of Michoacan, an ordinary Mexican cried out, "Viva the President of the Empire!" His Majesty smiled, and said that he would not object to the adoption of that title, but that the people in Europe might criticize it.

The revenue of His Majesty was at first fixed at one and a half million of dollars per annum, by the Regency. After the first year, it was reduced to one half of a million, at his suggestion. The first amount was the same as that allowed the first Emperor, Iturbide, by the Mexican Congress, December 28th, 1822. Although His Majesty drew a large amount of his revenue, yet he personally received no particular benefit therefrom, except a comfortable living. He was not extravagant; and the money unappropriated for his household affairs went to the poor. The greater part of his revenue was spent for charitable purposes, and the payment of the officers on the Civil List. All of it circulated in the country. So that its expenditure benefited the mechanic, the merchant, and especially the poor.

Thus it would appear, at first blush, that the sovereign head of the nation was oppressive in his financial demands upon a considerably exhausted exchequer, yet, after all, he was exceedingly frugal in fact.

The Emperor lived plainly. Nor could the articles of his household furniture be considered of too costly a character for a sovereign. He well knew that the greatness of a ruler was not measured by the value of the silver, gold, and brilliancies in his mansion; nor by the glitter of richly decorated equipage, with its long train of tinselled escort. It is true, that among his three elegant carriages there was one beyond the ordinary value and richness of vehicles which are made even for the conveyance of imperial sovereigns. But he obtained it by no expenditure from his own purse, nor the treasury of Mexico. It was presented to him by the citizens of the city of Milan, as a token of affection and esteem. One cannot view a gift of such artistic skill and of so much value, without being reminded of the fact, that Maximilian could not have been considered as a tyrannical Governor over the province of Lombard-Venice.

The exterior of that superb carriage is nearly all richly gilded—particularly the iron-work. The small part of the wood-work not gilded, is bright crimson. The exterior of the body is veneered with tortoise-shell. One large shell covers the door, on which is beautifully portrayed the Mexican coat of arms. The handles, hinges, buckles on the straps, the caps and rims of the hubs, a fabled griffin on the top at each corner, and the coat of arms surmounting the carriage on every side, are of solid silver. The top is about nine feet from the ground, curving outward a little, bell-shaped, and a foot wider than the centre. On each exterior corner is an angel some eighteen inches long, richly gilded all over.

The interior is of richly figured light-colored damask silk. It cost twenty-four thousand florins; which is less than twelve thousand dollars. It has been used but five times, twice in Milan, and three times in Mexico,—in the latter country, on the sixteenth day of September, 1864 and 1865, the anniversary of the Independence of Mexico, and on the sixth of July, 1865, the anniversary of Maximilian's birthday. It is now locked up in the carriage-house of the National Palace. It would suggest itself to refined minds of honor, that, inasmuch as it was a present from the people of Milan, the magnanimity of the conquerors ought to be great enough to cause it to be returned to the family of Maximilian.

The Emperor had forty mules, thirty of which were white; and six of the latter were usually driven in the carriage in which he rode. He also had sixty horses; several of which were expressly to be used under the saddle.

He was anxious to bring about harmony with the dissidents on the mildest terms. On the 27th of July, 1864, he issued a decree to the effect that those who felt disposed to lay down their arms, could do so, and return to private life, without being questioned as to their political views.

August 7th, 1864, he decreed that every one might freely express his opinion upon all official acts, with a view of showing their error and ill consequences.

Highway robbery became so frequent, that the Emperor issued a circular, September 16th, 1864, in which it was ordered that those charged with the crime of robbery should be tried before the French Court-martial. Many of those who were tried and executed for that crime have been considered by the Liberals as political prisoners, and the charge of cruelty therefor has been made against the Emperor.

Soon after the machinery of government under Maximilian was in good running order, he sought for a rural spot in which to repose—some place outside of the hum of the city walls, where he might survey Nature's beauty, reflect in silence upon the vastness and richness of his adopted home, and meditate upon the contemplated splendor that was to surround his new empire. And what could suggest loftier ideas than the sight of that bold, grand, and sublime mountain-pile, Popocatepetl, with its hoary head bathed in the summer cloud, while nearer and all around Nature was arrayed in her mantle of loveliest green, all studded with Flora's variegated colors. The Emperor found all this, coinciding in taste with Moctezuma, by selecting the famed hill of Chapultepec as his country-seat.

A little south of west, at a distance of two and a half miles from the city of Mexico, stands the palace or castle of Chapultepec, on elevated ground, nearly two hundred feet higher than the surrounding valley, which on the east side presents a porphyritic base, still bearing the prints of Aztec sculpture. The base of the hill from east to west is not far from fifteen hundred feet in length, and from north to south about one thousand, and oval in form. The eastern exterior line of the grounds is bounded by a long one-story stone house, nearly two hundred feet in length, near the centre of which is the entrance, through a large arched portal. Surrounding the hill for several hundred yards is a beautiful grove of elms, poplar, oak, and cedar. The latter class of tree has some among its number whose mighty trunks inform the traveller that they shaded the old chieftain Moctezuma from the noonday sun, while he plotted for the defence of his home against the advancing hordes of the Spanish invaders. The maguey, the narrow leaf pepper-tree, with its crimson berries, wild shrubbery, mingled here and there with some sweet-scented flowers, spread all over the steeps of that enchanted crest. An ancient road winds around its base, once only tracked by Indian foot-prints. Now is seen a superb macadamized road, that circles around from the east toward the right, until it reaches the summit of the terraced hill on the western side. This is one of the wise improvements of Maximilian. The building that faces the city is one hundred and twenty-five feet long, with two verandas, one above the other, supported by seven columns of the Doric order, between which is an iron balustrade three and a half feet high, richly gilded. From these verandas the view is perfectly enchanting. The great city in front, its cathedral, with its twin towers, catches the eye, as the great guiding object; the serrated mountains circled in the distance, the green lawns all around, studded with beautiful shade-trees, and variegated with the mosaic work of Art and Nature combined in its cultivated fields, present one of the most charming views to be witnessed anywhere. It causes the traveller to exclaim, "Who would not live in the valley of Mexico?"

The width of the front building is twenty-five feet. It has six rooms in the upper story, which was occupied by Their Majesties. There is nothing fine in the construction of this palace, nor did it contain costly furniture. The southern end has annexed thereto a tower ten feet in diameter, and about forty in height. The west side has also a veranda. The north end has a wing running west about twenty-five feet. About fifty feet in the rear of the centre of this building is another one, running west over two hundred feet, at a right angle with the former; on the east end of which is another tower thirty feet in diameter, and fifty high, having within it a spiral stairway, and surmounted by a gilded iron railing. In the latter building is a new dining-room one hundred feet long and twenty-five wide. It has five windows on each side, between which are two fluted

Corinthian pilasters; and the cornice, which is very neat, is adorned with a gilded crown and Mexican eagle alternate. The floor is of oak. This room, as well as the main part of the building, is not completed.

In the parterre in the rear of the front building, and running along on either side of the other structure, are exquisite groups of flowers, among which are the rose, the jessamine, the myrtle, the fuchsia, the honeysuckle, and countless others, mingling their ingredients in the balmy air, until intoxication from the sipping of the scented compound lulls the buzz of the numerous gaudy-plumed humming-birds. In front of the large tower is a fountain, throwing up its glittering spray, while the surrounding bronze statues are apparently silently listening to the music of its pattering drops. This was a favorite spot for Moctezuma, as it was for others who came before him in the same ancestral line.

While Maximilian was charmed with the interesting grounds of Chapultepec, he occasionally desired to wander where the sunbeams of the warmer clime of the lowlands bathed the tropical fruits; and where, in order to reach the spot, he would have to journey through wild mountain-scenery, receiving the pleasures of the ride, while he drank in the odors of the forest foliage, and photographed on memory's leaf the surrounding grandeur.

Cuernavaca, fifty miles south of the capital, was the attractive garden of the *tierras calientes.* Here he was surrounded by wild and cultivated flowers, aromatic shrubs, intermingled here and there with some stately and gracefully-bending tree, that cast a pleasant cooling shade beneath the burning sun.

It was a retreat particularly interesting and romantic to the Emperor and to the Empress, who not unfrequently accompanied him there. His Majesty visited that valley quite often, remaining there from three to ten days at a time. The climate is charming during winter and spring.

Bathing in the limpid waters, in the early morn, was a treat of which the Emperor availed himself. He expended no large sums of money there for costly mansions, nor for imperial show of grandeur. He first resided in an ancient building, formerly occupied by Cortez, which the Ayuntamiento tendered him. As it was considerably dilapidated, and not pleasant, he rented a better one, for which he paid $40 per month. He also purchased a tract of land containing about five acres, at Acapamzingo, a half-league distant, on which he erected a small house, with five rooms and a bathing place. He cultivated a little flower-garden near the house.

Cuernavaca had its charms for Cortez. He owned there an extensive estate, which may be seen to-day pouring forth its riches, in luxuriant growths of sugar-cane, coffee, and spangled all over with golden fruit.

Long before the traveller reaches that enchanting rural spot, the eye has been enchained by the sumptuous beauties of the road-side. The scenery is rich, beautiful, wild, and grand. You cast your eye downward, and you behold the slanting rays of the sun burnishing the deep ravines, fathomless to the eye; but from which, in countless places, shoots up exquisite foliage, apparently springing from an aerial base, or, as one might fancy, supported by some angelic hand anxious to bathe its paradisaical vegetation in the soft mellow light of the sunbeams. Amid the thickets, intertwined and embroidered with intoxicating flowers, is heard the various notes of the bird of Paradise and other sweet songsters, clothed in their mail of deeply-dyed plumage.

High above and around, massive rocks stand as sentinels, as if to guard the bewitching scenery from the touch of man, and sometimes curtain from his sight the deep-growing beauties that sparkle below.

And between those colossal walls float the glossy-plumed warblers in the ambient air, as gently as the sea-gull on the ocean's deep; and turn their golden hues to the glittering sun, and sparkle like the phosphoric gleam in its evening dance on the surface of a southern sea.

CHAPTER X.

Part of the "Provisional Statute" of the Empire—Laws of the Empire and Republic compared—Decree of October 3d, 1865—Why issued—Observations of a Mexican Journal—Death of King Leopold I.—Audience of grief—Address of Emperor thereat—Reduction of his revenue—His habit and dress—Ceremonies of Lavation—His address, Sept. 16, 1866.

IT will not be considered as deviating from the true course, to insert herein some of the principles which were woven in the warp and woof of the Imperial banner which Mexico flaunted in the breeze under the monarchy. They will be somewhat illustrative of the political views of him who stood at the head of that Empire. A knowledge of these is requisite to draw correct principles, from which we may judge with discernment of the character of that ruler.

If we hold them up to the light of jurisprudence, side by side with the fundamental basis of the Republic, together with the practice pursued under both, the piercing eye of justice will scarcely be able to distinguish and characterize more liberty, liberality, and equity under the latter than under the former.

If the word republicanism is in the least degree soothing to the thoughts, it exercises no influence in abating the rigor of the law that is actually applied under it, in Mexico.

On the tenth of April, 1865, at the Palace of Chapultepec, His Majesty executed the PROVISIONAL STATUTE, which is the substructure of the legislative fabric, as the Constitution is of a Republic. The following is taken from that Statute:

"The Emperor shall represent the sovereignty of the

nation; and while he shall decree nothing in the definite organization of the Empire, he shall act in all its branches according to his own will, or by means of the authorities and public functionaries.

"The Emperor governs by means of a ministry, composed of nine Departmental Ministers.

"The Emperor shall confer with the Council of State relative to the formation of laws and regulations; and upon consultation, when convenient, shall direct the same.

"Every Mexican has a right to obtain an audience with the Emperor, and to present his petitions and complaints. For this purpose he shall apply to the Cabinet in proper form.

"The magistrates and judges, in the exercise of their judicial functions, shall enjoy absolute independence.

"The military shall always respect and assist the civil authorities; they shall exact nothing from citizens except through the latter, and shall not exercise civil functions except when a state of siege or blockade is declared as provided by law.

"The Government of the Empire guarantees to all inhabitants of the Empire, in conformity to law, equality before the law, personal security, property, exercise of worship, and liberty of publishing one's opinions.

"No one can be detained without command of competent authority, made in writing and affirmed, which can only operate against a person when circumstantial evidence presumes him to be the perpetrator of an offence; except when a crime is committed in one's presence, in which case any person may apprehend the criminal and take him before a judicial or other competent authority.

"Property is inviolable, and cannot be used, except in case of absolute public utility, by means of prior and complete indemnity, and in the form prescribed by law.

"The confiscation of property is forever prohibited. All the imposts for the treasury of the Empire, shall be general and decreed annually.

"Taxes can be imposed only by virtue of the law. No one can be molested for his opinion; nor shall the freedom of the press be obstructed, but subject to the laws regulating the exercise of that right."

Who that has long lived in Mexico under the Republic, has not seen nearly every one of the foregoing principles violated?

Is property held inviolable, under the Republic?

I have just seen the Governor of the District of Mexico go stealthily, under the cover of night, with men, to demolish a citizen's property, in order to make a new street over the ground on which the building stood.

I have seen the President making laws, after the termination of the war, under a Constitution which prohibits him from so doing at any time.

Since the war, the liberties of the press have been curtailed by that same Executive, in violation of constitutional rights.

I saw Americans who had been arrested by the civil authority, and imprisoned, for three or four days, without trial, without a writ, or any complaint being made against them, but merely upon the verbal statement of a person, who requested the officer to make the arrest.

The inhabitants are taxed or forced to pay contributions, not according to regularly defined laws, but in accordance with the will of the Executive.

These facts and principles have not been stated herein, in support of the Empire; but that they may fall under the light of comparison—that the operations of those Republican officers may be seen, who have meted out their vengeance upon the head of the Empire, in retaliation for alleged cruelty and inhumanity.

It is not difficult for one familiar with Mexico to perceive that the Executive prerogatives exercised under republicanism, are not circumscribed within narrower limits than those claimed under imperial sway.

The formation of the political machine under the Republic cannot be considered as remarkably faulty; but the evidence presented to the world is conclusive that it has been ill-adjusted by the operators. Their unwise acts have so frequently obstructed and defeated the salutary effects of the fundamental basis of their government, that the rights of the citizens are lost sight of, and they no longer look upon it as a shield to their persons and property. It is to be regretted by every lover of republican principles; yet, the desire of our heart should not bridle the tongue from declaring the truth as to existing facts.

When there is in fact no constitutional restraint upon the will of the Executive, in a government that hoists the ensign of a Republic, it is like a false guide-board to the traveller in a foreign land; and the pirate that throws to the breeze the colors of a powerful nation, is not more deceptive and dangerous.

The decree executed October 3d, 1865, by His Majesty Maximilian has been viewed as extraordinary, and not within the pale of civilized governments, but fraught with that severity and inhumanity, the reading of which causes a shudder. The rule of the judiciary is to hear both sides of a cause before rendering a judgment. Let the public follow their example. Has the public ever read the infamous law of January 25th, 1862, made by the Liberal party of Mexico? That law will be hereinafter set forth and discussed.

The above-mentioned decree of October was issued at the instance of Marshal Bazaine. He appeared before the Council, and stated as a positive fact that Juarez had left the territory of Mexico, and that he was then in the

State of Texas, in the United States of North America. Bazaine said to the Council and to the Emperor that it was absolutely necessary to pass some severe law to put down the malcontents: that inasmuch as the leader of the opposite party had abandoned the territory, the remaining few were nothing more in the eye of the law than banditti; and therefore such a decree would be sustained by the law of nations. In the mind of the Emperor such a law was marked with too much severity, and he expressed himself decidedly opposed to it. But after much debate and consideration, together with a decided opinion of the ministry in support of the decree, he signed it, although reluctantly. It will be observed that this is one of the few decrees signed by all the ministers.

That the Emperor fully believed that Jaurez was actually beyond the jurisdiction of Mexico, there can be no doubt.

That great barbarity was practised by the Liberals, was a common remark in Mexico at that time. The people generally in Mexico believed that Juarez had left the country. At least, I have talked with many in the city of Mexico who said that they believed it.

As some evidence of the opinion prevailing in that city, I will insert here a copy of an article taken from "*The Mexican Times*," bearing date Saturday, February 24th, 1866:

"We are satisfied that the United States press, that have criticised so severely the order of His Majesty the Emperor, requiring all guerrillas taken with arms in their hands to be shot, are entirely ignorant of the state of things existing in Mexico. A long time before that decree was issued, the Imperial forces were suffering seriously from the conduct of the dissidents. Whenever they took a Frenchman he was immediately shot, while the prisoners taken by the French troops were released and sent back to their homes. The Emperor, in the kindness of his heart, has turned loose hundreds and thousands who, not appreciating his leniency, went straight into the mountains and joined again their old friends the robbers. This state of things lasted in Mexico for a long time,—the dissidents killing their prisoners without mercy, while the Imperial forces spared theirs. Although there has been no organized force in Mexico opposed to the Empire since the fall of Oajaca, still His Majesty did not issue this decree until Juarez had fled the country, leaving behind him no constituted legal authority whatever to carry on the war. President Juarez took with him his entire cabinet, leaving no head or leader in Mexico. As to Escobedo and Cortina, they were simply outlaws who rob friend and foe, and murder for filthy lucre. Witness the murder of General Parson of Missouri, and party, and the shocking barbarity committed on their persons. If these guerrillas are under the control of Juarez, he is responsible for this wholesale murder of those innocent men. We therefore request our brethren of the northern press to recollect:

"1st. That the dissidents (guerrillas) inaugurated this shooting of prisoners.

"2d. That there had not been for many a long month before the issuance of the decree by the Emperor, any organized force making war upon the Empire.

"3d. There is none now.

"4th. Ex-President Juarez, with his whole court and cabinet, had abandoned Mexico before the decree was issued. The only force in arms against the Empire at the time the decree was issued, were irresponsible guerrillas, who robbed friend and foe, old and young, women and children."

Under the foregoing state of facts, and the provisions of the law of 1862, made by the Liberals, it could hardly be expected by rational men that some law in retaliation of those acts of savage barbarity would not be created by the Empire. The surprise well might be, that the Emperor waited so long before executing some decree that would be considered a sufficient punishment to deter further inhuman acts.

Soon after the issuance of the said decree of October 3d, near the latter part of the said month, twenty-eight persons were taken prisoners by General Mendez, in Morelia, in the Department of Michoacan. Four of them were shot; namely, General Arteaga, Colonel Salasa, and two whose names are unknown to me. When information reached the Emperor that the four had been executed, he felt exceedingly grieved, and despatched a courier to inform Mendez that he disapproved the act, and that he must shoot no more. The Emperor immediately issued orders to the commanders of the different divisions to execute no prisoners until orders were received from him to that effect.

Although the decree was in force, it was not the intention of His Majesty to carry it out; but only to hold it as a terror over the enemy, in order that it might have a tendency to stop bloodshed.

With a view of preventing executions under that decree, the Emperor ordered the telegraph-office to be kept open nights. And he further ordered that the operators should wake him, whenever a message came which reported a capture of prisoners. He was frequently awakened under that order, and he never failed to send an order prohibiting the execution of prisoners.

Further comment will be made upon the October decree, in connection with the trial of Maximilian.

A sad event occurred in December, 1865, in Europe, information of which reached Mexico in the first part of the following month, and mantled Their Majesties with mourning and sorrow. King Leopold I., of Belgium, the father of the Empress Carlota, had expired.

In memory of the departed, and respect to the living, an "audience of grief" was held, January 15th, 1866, in accordance with the programme previously published. The Diplomatic Corps and the great dignitaries presented themselves in full mourning, to offer condolence to Their Majesties, on account of the sad bereavement which had befallen them. In the midst of that solemn audience, one of the Ministers of State, Señor D. F. Ramirez, addressed Their Majesties in a becoming style, with much dignity and with tender feelings of sympathy.

His Majesty, with great kindness of heart, responded. On this occasion, he expressed his feelings and opinions relative to his government, which will not be uninteresting, as expressive of the sincerity of his views and the rectitude of his actions. That response was in the following language:

"Gentlemen:

"I am thankful to you for the participation you have taken in the sad event which has just wounded the Empress and myself.

"In such a great misfortune it is, however, a consolation to remember the great and laudable example which, as a most sacred inheritance, the King of Belgium bequeaths to us. He, as ourselves, in accepting the throne which a people offered him, met a nation to constitute and a government to establish. The uninterested intervention of France enabled him to restore peace, and he dedicated himself to very important internal reforms. He promised liberty to his people, and during the lengthy period of twenty-five years, he fulfilled his engagement. He promised security and tranquillity to the country, and they were given, and with them their independence,—thus placing Belgium in a high rank among the nations of Europe, especially in a commercial point of view, and leaving spotless its noble motto and banners.

"We will know how to follow that great example, by which God has taught us that Providence never abandons the honest and just monarchs in their noble enterprises.

"The Empress, his daughter, has just returned from a laborious journey in distant lands and in dreadful climates, without other guard than the love of the people, and everywhere meeting a frank and cordial reception, which shows once more the sympathy existing between the nation and its rulers. This fact proves beyond a doubt the error in which were laboring many ill-intentioned parties who had rumored a departure of the Empress for Europe, and predicted and wished her a hostile reception in the country she was to travel through.

"It is gratifying to me to express on this occasion my profound gratitude to the heroic Vera Cruz and the beautiful Yucatan, which received the Empress with such solicitude, that its memory will ever be graven upon my inmost soul.

"As to me, Gentlemen, you have witnessed my labors. Discarding the dangerous theories which lead to anarchy, I devoted my time to the organization of public administration, to the development of all the elements of prosperity and wealth of the country, and to the solution of the questions which most interest it.

"In this arduous labor I have resisted the importunities of some and the discouragement of others, knowing that the wounds inflicted during fifteen years of civil war do not heal in one day; but, firm in the consciousness of my duty, I will follow unhesitatingly my path with indefatigable perseverance. My strength may fail—my courage, never!

"I will endeavor to maintain the democratic habits of the nation. I am convinced that they elevate the minds of the citizens, impressing them with consciousness of their dignity and valor.

"I have protected the liberty of the press as long as it did not degenerate into unlimited license; at the same time having the authority of the law exercised.

"Very blind is he who does not see that a strong authority is the only anchor of salvation for our country.

"You have been able to observe our calm attitude during that storm of calumnies raised against us abroad. On, Gentlemen! the calumnies will pass over, and our work will stand.

"Strongly supported by my conscience and the uprightness of my intentions, I quietly contemplate the future. Mexico has placed her honor in my hands, and she must know that this honor will be kept unstained and unspotted."

The reduction made by the Emperor in his own revenue, which includes all of that expended for the Imperial House, known as the Civil List, is adequate proof of his economy. On the 15th of March, A. D. 1866, he wrote from Cuernavaca, to the Minister and Intendent-General of the Civil List, a letter which contained, among other things, the following:

"In view of the present exigencies of the treasury, and while the condition of the public treasury is so burdened, it is our firm resolution to receive only from the State for the Civil List the third part of the annual revenue which belongs to it, according to the said decree of the Regency; that is, the sum of five hundred thousand dollars for all the said expenses."

He further observed in the same letter, that—

"This reduction in the expenses is preferred by us, through choice, to the customary splendor and greatness of the European Courts; because simplicity and moderation better accord with the democratic ideas which animate us; and besides, it raises the prestige of the monarchy as much as the brilliancy of a splendid Court."

The Emperor was quite regular in his habits. He retired from eight to nine o'clock. When in the National Palace he frequently went to bed at eight, and at Chapultepec usually at about nine o'clock. He sometimes read while in bed for a half-hour, and sometimes would require his *valet de chambre* to read to him from some German work until he fell into slumber. While at Chapultepec he rose at three o'clock in the morning, and immediately commenced writing,—answering letters, signing documents, etc. At half-past five he took a cup of coffee. At seven he rode out for an hour. He breakfasted between eight and nine. He drank seidlitz water with ice at the table. He dined at half-past three, never eating fruit at his meals, nor drinking coffee at dinner. After dinner he smoked, then rode out in his carriage, usually drawn by six white mules, with coachman and groom, and one mounted escort in the advance. The three servants dressed in apparel made of soft leather. After the ride he would generally call his secretary, or an officer, and play billiards. His breakfast and his early coffee were usually taken without the company of the Empress,—that is, the coffee particularly, as it was not a convenient hour for her. They invariably dined together. Whenever they ate separately, he was accompanied by his secretary, or some officer, and the Empress by her maid of honor, Señorita Josefa Varela.

From one o'clock to half-past two, in the afternoon, was the time designated for his ministers and visitors to call.

He wore, generally, light-colored pants, a black frock-coat, black vest; and while at Chapultepec, a soft white hat, with a low crown;, and when in the city, a high-crowned hat, white or gray. His overcoat was gray. He also wore a set of studs and sleeve-buttons, set with blue stones, which he had used for many years without any change for others.

On the second finger of his right hand were two heavy plain gold rings. One of them had the following inscription on the interior surface: "Prince. M. Charlotte, 27th July, 1857. G. G. G." On the little finger of his left hand was a gold ring with a large blue setting, having engraved thereon the Mexican coat of arms. When he retired at night, he took off one of his plain rings; and after washing the next morning, placed it again on his finger. Which ring it was, or why he did so, I was not able to learn. While at Cuernavaca he dressed in white linen, and Panama hat. At parties, he sometimes dressed in citizens' clothes.

Their Majesties were both devout in their attachment to the Roman Catholic faith, and in attention to its precepts. They performed the ceremony of the Lavation, on Holy Thursday, at noon, in 1866, at the National Palace, in the reception-saloon. Tickets were issued inviting a large number to attend; and the apartment was quite crowded. Twelve old men, of humble position in life, were seated on a bench with a table before them, furnished with a white cloth, twelve plates, and knives and forks. On the opposite side of the room stood another table prepared in like style, with twelve women seated thereat. The Emperor wore the uniform of a Mexican General, and was accompanied by his aids and household officers. The Empress was dressed in black, wearing black earrings - assisted by her maids of honor. The twelve men and women were in black apparel, with white collars. The table was served in courses, brought in on wooden trays, by the guard palatinate.

The dishes were taken therefrom by Count Bombell and Princess Iturbide, and handed to the Empress, who served the twelve women with the same, at the same time conversing with them. She poured out the water and wine for them; changed their plates as the different courses arrived; handed the used plates to Count Bombell—and thus continued until the conclusion. The Emperor went through the same ceremony with the twelve men, assisted by his household officers. Neither men nor women appeared to eat very heartily, although requested so to do, until the *frijoles* (beans) were served; and as that dish is the favorite of the Mexicans, they could not resist temptation.

After the eating was finished the tables were removed, but the parties remained seated, and were covered with a long white cloth from their laps down to the floor.

Behind the twelve women stood an equal number of girls from ten to sixteen years of age; and behind the men the same number of boys were arrayed.

The girls and boys advanced in front of the men and women respectively, and turning towards them took from them their shoes and stockings. The Emperor and Empress, taking off their gloves, each receiving a bowl of water from their respective assistants, bent down upon their knees—the Emperor before the twelve men, and the Empress before the twelve women—and washed the feet of the twelve respectively; and as they finished the washing, they kissed one foot of each person so washed.

Thus ended that religious ceremony, which is performed by His Holiness the Pope, in imitation of our Saviour.

On the sixteenth of September, 1866, the anniversary of Mexican Independence, an address was delivered to Their Majesties by D. José Fernando Ramirez, Minister of Foreign Affairs; on which occasion the Emperor made the following expression, showing how truly he felt himself identified with the interest and welfare of Mexico :

" MEXICANS :

"This is a family rejoicing. It is to rejoice together as brothers, that we meet each year on this celebrated day around our glorious banner. The day on which our immortal Hidalgo, raising his patriotic voice with noble courage, assembled the heroes of a new era for Mexico, will always be for the children of our country a day of rejoicing as well as a day of duty;—of rejoicing, because we celebrate in it the anniversary of our nationality ; of sacred duty, because every good Mexican ought to renew on that day the oath to live only for the greatness, the independence, and the integrity of his country, and to be ever ready to defend it with all his courage and energy. The words of this oath are the first which I uttered as a good Mexican. I solemnly repeat them to-day to you. My heart, my soul, my labors, all my loyal efforts belong to you and to our dear country.

"No power in this world will be able to make me vacillate in my duty. Every drop of my blood is now Mexican, and if God were to permit that new dangers should threaten our dear country, you would see me in your ranks fighting for its independence and its integrity. I may die, but I will die at the foot of our glorious banner, for no human force can make me abandon the post to which your confidence has called me.

"What I do myself every true Mexican must do; he must extirpate past feuds, he must bury past hate, and live only for the good and the prosperity of our beautiful country. Thus united in sentiment, and following the same path indicated to us by duty, we shall be strong, and we shall make those principles triumph which form the main object of our labors.

"Let us take advantage of each day to develop and

strengthen them. Let us unite ourselves closely to our noble allies and their glorious flag, and we shall thus see, growing in strength and bearing fruits, the beautiful tree of our independence, the seed of which was sown more than half a century ago by the great Hidalgo and his illustrious companions. Long live Independence! Long live the remembrance of its great heroes!"

When "new dangers" did arise, the Emperor was true to his promise. How well can his brave officers and men, who were around him in Queretaro, attest the truth of that averment! He asked no man to run any more risk than he was willing to incur himself. The true soldier, the true man, was prominent in all his bearing. He was a nobleman of Nature, wanting no indorsement of man to perfect the title.

About the eighth of October, 1866, the Emperor received the sad intelligence of the derangement of the Empress Carlota. It completely prostrated him. It was about two o'clock in the afternoon when the news reached him. He immediately rode out to the palace of Chapultepec, where he shed tears all that day. He remained there over ten days, confining himself closely to his apartments, scarcely seeing any one during that time. It was a sudden as well as a terrible blow of affliction to him. Her physical condition had been so good, that he never for a moment thought that such a misfortune could befall her.

Smarting under the late bereavement, perplexed by the course pursued by Bazaine, and believing that the jealousy and discord of the latter had so weakened the political ties around him, that nothing but danger and misfortune could be seen looming up in the future—with all these thoughts pressing on his mind, the Emperor went to Orizaba, about the twentieth of October, with a view of leaving the country. These were trying circumstances, which called for the utmost vigor of thought and resolution to determine what method to adopt. But after a short reflection his drooping spirits became aroused, and his inclination became strongly in favor of a resolute defence till the last. Honor inspired his martial spirit to the highest pitch. He began to meditate upon the fact that they who had solicited his presence as their ruler, would be left in no agreeable or safe condition after his departure; that they had been, with him, joint actors in the great work of building up the Empire, and that he could not go out of the copartnership until the contemplated work should prove to be an impossibility, and the framework already erected should be annihilated.

But anxious that the work should proceed in harmony with the majority, he was desirous of testing the will of the Mexican people. The same rule that governed his actions in coming to the country was still adhered to. That is, he required the support of a majority of the Mexicans in order to sustain his conscience in consenting to be their head.

The fact that armed dissidents were in the field was no proof that such a majority was against him. He was not ignorant of the historical fact, that the supreme power of a nation is possessed by those who have the implements of war in their hands; while at the same time it may be true, that they are far in the minority. That such a state of things has existed in Mexico, more than once, will not be questioned by those well versed in its history.

He therefore expressed his views clearly to his Council, to Generals Miramon and Marquez, and Father Fischer, his secretary, while at Orizaba. He desired to receive an explanation of the will of the people; and if that will were against him, he considered that honor would no longer compel him to remain for the purpose of soliciting the people to yield to his reign, nor to force them by arms.

With a view of hearing the voice of the people, he issued the following proclamation:

"MEXICANS: Circumstances of great magnitude, relating to the welfare of our country, and which increase in strength by our domestic difficulties, have produced in our mind the conviction that we ought to reconsider the power confided to us.

"Our Council of Ministers, by us convoked, has given as their opinion that the welfare of Mexico still requires our presence at the head of affairs, and we have considered it our duty to accede to their request. We announce, at the same time, our intention to convoke a National Congress, on the most ample and liberal basis, where all political parties can participate.

"This Congress shall decide whether the Empire shall continue in the future; and in case of assent, shall assist in framing the fundamental laws to consolidate the public institutions of the country. To obtain this result, our Councillors are at present engaged in devising the necessary means, and at the same time arranging matters in such a manner that all parties may assist in an arrangement on that basis.

"In the mean time, Mexicans, counting upon you all, without excluding any political class, we shall continue with courage and constancy the work of regeneration which you have placed in charge of your countryman.

"MAXIMILIAN.

"ORIZABA, Dec. 1, 1866."

On the 12th, His Majesty, His Council of Ministers, General Marquez, and Father Fischer, left Orizaba, and on the 18th reached Puebla. His Majesty and Father Fischer there remained until the 3d of January following. The Ministers and Gen. Marquez proceeded on to the city of Mexico. On the 5th of January, His Majesty and Father Fischer arrived at the Capital.

The contemplated session of Congress did not take place, for the reason that the state of the country was such that an election was impossible. No blame can be attached to his Majesty on that account. He was heartily desirous of bringing about an election, at which all parties might express freely their wish, uninfluenced by his own bayonets.

Inasmuch as vituperations have been profusely uttered against His Majesty for the alleged cruelties perpetrated under his sway, it will not be improper to state certain facts as to the regular course of justice pursued during a part of the time, considering that I have procured positive proof of what I am about to relate.

During nine months of the year 1866, in the city of Mexico, the court-martial, of which Colonel Luis Reyes was president, tried twenty-seven persons, most of whom had been guilty of robbery and other felonious crimes. Three of them only were convicted of political crimes, and not one of the latter was executed, but all were released.

Cruelty was not an ingredient mixed up in Maximilian. It was as impossible for him to be cruel as it is to mix oil and water.

CHAPTER XI.

Maximilian goes to Queretaro—History of the city—Maximilian's opinions—His habits—Battles—Taking of the city by the Liberals—His surrender and imprisonment.

"Before my breath, like blazing flax,
Man and his marvels pass away!
And changing empires wane and wax,
Are founded, flourish, and decay."

ON the 6th day of February, A. D. 1866, the French troops left the city of Mexico. Their connection with the government of Maximilian had ceased. His Majesty, fearing that the clouds of despair might darken the views of his forces within the city of Queretaro, concluded, after receiving the opinion of his Council, in unison with his own, to appear in person at that point, hoping that his presence might stimulate the soldiers, and give them new hope. Consequently, at the head of a force of not far from eighteen hundred men, composed of cavalry, infantry, and artillery, accompanied by General Marquez and Señor Aguirre, Minister of War, he took up his line of march February 13th, for Queretaro. On the first and fourth day he had light skirmishing with a party of guerrillas, the latter day's fight lasting several hours; a few were killed, and several were wounded on both sides. He reached Arroyo Seco on the 18th, distant from the latter city four leagues. Very early the next morning he was again in the saddle, and at about ten o'clock he, with his little army, entered Queretaro in the most triumphal manner. Before entering, he was met by Generals Miramon and Mejia, their staffs, and the whole force at Queretaro, numbering over three thousand men. The entrance was grand and imposing. His

Majesty sat upon a large elegant white steed, dressed in a dark blue uniform as a Mexican general, with military boots over his pants, and a small cap, called a *kepi.*

All Queretaro seemed to be out of doors. Both sides of the road were lined with people, crowding almost on to the soldiery. Shouts of "Long live the Emperor" went up from every direction, as though by one united voice. Church-bells chimed without cessation, as if they were calling the whole nation together; hats, handkerchiefs, and gay ribbons were waving, while bouquets were falling all around His Majesty in showers, thrown by smiling señoritas, as fresh as their garden-flowers. One would have concluded, while gazing at that enthusiastic mass, that they supposed a new era of perfect bliss had appeared. His Majesty, with his accustomed affability and general good-nature, was bowing, first on this, then on that side, amid the universal applause of the multitude. Surely Maximilian thought he had fallen among friends. That friendship was genuine. The citizens of Queretaro have given ample evidence of their friendship for him during all his misfortunes. Would that the same could be said of his own officers! Those citizens smiled when fortune surrounded His Majesty—they wept when sorrow lighted upon his brow.

Queretaro is situated in latitude twenty degrees and twenty-three minutes north; and in longitude one degree and five minutes west from the meridian of the city of Mexico, and distant from the latter place fifty-seven leagues. It was founded about the year fourteen hundred and forty-five, and formed a part of the Empire of Moctezuma I. It was conquered by D. Fernando de Tapia, July 25th, 1531, who gave it the appellation of Santiago de Queretaro. In the Tarasco idiom—whence the name of Queretaro—it signified a place where ball was played; probably not those leaden balls of death, which have played so important a part in this century.

8

In the year 1655, it was raised to the rank of a city, by King Felipe IV. It contained, a few years ago, about fifty thousand inhabitants. Now, half that number would be nearer a correct estimate of its population. Empty houses are very abundant, as well as many half annihilated from the storms of battle.

During the war with the United States, Mexico held its congressional sessions there; and there executed the treaty of Hidalgo, made between those two Governments in the year 1848.

On the arrival of His Majesty in that city, the Queretaro Club offered him their apartments, in the building known as the Casino, which had been elegantly fitted up by them. It was the most comfortable quarters that could have been tendered him. There was ample room for him and his staff. He accepted the generous offer.

On the twenty-fifth of February, the Emperor received a re-enforcement of four thousand men, under Gen. Mendez.

Soon after taking a survey of that city and its surroundings, the Emperor commenced erecting fortifications on *El Cerro de las Campanas* (the Hill of the Bells), which is a little over a mile northwest of the city. He was of opinion that that position would be first attacked by the enemy. He attended to that work in person. He remained there night and day, from the sixth of March until the thirteenth. The first three nights he slept upon the ground. The fourth day, Gen. Mejia arranged an elegant Turkish tent for the Emperor, in which he rested the last four nights. It had been purchased by Gen. Almonte in Paris, and by him presented to Mejia, who tendered it to his Majesty.

The Emperor wrote the following letter as explanatory of his acts and wishes, in order that erroneous views might not be taken relative to his intentions:

"QUERETARO, March 2d, 1867.

"MY DEAR MINISTER:

"As my departure for Queretaro, where I have come to place myself at the head of the army recently formed, might be falsely interpreted by persons badly disposed, in the country as well as out of it; and as my reasons for it ought to be known, in view of the many calumnies which our enemies propagate with so much promptitude upon the conduct of our Government, I am of opinion that it is necessary to make some brief observations, which may serve as explanations, and also as a rule of conduct in the difficult circumstances through which we are passing.

"The programme which I adopted in Orizaba, after having heard the frank and loyal opinion of the consultative bodies of State, has not been changed a particle. My prevailing thought continues to be the calling of a Congress, which I always thought to be the only means of founding the future on a durable basis, and to form a point of cohesion where may be united successively all the parties which now cause the ruin of our unfortunate country.

"I have not wished to emit this idea of a Congress (which I have always supported since my arrival in this country), until there would be a security that the representatives could assemble free from exterior influence. During all the time that the French maintained under their authority the Central provinces, it was impossible to assemble a Congress which could have deliberated freely. My trip has hastened the withdrawal of the troops of the Intervention, and thus the time has arrived when I am able to express myself openly upon the thought of a constituent Congress. The best proof that I was not able to make this resolution before is, the sad opposition which I met with in the French authorities, when I mentioned it on their departure.

"A Congress elected by the nation, a real expression of the majority, with full powers to work, and a complete liberty to deliberate, is the only possible means of terminating the civil war, and of stopping the effusion of blood so prolonged. As Sovereign and Chief, called by the nation, I shall submit with pleasure to their will, having the most ardent desire to terminate promptly this desolating struggle.

"I have done more, even. I have communicated personally with the chiefs who pretend to fight in the name of liberty and of the principles of progress, to induce them to submit themselves, as I have the intention of doing, to the national vote. What has been the result of these negotiations? Those men who invoke progress have not wished, or have not dared to accept that judgment. They have responded to me by ordering loyal and distinguished citizens to be executed; they have repulsed the fraternal hand which was extended; they have worked as blind partisans, who know no other means of governing but the sword.

"Where then is the national will? On the side of whom exists the desire of true liberty? Their only excuse is in their blindness.

"It is impossible for us to rely on such men, and our duty is to work with the greatest energy to restore the liberty of the people, so that they may express voluntarily their will.

"This is the reason why I have hastened to come here, in order to try all means to establish order, peace, and to prevent another and more terrible foreign intervention in this country. The French bayonets have marched; it is necessary then to impede the action of every influence which directly or indirectly might threaten our independence and the integrity of our territory.

"In this moment our country is for sale at public auction.

"It is necessary to employ all the means possible to free us from a situation so critical, and to place Mexico safe from every oppression, come whence it may.

"In a word, the National Congress will determine upon the destinies of Mexico—also upon the institutions that it may see proper to establish, which may exceed the present form of government; and if this Assembly cannot be invoked, because we, who wished to call it, have succumbed in the struggle, the opinion of the world will do us justice at least, and will acknowledge that we were the true defenders of the nation, that we have never sold the territory of the nation, that we have tried to save it from a second and oppressive intervention, and that we have sincerely used all our efforts in order that the principle of national suffrage might triumph.

"MAXIMILIAN."

The foregoing letter is another proof of the Emperor's desire to ascertain, and to be governed by, the will of the Mexican people.

The Liberals, under Escobedo, attacked the city of Queretaro, on the 14th of March, with a superior force of nearly thirty thousand, while that of Maximilian numbered less than nine thousand. The Emperor, on that day, saw not a moment's rest. He was in the saddle during the engagement, riding here and there, where danger was greatest, and where observation was most needed. He never seemed to think of personal danger; the defeat of the enemy was uppermost in his mind; and that was the result of the action, although accompanied by a loss on his part of about two hundred killed and three hundred wounded.

After that battle, he moved his quarters into the church called La Cruz. The comforts of life he abandoned. In fact, many of his officers had better rooms and food than he. His new apartments were a room of about twelve feet by eighteen; and another one adjoining for his servant. The furniture that adorned his place of rest was composed of a camp-bed, two common tables, and six camp-chairs. Most officers of the rank of captain would not have considered such quarters as suitable even for them, in a city where elegant apartments could have been obtained by a written order from His Majesty. But that position was considered the best for observation; and to be there day and night, was viewed by His Majesty as extremely important. Inconveniences and the want of present comforts were considerations that did not trouble him.

His men saw no evidence that he was not willing to share hardships and deprivations equally with them. He looked upon it as a joint cause: the salvation of the army was his own success.

On the 22d of March, General Marquez left Queretaro, with orders from the Emperor to march with his thousand mounted men, selected for that purpose, to the city of Mexico, to obtain a re-enforcement of men and procure provisions and munitions of war—and to return within fifteen days: if there were not men enough to hold the city of Mexico, and also increase his force sufficiently for the defence of Queretaro, to abandon Mexico, and return to the latter city with all the men he could raise. Such a concentration of the Imperial forces at Queretaro would have saved the Emperor, and probably destroyed the army of Escobedo.

The Emperor conferred upon Marquez the title of Lugar Teniente, which is usually translated "*Lieutenant-General,*" but which means something more. Such an officer takes the place of the Emperor, with full power to act as he sees proper. The Emperor deemed it important to place unlimited power in Marquez, in order to carry out his plans. It was an unfortunate selection on the part of His Majesty, of a commander for such a duty; and it has been cited as an instance of his erring judgment as to human nature. Whether the Emperor did honor Marquez with the above-mentioned title, has been seriously doubted. When the latter arrived in the city of Mexico, he exhibited his authority to act in that capacity; but the question as to its genuineness was raised in the minds of many. I was informed of the fact of the appointment by His Majesty's secretary, who said he himself drafted the order empowering Marquez thus to act. And as I suggested to him the importance of knowing the truth, I cannot have any suspicions of the authenticity of Marquez's title of Lugar Teniente. The latter evidently abused his power—acted far beyond what justice and honor would dictate, and much to the regret of and injury to Maximilian.

On the 27th of March the Emperor attacked the enemy, captured two pieces of artillery, and nearly two hundred prisoners. He was on the field in person, urging on his men with great enthusiasm. Where the balls fell the thickest, there he was found doing duty. His loss was quite small.

Marquez did not obey orders. After reaching Mexico, and increasing his forces to four thousand, eight hundred of which were European soldiers, he advanced slowly on Diaz, who was besieging Puebla. That city was then held by about three thousand Imperial troops. Diaz had nearly fifteen thousand men.

It was the hope of Marquez that Diaz would sally out and open an engagement with him, which would have relieved the Imperial force within Puebla. General Diaz was short of the munitions of war, and he viewed an attack by him upon Marquez as extremely hazardous. He also considered inaction on his part equally dangerous. He therefore saw no probable chance for success but in an attempt to storm the city of Puebla, which he did on the second of April, in the morning early, with a force of eight thousand. He was soon in possession of the city, although meeting with a considerable loss on his part.

Some of the prisoners which he there captured were wheeled into his own ranks; and he hurriedly prepared to follow Marquez. On the fourth of April he sent out three thousand cavalry under General Toro, who met Marquez on the sixth, at the Hacienda de San Diego de Notario, about fifteen miles from Apizaco. General Toro formed for battle on a not very advantageous ground, the place being surrounded nearly by ravines. He brought on an engagement with ill success. The first charge of Marquez sent his men flying in confusion, who were only saved by the force of General Leva, who attacked the left flank of Marquez.

The Liberals drew off and re-formed within three or four hours thereafter. Marquez retreated toward Apizaco.

At half-past three he was discovered moving on the left flank of the enemy, and in half an hour he was in front disputing his passage.

General Leva formed three thousand cavalry in line of battle, himself commanding on the right. His centre rested on a hill. His cavalry were ordered to dismount. Marquez charged up the hill, and the Liberals fell back seven leagues to Piedra Negra, where they rested all night.

The next day, Diaz having arrived, went out with his full force of over twelve thousand men near Apam, formed in line of battle, and advanced in that form five leagues.

On the eighth, at four and a half o'clock, he halted. His cavalry horses were then double-mounted, by placing one of the infantry behind each horseman. Six thousand men thus mounted advanced on a walk, as the roads were wet and bad. Light mountain-pieces were mounted on mules. At six o'clock, in sight of San Lorenzo, Diaz formed in line of battle; and with four pieces of artillery he pushed on rapidly to engage the enemy's right flank. Diaz carried the position. He formed a line of battle around the Hacienda of San Lorenzo, and gave orders for the men to be ready at half-past four the next morning,—thinking that the enemy could not get away in the night, and that the following day would be a victorious one for him. The morrow came and found Marquez and his force absent and out of sight. Diaz followed on with cavalry at a gallop. Marquez came to a broken bridge, and not having sufficient time to repair it, ran his artillery into the ravine, and there abandoned it. He had placed his European troops in the rear, and the cavalry of Diaz never but once approached within pistol-shot of them. The foreign soldiers retreated in excellent order, losing but a few killed, and a few who were taken prisoners from weakness and sickness, which prevented their keeping up with the command. Marquez, however, with a small escort, soon deserted his men, and went flying back to the Capital like a coward. There was a narrow passage in the road where he could have held the enemy in check, but his cowardice would not permit the attempt. He afterward assumed command in the Capital, where he remained until that city also fell into the hands of the Liberals. His force followed after him, reaching the city a few days later.

Marquez considered it of the utmost importance to hold the large and opulent city of Puebla, if possible; but his force was inadequate to make an attack upon Diaz. If Diaz had had sufficient ammunition (his want of which was unknown to Marquez), he could have engaged Marquez, and considering his men equal, the probability was, he could have conquered; while at the same time his remaining forces would have been able to support and hold good the siege of Puebla.

I apprehend the soldier may question Marquez's wisdom, under the circumstances, in disobeying the order of the Emperor.

On the 14th of April, the Emperor's forces in Queretaro, numbering but little over six thousand, made a sortie, took nineteen guns and six hundred prisoners, with a loss of a very small number. At that battle, the Emperor was also at the post of danger.

This action produced great havoc and consternation among the enemy. He was routed at all points. The opportune arrival of General Treviña, with a cavalry re-enforcement of five thousand, prevented a general rout of the enemy. In order to prevent a complete stampede of the Liberals, the force under General Treviña was employed in surrounding the scattered regiments, that hardly knew which way to go, or where or when to stop.

It is difficult to say what force the Liberals had in that action. It has been estimated from seventeen to thirty thousand. They made no morning or monthly reports of their number.

Even with this re-enforcement, the Liberals felt no inclination to renew the engagement; but were content to exercise their ingenuity and skill in checking, in some degree, the wild fury and the escape of a completely disorganized army.

On the morning of that day, before the attack, everything was in readiness for a final departure from that city, with all the Imperial forces. But on reviewing that brilliant victory, His Majesty saw that he enjoyed a more signal triumph than he or his officers had anticipated,—far greater than they believed possible, when they considered the numerical superiority of their adversaries.

His Majesty, flushed and animated with the victory his daring blow had produced, reconsidered his opinion of the morning, and resolved to remain longer in that city, and save its inhabitants from what they believed to be a plundering and sacking party. The number of foreigners in the Emperor's service there did not number over two hundred, all told. But his men were better officered and better drilled than the opposing army.

As General Marquez had not made his reappearance in Queretaro, according to the Emperor's positive instructions, and more than ten days had elapsed since his contemplated arrival, the Emperor was quite uneasy, and harbored grave misgivings as to the real intent of Marquez. Consequently, with a view of ascertaining the true condition of the Capital and the movements of Marquez, His Majesty, on the 17th of April, issued orders to Prince Salm Salm, requiring him to leave for Mexico, in pursuit of Marquez, and to obtain full information as to the situation of affairs; to tell Marquez, in the name of the Emperor, to bring all of his forces forthwith to Queretaro, and, if necessary, to give up the Capital: and that if Marquez should refuse to comply with these commands, then the Prince's order was to arrest him, and to hasten back to Queretaro with him and the cavalry, particularly with the Hussars. At twelve o'clock that night, the Prince, with five hundred men, sallied out, and advanced about one half of a league, when he was attacked, and wounded by a shot in his left foot, though not seriously. His intention was to take the Cerro Gordo road. But on examining the position and number of the enemy, from whom he was receiving a heavy fire, near the Campana, from artillery and cavalry, he saw that it was impossible to break his lines, and therefore returned into the city, without making another attempt. The enemy was so strong, that a sortie, with a small number of men, was but a waste of force, material, and time.

The Imperialists made an unsuccessful attack on the 1st of May, retreating with a small loss. It was said that the blame was due to Miramon. Their number did not exceed five thousand, while the Liberals were twenty-five thousand strong.

Immediately after a battle, the Emperor would visit the hospitals in person, seeing every sick and wounded man, inquiring of him how he felt, how he was treated, and, as he parted, a kind word of hope fell from his lips. This visit was daily made for several days following a battle, and never more than three or four days passed without his visiting them. He gave each widow of his deceased soldiers, who was there to receive it, ten dollars out of his private funds, as long as they lasted. He also paid visits to the prisoners, not passing one without speaking to him.

He was not unmindful of those who had rendered him important service. Mr. Edwin R. Wells, from Texas, formerly from New York, who had paid some attention to medicine and surgery, though not a physician, made himself exceedingly useful in the hospitals. He received some poisonous matter in his finger, and came near losing his hand while thus employed. His Majesty did not forget him. On the 22d of March he bestowed upon him a gold medal of the Order of Guadalupe.

The Emperor kept no carriage in Queretaro. He rode on horseback. Frequently he would go on foot to visit the different posts. Many mornings he was observed returning on foot, between six and seven o'clock, having, at that early hour, visited all the outposts. He superintended the placing of nearly all of the batteries, sighted the guns, and saw that all the requisite work was done. He wore a broad-brimmed Mexican white hat, high military boots, and a white blouse, generally, in going the rounds.

He retired and rose early. He took exercise every day. If he deemed it unnecessary to visit in person the different batteries every morning, he walked at sunrise one hour in the square in front of the church La Cruz. He likewise performed the same exercise at sunset, in the same location. Usually, on those daily walks, he was attended by his secretary, or one of his aid-de-camps. When thus promenading he was not unfrequently accosted by some one who had some complaint to make, or some favor to solicit. Were they rich or poor, high or low, he never turned a deaf ear, but most patiently listened, and clothed his answers in kind words. In order that the matter should not be forgotten, he would order his secretary or aid-de-camp to enter the matter in a memoradum-book. He never failed to examine the complaints and requests, giving them due consideration.

Whoever desired an audience with him could obtain it, when he was not otherwise occupied. When saluted, he bowed, however humble the individual whence came the salutation. His disposition was such, that mildness and gentleness were his natural elements.

Whatever lofty ideas of Imperial prerogative he may have imbibed, in unison with other sovereign heads, a violation of the right of petition could hardly be imputed to him. The sincerity of his professions and declarations was among his shining qualities. One was more inclined to look upon him as a President than an Emperor.

The tower on La Cruz church was His Majesty's observatory, until it became too dangerous. Near the close of the siege, General Escobedo's guns were nearly opposite, scarcely a mile distant, and, in fact, some were within six hundred yards. General Escobedo having ascertained that the tower was the point of observation, did not fail to have guns bearing directly upon it continually. No person could place himself within that tower without being immediately discerned through the spyglass of Escobedo. On one occasion the Emperor and five of his officers were in the tower, making close observations; suddenly there came a shell, which fell in their midst, bursting, and, most miraculously, killing no one, but wounding very slightly one of the officers. After that it was walled up, and no more views taken therefrom.

About the 1st of May, it was quite apparent that great suffering among the poor was near at hand on account of the scarcity of edibles. His Majesty therefore issued an order that persons who had large stocks of provisions should sell them at reasonable rates, so that they would be within the reach of the poorer classes. The order contained the prices which specified articles should not exceed.

After that date the army learned the flavor of horse and mule meat. Whether the latter was as refractory in mastication as it generally is in the harness, is a subject upon which I received no information.

Had the name been unknown to them, doubtless a fat horse-steak would have been more palatable than poor beef. About the tenth of the month, the citizens were reminded of the fact, that they would be no longer the recipients of animal food, unless they too could relish the viands taken from the flesh of the same class of four-footed beasts. The Emperor fared no more sumptuously than the rest. He was favored with the same elegant and rare dishes. Every action and move he made there proved him to be quite as democratic as any one who was nursed in republicanism.

Both the political and military condition of the Empire had attained that state in which everything was viewed through the greatest doubt; and as Maximilian was in the field in person, there was no certainty among the chances of war that he might not some day, not far distant, be found among the fallen. He deemed it requisite to be prepared to meet such emergencies as were within the range of possibilities. He, therefore, on the 11th of April, created a Regency, by a decree to take effect in case of his death. That decree is in the following words:

"*Maximilian, Emperor.* Considering that if Our death should happen, the Government of the Empire would be without a head, on account of the absence of its Regent, Our august spouse, the Empress Carlota:

"Considering that, in order to obviate such a misfortune, and to procure on Our part the well-being of the Mexican nation, even after Our death, it is indispensable to leave a Government which the nation may recognize as the head of the Union:

"Considering that, in the mean while, if this nation, through the means of its Congress, freely convoked and assembled, should not declare the form of government which it will adopt, the present one will exist—which is the monarchy; and therefore, in case of Our non-existence, the government ought to be deposited in a Regency:

"We decree:

"Art. 1. In case of Our death, D. Teodosio Lares, D. José M. Lacunza, and General D. Leonardo Marquez, will be the Regents of the Empire.

"Art. 2. The Regency will govern in subjection to the Organic Statute of the Empire.

"Art. 3. The Regency will call a Congress, which must definitely establish the nation, as soon as the war may be determined either by arms or armistice. The free and legitimate election and meeting of that constituent body shall take place.

"ART. 4. After the instalment of Congress, the Regency will cease, terminating, with that act, the power which We confer upon it by this decree.

"Our Minister of Public Instruction and Worship is charged to make known this decree to the Regents whom We have appointed, in case of Our death.

"Given in Queretaro, May 11th, 1867."

On the morning of the 13th, preparations were going on for a final departure that night, but as the three thousand citizens who were to have been armed, had not that day received their implements of warfare, the movement was postponed. The following morning, General Miramon consulted the Emperor as to the propriety of leaving that night. Their views coincided in favor thereof, but the latter desired first to hold a council of generals and to discuss the mode of procedure. The council having assembled, discussed the matter, and decided to leave that night at eleven o'clock. General Miramon, accordingly, notified the chiefs of the different corps to appear at his quarters, which was done; whereupon he advised them of the intended departure. He also notified Colonel Gonzalez, commander of the Regiment of the Empress, that that regiment had been detailed as a special escort to the Emperor.

About the time for the move, on the night of the 14th, it appeared that only twelve hundred of the new volunteers had received their arms; in consequence of which, some of the generals were in favor of another delay. And besides, General Mendez had sent Colonel Redonet with a petition to the Emperor, asking a delay for another day, saying that he was quite unwell, and that he wished to command in person his old brigade, in which he had great confidence; and that if His Majesty would make the concession, he, Mendez, would be responsible for a safe exit. In view of the foregoing facts, the Emperor called Generals Miramon and Castillo for another council, when it was determined to positively leave the next night at twelve o'clock. General Miramon notified the chief officers to remain quiet until further orders.

The west side of the city, where the forces of General Corona were stationed, was considered the best point on which to centre the whole body of men in making the sortie.

At the Imperial headquarters, staff department, orders were issued by General Castillo, secretly and verbally, to the various officers of the army to be ready for action at the time designated. No fires were to be lighted, and strict silence was to prevail.

The infantry were to carry nothing but their blankets and tin pots. All of the cannon on the fortress of the Campana were to be spiked, and the magazines to be flooded. The light mountain-pieces of eight and ten pounders were to be dismounted and packed on mules, together with light supplies of grape and canister.

The men were ordered not to burden themselves with anything not actually necessary, or that might be disadvantageous in a forced march, which it was anticipated they would be compelled to make through the defiles and mountain gorges of the Sierra Gorda. That route, with light accoutrements, would have defied the rapid pursuit of the enemy.

General Mejia had armed twelve hundred citizens of Queretaro, who were ordered to remain behind to protect the city and to keep order. They were further ordered to surrender to General Escobedo at discretion, at any time they should think proper, provided they first allowed twenty-four hours to pass after the evacuation.

Complete orders having been issued, and all arrangements having been made in accordance with the projected plan, the Emperor retired. His accustomed hour was eight o'clock, but the business of that eventful night extended his hour of slumber until a quarter past one o'clock.

Prince Salm Salm was working until after twelve o'clock that night, arranging the Emperor's archives, after having packed them the day before into small canvas sacks, ready to be strapped to the escort saddles.

Many of the men occupied a short time in writing to their relatives, saying a parting word to their families and friends. As lights were prohibited, they assisted each other by smoking cigarettes close to the paper. One would puff his exhilarating weed, while another would scribble a few words by the glimmer thereof.

Between one and two o'clock, the traitor, Colonel Lopez, who had previously plotted with the enemy to betray his own party, silently crept out of his quarters, and threaded his way through the dark and narrow streets of the city, in pursuit of General Escobedo. He first met Colonel Garza, who was in command of the advance guard of the enemy. Garza took Lopez to General Veliz; the latter and Lopez went to see Escobedo: after which interview the two returned to meet Garza. General Veliz ordered Colonel Garza to take his command and follow Lopez, who guided him to a hole in the wall near the church called La Cruz. General Veliz himself proceeded to this opening in the wall, and there remained for a while; at which time he ordered Colonel Garza to proceed further under the guidance of Lopez. The latter was the officer of the day. On arriving at the nearest station of the Imperial troops, Garza's command halted. Lopez asked an Imperial officer if there were any news; to which the latter replied, none. Lopez then ordered the Imperial officers at that post to be paraded, and that the roll be called. That was done, the officers standing up in a line. Lopez then ordered the command to be formed and marched to the rear of Garza's forces, leaving Garza in possession of that post. Lopez immediately escorted other Liberal officers to the different posts under his command, in order that the same plan should be executed, until the enemy had possessed themselves of all the points within the control of Lopez.

When the Liberal forces entered the city, quite a number of the Imperial officers were awake, with the excitement of the expected engagement, and were cleaning their arms and making preparations for their contemplated departure. As they saw Col. Rincon's regiment pass their bivouacks, they supposed it was a part of their own forces moving toward the Casa Blanca, for some reason unknown to them, before the designated time. It being in the darkness of the night, and the dress of the two armies being so near alike, it was quite difficult to distinguish the one from the other.

By half-past three o'clock, nearly one half of the city was in the almost noiseless possession of the Liberals. Soon thereafter nearly all of the church bells commenced, almost simultaneously, to ring with great force. The Imperialists were much confused. Many of them were of opinion that Marquez had arrived from the city of Mexico, attacked and defeated Escobedo: hence the great rejoicing. What a sad deception!

Commander Yablonski, an adjutant of Lopez, was in the treasonable plot with him; but he did not wish any harm to fall upon the Emperor. He went to the room of Don José Blasio, Secretary of His Majesty, which was in the convent of La Cruz, and near that of His Majesty, and awoke him, and said, "The enemy are in the garden; get up!" Blasio immediately dressed himself, went to the room of the Emperor, called him, and informed him of the condition of affairs. He then notified Gen. Castillo and Col. Guzman, who roomed together; also Prince Salm Salm and Col. Pradillo,—all of whom were in that convent and came to the Emperor's room. Colonel Pradillo informed the Emperor that the enemy occupied that convent, and had taken eight or ten pieces of artillery in the plaza of La Cruz; and that it would be useless to attempt to defend it. The Emperor gave Col. Pradillo one of his pistols, and holding another in his hand, went to the door, followed by Pradillo, Prince Salm Salm, and Blasio, and then said, "To go out here or to die is the only way." They crossed the corridor, and on the stairs met a sentinel, who ordered them to go back; but an officer of the Liberals, said to be Colonel Rincon, saw them, and said to the sentinel, "Let them pass, they are citizens." As the Emperor and party advanced a little further into the plaza, they were met by a party of Liberal soldiers, who were about to stop them, when Colonel Rincon came up, and said to the soldiers, "Let them pass, they are civilians!" They then hurried on to the quarters of the "Regiment of the Empress," which were the Emperor's escort, and ordered them to prepare and mount, and to advance with all speed to El Cerro de las Campanas. In the mean time the Emperor said to Colonel Pradillo, that it would be more convenient for him, the Emperor, to have his horse. Pradillo then went for it. The Emperor, Prince Salm Salm, and Blasio immediately proceeded to the Departmental palace, where Pradillo soon met them with the Emperor's horse. General Castillo had just met them also, when Lopez came riding up to them, of whom His Majesty asked what was going on. He replied, "All is lost. See, your Majesty, the enemy's force is coming very near!" Just then a body of infantry were entering the plaza, which the Emperor thought were of his own army; and he exclaimed, "Thank God, our battalion of Municipal Guards are coming." One of his officers advanced toward them, and ascertained that they were a part of the enemy, and returned to notify the Emperor, who, with his little party, started again; and when near the house of Señor Rubio, Lopez said to the Emperor, "Your Majesty ought to enter this house or some other, as it is the only way to save yourself." The Emperor refused to do so, and was determined to go to the hill (El Cerro), as first contemplated. In front of the Casino, they met Capt. Jarero, Adjntant of Gen. Castillo, whom the Emperor ordered to notify Gen. Miramon to bring all the force he could gather to El Cerro de las Campanas. The Emperor was implored by Lopez to mount the horse that was saddled; but his Majesty refused to accept of that comfort, so long as Gen. Castillo and his other surrounding friends had no horses to ride in his company. They all proceeded on foot to El Cerro. When they reached that position, they found about 150 men of their forces there. Soon the Regiment of the Empress reached them. His Majesty was anxiously waiting the arrival of General Miramon, and frequently remarked, "See if he cannot be distinguished in the crowd that is coming." General Mejia had rallied a few men in the plaza del Ayuntamiento, and rushed on to El Cerro.

General Mendez was surprised in the Alameda, and surrounded. He opened fire on the enemy, which was returned. His men were cut down rapidly; but he tried, notwithstanding the havoc made among his men, to rally them, with a view of cutting his way through the enemy's lines to the convent of La Cruz, to save the Emperor. The enemy's force met him on another point, and being between two fires, his men falling rapidly, he surrendered at half-past five. He was shot the next day at six in the morning.

General Miramon, awakened by the ringing of the bells, rushed down, with an aid-de-camp, into the street, was surrounded by soldiers whom he took to be his own men, and told them that he was General Miramon. An officer on horseback fired at him, and he received the ball in his cheek. He returned the shot, and a running fight ensued along the street. Finally, he saw a door ajar; he entered the house, which he learned was that of Dr. Samaniegos, who hid him, as he was weak from loss of blood. The owner of the house rushed into the street, met a party of Liberals, and informed them that he had captured Miramon. After the Liberal force had discovered him, they tied him, dragged him away, and placed him in the convent of Terrecitas.

For nearly half an hour after the arrival of the Emperor and his small force at El Cerro de las Campanas, a fire from two different batteries of the Liberals, that of San Gregorio and the one at the garita of Celaya, poured their shot in that direction.

The Emperor, considerably excited, exclaimed in German to Prince Salm Salm, "Oh, Salm, how much would I give now for a friendly shell!" wishing that one might end his life.

When Colonel Gonzales reported the arrival of his regiment to the Emperor, and that Miramon was wounded, the Emperor took Castillo and Mejia one side, and asked them if it were possible to break the lines of the enemy. Mejia took his glass and surveyed quite accurately the position of the enemy, and then replied to His Majesty, "Sire, it is impossible; but if Your Majesty orders it, we will try it: for my part, I am ready to die." His Majesty immediately took Colonel Pradillo by the arm, and said, "It is necessary to make a quick determination, in order to avoid greater misfortunes." He then put up a white flag on the fort on the hill, and ordered Colonel Pradillo and Ramirez to go and have an interview with General Escobedo upon the following basis: "First, that if he wished another victim, he could take him, the Emperor; Second, that he wished that the men of his army should be treated with all the consideration that their loyalty and valor merited; and, Third, that he and the men of his personal services should not be molested in any manner."

The Emperor saw in the distance a small squadron of soldiers dressed in scarlet, riding at a rapid speed toward the Campanas; and as he descried them, he exclaimed, with tears in his eyes, "See! see! my brave hussars! How fearful a risk they run, exposed to the full fire of the enemy's batteries! Who would not be proud of being their chief?" But, alas! what a terrible disappointment! He soon learned that they were a part of General Treviña's cavalry, of the Liberal army. The firing soon ceased. A squad of cavalry rode up, and an officer among them asked where the Emperor was, using at the same time a vulgar epithet. His Majesty stepped outside of the fortification, and said, "I am he." The officer declared that Mendez had been taken, and demanded that the Emperor should deliver up himself and all his officers as prisoners. The Emperor consented, and was taken prisoner by General Echegary, and said to him: "If you should require anybody's life, take mine, but do not harm my officers. I am willing to die, if you should require it, but intercede with General Escobedo for the life of my officers." Soon General Corona appeared, to whom the Emperor said, "If you wish another victim, here he is," meaning himself. General Corona replied that it did not belong to him to treat upon that question; that until he could deliver him to the general-in-chief, his person and the generals around him would be safe.

The Emperor had on his overcoat when taken. He opened it to show his uniform and rank. He, Generals Castillo and Mejia, and Prince Salm Salm, accompanied by General Echegary (Liberal), mounted horses, which were furnished them by the Liberals, and rode down the hill several hundred yards, where they met General Escobedo, with whom they returned on to the hill, and into the fort, where they dismounted. His Majesty, General Escobedo, and two of his officers, and Prince Salm Salm entered a tent. The Emperor shook hands with Escobedo, and said to him: "If you wish more blood, take mine; and I ask that the officers, who have been true to me, be well treated, and that I may not be insulted by your officers or men." Escobedo replied that the Emperor should be treated like a prisoner of war, and that he should not be insulted. Shortly after that, Escobedo delivered the Emperor, Generals Mejia and Castillo, and Prince Salm Salm into the hands of General Riva Palacio, who conducted them to La Cruz Convent, passing around the city by Casa Blanca, through the Alameda, thence through the ruined part of the city to the convent.

The Emperor was placed in the same room which he had previously occupied in the Convent of La Cruz. That day he requested General Escobedo to permit the officers of his house to remain in the same convent, which was granted. Those officers were Prince Salm Salm, Colonel Guzman, the Minister Aguirre, Colonel Pradillo, Doctor Basch, and Don José Blasio, secretary. They remained four days there; three of which His Majesty was sick with the dysentery. The fifth day they were removed into the Convent of Terrecitas, which place they occupied seven days; thence were taken to the Convent of Capuchinas, where were also imprisoned all the generals of the Imperial army. They all occupied the first floor until the third or fourth day, when the Emperor and Generals Miramon and Mejia were placed in the second story, where they remained until their execution.

His Majesty lost everything the day the city was taken, except the clothes he had on.

No form of speech could express His Majesty's astonishment at the acts of Colonel Lopez. A man in whom he had placed the utmost confidence, whom he had treated like a brother, as it were, stabbed him in the dark. And it would hardly be considered an error in judgment, in placing entire and confident reliance on the fidelity of the man whose interests, he supposed, were united with his, in asserting and maintaining a cause and rights common to both. His Majesty was the godfather to Lopez's child. He laid his heart and cause open to Lopez, with all the confidence of a child in its mother; and in consequence thereof lost his life. Had the Imperial party not been betrayed, they would have undoubtedly broken through the enemy's line, and made their way down to Vera Cruz.

Lopez is equally despised by both parties in Mexico; yet he has the effrontery to attempt to write himself innocent, by filling one or two journals with his evidence, which, closely scanned, proves him guilty. He ought to hide his face in shame, from the view of heaven and earth. He has at last succeeded in obtaining a few of the Liberals to assist him, while the others, who were eye-witnesses to his work of betrayal, stand back and laugh.

The Emperor had often gallantly steered his bark upon the sea-waves; but he had never been baffled by the waves of duplicity before; they were too strong for him; they washed him from the deck, and stranded his ship of state; and the Mexican eagle sprang from the Imperial and lighted upon the Republican banner, save at the Capital of the nation, where for a short period thereafter, Imperialism held sway through the cowardly oppressor, Marquez, who was as little friendly to his Sovereign as he was to his open foe.

But few sovereigns ever found themselves so completely surrounded by bad faith and treachery. And the ruler who shall stand at the head of that nation, whence fell Maximilian, and succeed in preserving fidelity and attachment to his administration, for any considerable length of time, will have exhibited greater skill in the art of government than has been the fortune of any preceding one to manifest. Let us hope, for the sake of humanity, that in the future the banner of peace may spread its ample folds all over the broad lands of Moctezuma.

Imprisonment, and even death, were insufficient for the gallant and ill-fated Emperor, in the estimation of his enemies. They must endeavor to tarnish his honor by the breath of falsehood. Hate was so engendered in them, that it was bound to show itself in every conceivable form. It came from the depths of their hearts to their mouths like the bubbles that rise up from the bottom of the seething kettle to its surface. All kinds of foolish statements have been circulated as coming from the Emperor's lips. Such a course of revenge only springs from those who, by mistake of the authorities, have not worn the halter—contemptible and cowardly hearts who never remember that true honor strikes not a fallen foe.

Not long after the imprisonment of His Majesty, an article purporting to be a proclamation from him to the inhabitants of Mexico, was circulated in every newspaper within the territory of Mexico, but which bears no date. Some of its circulating mediums had the effrontery to guarantee its authenticity.

No writing of a public character was issued by His Majesty after his capture. That false proclamation is in the following words:

"The Archduke Ferdinand Maximilian of Hapsburg, ex-Emperor of Mexico, to all its inhabitants:

"Compatriots:

"After the valor and the patriotism of the Republican armies have brought about the end of my reign in this city, the obstinate defence of which was indispensable to save the honor of my cause and of my race; after this bloody siege, in which have rivalled in abnegation and bravery the soldiers of the Empire with those of the Republic, I am going to explain myself to you.

"Compatriots: I came to Mexico animated not only with a firm hope of making you, and every one of you, individually happy, but also protected and called to the throne of Moctezuma and Iturbide by the Emperor of France, Napoleon III. He has abandoned me cowardly and infamously, through fear of the United States, placing in ridicule France itself, and making it spend uselessly its treasures, and shedding the blood of its sons and your own. When the news of my fall and death will reach Europe, all its monarchs, and the land of Charlemagne, will ask an account of my blood and that of the Germans, Belgians, and French, shed in Mexico, from the Napoleon dynasty. Then will be the end . . . . . .

"The whole world will soon see Napoleon covered with shame from head to foot.

"Now the world sees H. M. the Emperor of Austria, my august brother, supplicating for my life before the United States, and me a prisoner of war at the disposition of the Republican government, with my crown and heart torn to pieces.

"Compatriots: My last words to you are these: I ardently desire that my blood may regenerate Mexico; and that as a warning to all ambitious and incautious persons, you may know how, with prudence and true patriotism, to take advantage of your triumph, and through your virtues ennoble the political cause, the banner of which you sustain. May Providence save you, and make me worthy of myself.

"MAXIMILIAN."

It is quite clear, from the reading of the foregoing pretended proclamation, that the feeling that prevailed in the mind of its author was based upon a deep-rooted hatred, and void of that magnanimity which flows from a brave and noble-minded conqueror.

On the 20th of May, the Emperor was permitted to visit General Escobedo. He went accompanied by Prince Salm Salm and wife. He empowered the Prince to treat with General Escobedo; and in order that the latter might show his authority thus to act, the following written power was executed by the Emperor:

"I authorize Colonel and Aid-de-camp Prince Salm Salm to treat with General Escobedo, and I acknowledge the acts done by him as done in my name.

"MAXIMILIAN."

Prince Salm Salm, accordingly, wrote down certain propositions which were presented to, and rejected by, General Escobedo. One of the main ones was, that the Emperor, if permitted to leave Mexico, would never return to it again.

CHAPTER XII.

Convent—Prison of Maximilian—Author's visit and conversation with Maximilian—Arrival of lawyers from the city of Mexico—Foreigners ordered to leave Queretaro.

THE convent of the Capuchinas, in Queretaro, is an ancient, spacious building, all over which the hand of Time has drawn its dingy strokes; and as you gaze at its exterior, observing its dimensions, its domes, its statuary, and carvings, you are reminded that the pile of silver and gold that reared that massive temple, could be enclosed in no small compass.

Year after year, mite after mite, was contributed by rich and poor, to raise its lofty dome toward the heavens; beneath which, the ever faithful daily gathered to offer up, on bended knee, thanks to our Maker for the many blessings they had received. Those who gave their mite, those who laid stone upon stone, upward, upward rising in the sky, little thought that they were walling in their descendants for sustaining political opinions honestly formed, and conscientiously advocated. They never dreamed that they were erecting warriors' abode, a depository for bristling bayonets, polished swords, powder and balls;—where the bugle, the fife, and drum were to summon the inmates to service; where the armed sentinel paces to and fro, with a measured tread. Those workmen reared that costly structure for a house of Peace; where the multitude, armed with the word of God only, were to be taught, "Vengeance is mine, saith the Lord."

As you approached the door of that temple, after the taking of Queretaro by the Liberals, you observed two sentinels at the door, armed with muskets and fixed bayonets. If you passed there in the day-time, they said not a word; but if darkness had overspread its folds, you heard at a distance of fifty yards therefrom, "*Quien Viva?*" ("Who comes there?") You then answered, "*Libertad*," or "*Amigo*." ("Liberty," or "Friend.") If you wished to enter there, to visit His Majesty, you first reach a not spacious room; then, turning to the left into another of like dimensions, and going straight ahead in the same direction as you first entered, a distance of about twenty feet, you there meet two other sentinels; passing still onward into the court to the stairway, two more persons stand in armor arrayed. No questions are yet asked you, and you wind your way up that pair of stairs; at the top thereof you turn to the right, and walk straight on in a direction at right angles with that which you pursued in entering, until a promenade of fifty feet or more brings you to the end of the passage-way, where stands another sentinel, who exclaims, in a stentorian voice, "*Cabo!*" ("Corporal!") The corporal appears, asks you your business. If you expect to proceed further, you must present a written order. The corporal calls the captain of the guard, who reads your order, and if correct, the soldier is ordered to let you pass. In advancing, you turn half around to the left, in the opposite direction from that which conducts you to the first entrance of the building. You enter the corridor around the court,—passing first, before reaching the court, on the right, a small room occupied by the captain of the guard. On the left you pass two doors—one enters the room of His Majesty's servant, the other into that of his physician, Dr. Samuel Basch. The corridor is six or seven feet wide, running on two sides of the court only, protected by a balustrade about three and a half feet high. As you first enter that corridor, on the opposite side of the court, a door is seen directly in front of you; that leads to the room of the Emperor. As you advance a few feet further, at your right, on the opposite side of the court, two more doors are observable in a line with that of the Emperor's;—one of them, which is nearest to that of His Majesty, opens into Miramon's room; the other, into that of Mejia. In front of the Emperor's room is a vacant space, nearly fifteen feet square. In front of the other two rooms, the space is only of the width of the corridor.

The apartment of the Emperor is about eighteen by twenty feet, measuring to the ceiling nearly twenty feet. In front, and to the left of the door as you enter, is a window, which opens out to the vacant space in the corridor. The door and that window were the only apertures that gave light and air. When clouds darkened the sky, his room was not as light as one would have desired; and on warm days the space in front was more comfortable than the room itself, in which he found a fan an agreeable article.

The furniture of His Majesty exhibited no proof that it was prepared for an Imperial mansion. It consisted of an iron bedstead surmounted with brass, and a tolerably comfortably bed; a pine table twenty by thirty inches in dimensions, another double its size, one rocking-chair, three or more common ones, and a small box which contained some private articles.

The room itself had a brick floor, plastered walls without any ornaments, and as much the appearance of a prison as though it had been built for that purpose. The rooms occupied by Generals Miramon and Mejia were once used as chapels, and presented a little better appearance than that of His Majesty. The space in front of the latter made that one a little more desirable. The three prisoners were allowed to visit each other, and to walk in the corridor, or sit there, all of which they frequently did.

That convent contained all the prisoners who were of the rank of general. Prince Salm Salm, who was registered as a colonel when taken, but who had been commissioned as a general a few days prior to the capture of Queretaro, was permitted, at the solicitation of His Majesty, to occupy the same building on the first floor. As the Prince was German, and a person in whom the Emperor had confidence, it was a favor to him to be allowed the company and service of the Prince. Although the latter was below, he had the permission to ascend to the room of His Majesty when the latter requested his presence. The consequence was, the Prince spent a great deal of his time with the Emperor. At or near each door of the three prisoners stood a sentinel. The prisoners were thus guarded day and night. A battalion of soldiers was quartered in the convent also.

On Tuesday morning, May 28th, 1867, I left San Luis Potosi, and reached Queretaro on the following day at five o'clock, P. M. I there met, at the hotel, Mr. Bansen, the Hamburg Consul resident at San Luis Potosi. Wednesday morning, the day after my arrival, he observed to me that the Emperor was desirous of seeing me. A few hours later the wife of Prince Salm Salm met me, and remarked that she had just come from the room of His Majesty, and that his request was that I should visit him. I therefore escorted her to the convent where the Emperor was, first obtaining a written permit from the Fiscal, the law-officer of the Government, who had charge of the prosecution of the three mentioned prisoners. It appeared that the Fiscal was the proper officer to grant that permission, rather than the commanding-officer of the division. I was requested to converse with His Majesty in Spanish, so that the officer of the guard would be able to understand all that I said. The Emperor met me most cordially, and as though it was a treat to see anybody who was friendly disposed towards him.

After quite a long social conversation, he commenced to relate some facts pertaining to himself and government, first prefacing his remarks with the observation, "I wish to tell you all, that the world may know the truth." He further remarked, that when he came to Mexico it was with a sincere belief that he was called by the will of a majority of the people; that he told the Mexican deputation, when they first visited him at Miramar in the fall of 1863, that he would not accept the throne of Mexico until he was satisfied that the majority would sanction it. That the deputation then said to him that they believed that the majority were already in favor of his coming. The evidence at that time was inadequate to convince him. He observed that when the deputation appeared the second time, in the following April, the proof which they presented left no doubt on his mind as to the condition precedent having been complied with. His consent to accept the crown was based upon that belief. He further stated upon that point, that when he arrived at Vera Cruz, and witnessed the demonstration in his favor, which continued to the capital of the nation, he was more convinced than ever of the truth of the statement made by the Mexican deputation. He said, that on the way to the capital he remarked to the Empress, "Surely the deputation were right when they said a majority of the Mexicans were in favor of our coming to be their ruler." He then added, "I never in all Europe saw a Sovereign received with such enthusiasm as greeted us."

I might well testify in his behalf that, according to the statements related to me by many persons who witnessed parts of that demonstration, the Emperor could not have come to any other conclusion.

I do not think there is the slightest room for doubt that His Majesty was perfectly sincere in his reported belief.

He said, in speaking of his capture, that General Escobedo promised that he should be treated like a prisoner of war. If that promise had been carried out, he never would have been shot.

As to the decree of October 3d, 1865, issued by him, he remarked that it originated with Marshal Bazaine; that Bazaine appeared before the Council and pressed the matter, saying some severe law was necessary to put down the dissidents; and that Juarez was then in Texas. He said further, that he himself was opposed to the decree; and putting up his hands in the attitude of surprise at the severity of the decree, said: "That is against all rules of warfare in Europe; and I did not wish to sign it; but the ministers being also in favor of it, and believing Juarez to be out of the country, I signed it." Statements had been so made to him that he did not for one moment doubt that Juarez had been, and was, in Texas when he signed that decree. In fact, he said to me that he was almost certain that there was documentary evidence to prove that Juarez had been out of the country. He further remarked, "That is what makes Juarez mad, to think that it can be proved on him."

I asked him if he had ever signed a decree or order to have any particular person or persons executed for a political crime? He replied, "Never."

He then observed that he ordered the telegraph office to be kept open day and night; that an operator should be there at all hours, and should immediately deliver dispatches which contained a statement of the capture of prisoners, whether received in the day or night; and if during the latter period, to wake him up, so that he might forthwith send orders that none of the prisoners should be executed. He observed that he had frequently gotten up in the night for that purpose. He said, in speaking of executions, that the trouble with himself was, that he was too tender-hearted; that he had been told by the Empress that he was not willing to punish when justice demanded it.

He felt very much annoyed at the many acts of cruelty which had reached his ears, and which were alleged to have been committed by the French.

I think I never saw a man more opposed to cruelty than the Emperor. In that regard his feelings were as tender as those of a lady. Yet, in battle, he was as brave as Cæsar, as all who saw him in that position will testify. We were speaking about some battles; during which time the names of Prince Salm Salm came up. His Majesty said of him: "He was as brave as a lion, Sir." He had no good feelings toward Marshal Bazaine, nor his own general, Marquez. He considered that he himself had to suffer, and perhaps to lose his life, through the actions of Bazaine.

I said to him, "The treaty of Miramar placed Your Majesty in an exceedingly difficult position; while it gave the French commander full control over the military actions and movements of the French troops, as well as over any body of mixed French and Mexican forces: it made the Sovereign head responsible for their acts." He replied, "Yes, I know it, and I am almost ashamed of it; but I submitted to it, thinking it would be the best for the country."

In speaking of President Juarez, he said, "I believe he is a good man." I never heard him say any unkind words of Juarez.

After my two first visits, I requested the Fiscal to allow me to speak in English or French, as I could therein best express the law to the Emperor, inasmuch as I was one of his counsel; to which he assented. In speaking in English, he sometimes hesitated for a word, and would place in its stead a French one, when I would give him the English of it. After a few days' conversation, he remarked, "Since my practice with you, I speak better

English. I do not speak as well as I did fifteen years ago: when in the navy, I was in the habit of meeting officers who spoke it." He spoke English very well, and read it better. He had but two books, I think, in his room to read. One was a Universal History in Spanish, and the other I have forgotten. I carried him, "*Wheaton on the Law of Nations*," in Spanish. He asked if I thought the translation good. I replied, "Very good."

When conversing about his case, he remarked, on several occasions, placing his hand on his heart, "I have never done anything against my conscience." He spoke it with such a sincerity of expression, that no man could have heard him say it without believing it. Two or three times he said to me, "I should like very much to see the Empress, my dear wife, my mother, and other relatives; but my honor before life." The name of her Majesty Queen Victoria was mentioned in conversation between us alone, on one or two occasions, when he spoke in a very kind and brotherly manner of her. His expression indicated that he looked upon her as a warm friend.

He held Americans in high estimation. He said: "The Americans are a great people for improvements. And besides, they are great lovers of justice. They pay such respect to the laws, that I admire them. And if God should spare my life, I intend to visit the United States, and travel through them." He further said of them, "You can rely on the word of an American gentleman." The idea of improvements and progress seemed to occupy a good deal of his attention. He was anxious to see Mexico advance. He frequently alluded to the lavish bounty of nature to the country: he was much delighted with its natural beauty and resources. We were much in hopes that the point raised as to the jurisdiction of the court would be decided against it, in order that more time might be obtained, as that would decrease the excitement against his Majesty; and that after such a favorable point gained, the government might determine to bring the matter before Congress. His Majesty said: "If my case can go before the Mexican Congress, I am not afraid. I will speak myself, without any lawyers." He then turned towards me, and smiled a little, and observed, "I might need a lawyer to point out some of the law, but I would do the talking."

When I pointed to several articles in the Mexican Constitution, which were in his favor, he took his own copy of it, and marked the articles with a red pencil, read them carefully, and became quite animated. They had not been suggested to him before. He sent immediately for Mr. Vasquez, one of his lawyers. When he came, he alluded to what I had said in regard to the unconstitutionality of certain laws. Mr. Vasquez replied that he believed that I was correct in my opinion; but as the Government was still, in some respects, acting contrary to the Constitution, he could not say what view would be taken of those questions. He further said, that the Minister of Foreign Affairs, Señor Lerdo Tejada, when a member of Congress, had expressed his opinion upon the Constitution in conformity with mine.

Afterward I set forth my opinion upon the case, in a written document, which was translated into Spanish. This, he said, he would like to have sent to the United States and Europe: a copy thereof is inserted herein among the papers of his cause.

After I had read the accusations in the law-office of Señor Vasquez, I visited His Majesty, and found him in bed, not very well, but sitting up. I said to him, "I have just read the accusations." "Have you?" he observed; and smiling, said, "When they were read to me, I had to put my hand over my mouth to keep from laughing, they were so silly." I remarked that I could not say that they appeared to be written in a lawyer-like style.

On Tuesday morning, June 4th, soon after I entered his room, the Emperor said, "We must hurry with business. I have been talking with Miramon. He has counted up the time, and says that he thinks they will shoot us Friday morning." I replied to him that I thought not, that more time would be given by the President. We had been anxiously waiting the arrival of the lawyers from the city of Mexico. They had been expected for several days, and what detained them we could not learn. As the city of Mexico was besieged, we thought it possible that the difficulty might be that they were not permitted to pass the lines. They arrived that evening, the 4th.

For two days the wife of Prince Salm Salm had been doing her utmost to procure mules or horses to convey her to the city, to ascertain the reason of the delay of the lawyers. She had been able to obtain a carriage, but no animals. I went in search of animals. I called on General ——, of the Liberal army, whom I knew, and solicited animals of him, saying that I wished them to go only to the first station, where the stage line changed. He replied that he had not sufficient for his own use. At first I did not tell him the urgent reason of my desire for the animals. After I ascertained that he had none to spare, and as he asked me why I wished them, and if I were going to Mexico myself, I told him that I wished them to send for the lawyers whom the Emperor was desirous of having to assist in his defence. He then observed to me, that if he had a thousand to spare, he would not let one go for that purpose. In other words, he would deprive the Emperor of any defence, if he could. That class of officers caused the death of the Emperor. General Escobedo is among that number. It has been said by those in Mexico, that he could have saved the life of Maximilian if he had desired it; notwithstanding, he communicated the statement to the President, that if Maximilian was not shot, that he, Escobedo, could not hold his army together. The truth will some day make its appearance. It has already to me, on good authority. And I attach more blame to Escobedo than to Juarez. When Escobedo appointed the members of the court-martial, he knew what their decision would be. There were many officers of the Liberal army that would have rejoiced at the verdict of not guilty, in the Emperor's case.

On one occasion I visited the convent about the middle of the day. I found the Emperor, Generals Miramon, Mejia, Prince Salm Salm, and Dr. Basch, around a table in the space in the corridor, in front of His Majesty's room, playing dominoes. As I entered, they were about to stop, through politeness; but I insisted that they should proceed with the game. They requested me to join them. I did so—placing myself between General Miramon and Prince Salm Salm, and opposite the Emperor. They all smiled a little, and His Majesty looked up at me and said, "This is a stupid game; it's like children's play." He seemed to be impressed with the idea that I might think it was a silly occupation for men of talent to be engaged in. He made that same remark twice. I replied that it was by no means stupid; that it occupied the mind, and made the time pass pleasanter than sitting idle. I think we played an hour. The Emperor asked me one day if I thought that he and his two generals, Miramon and Mejia, would be justified in escaping, if they could. I answered him, "Certainly, by all means; I have no idea that the court-martial will do you justice: the law is clearly in your favor; but from my discussion on some of the principles of law with the officers of the government, I am quite satisfied that the determination is to convict you at all hazards." He preferred to have a fair trial before Congress, rather than to have escaped; but believing that they were anxious to murder him, he had no scruples about saving his life the best way that might be provided. He remarked, "I have never given my word that I would not escape; I was clever about that." But if he had ever promised not to escape, he would have kept his word. He was punctilious about his honor.

He then told me of a plot formed to save them. One Henry B. del Borgo, an Italian rascal, a captain in the Liberal army, had received two thousand dollars of the Emperor's money to purchase six horses, saddles, equipments, and pistols. He purchased that number of horses of an ordinary class, and the accoutrements. I do not think, from an examination of them, that they could have cost over seven or eight hundred dollars. The horses were to be ready on the night designated, at a given point, and the three prisoners were to be let out at the proper time, to mount their horses, and to rush for the mountains. It was known that Mejia was well acquainted with the whole country, and that with him, there would be no danger of being lost. Much to the surprise of us all, the Italian left one morning early, taking with him the balance of the money; and it was believed that he had made known the plot: but as to that, we did not positively know. I think he left on the morning of the 5th of June.

That night the guard was increased, and a light kept burning all night near the Emperor's room. We began to conjecture as to the cause. Finally, it was rumored that Miramon's wife had attempted to bribe the officers; that she had succeeded with several, but one of them had told the secret. We therefore considered that the Emperor's plot was yet undiscovered.

The getting out of the convent was the difficult part.

They considered that once out, there would be no danger. How to pass the officer and nine or ten sentinels, was the great question. The Emperor once said to me: "Cannot we get out with ropes—putting one hand over the other, like sailors in climbing? You know I am good at that—I have been in the navy." I answered him, perhaps that might be done, but I thought it would be difficult, as there was no outside window to his room. I did not think it feasible, as the most difficult part would be to pass the first guards in the corridor, which he would have to do to reach any opening.

After the foregoing had taken place, I was requested by the officer of the guard to speak entirely in Spanish to His Majesty. He said that was the order which he had received. As he remained near us when we conversed, I was compelled to talk in that language. At one time I knew that the wife of Prince Salm Salm was to be there within a half-hour or more; I therefore prolonged my visit, knowing that she could talk but little Spanish, and was under the necessity of speaking in English to the Emperor. As they conversed I joined in, of course in English; and then I availed myself of the opportunity of saying to His Majesty what I did not wish the officer of the guard to understand.

The lawyers from the city of Mexico visited His Majesty the next day after their arrival. They suggested that the laws were unconstitutional, and that they would attack the laws on that ground.

His Majesty said to me on the following day, that when they made those observations to him he immediately said to them that those points, as to the unconstitutionality of the laws, had already been made. They inquired, "By whom?" "By an American lawyer." They exhibited a little surprise, His Majesty said, that a foreign lawyer should be so familiar with their constitution and laws. The Emperor pointed out the favorable positions which I had assumed, and gave them a translation of my legal views. They did me the honor to say that they agreed perfectly with all my opinions. They requested that I should meet them in consultation the next day at ten o'clock in the morning. Before that hour arrived, they thought it best for Messrs. Palacio and De la Torre to go forthwith to San Luis Potosi to see what could be done with the President and Cabinet.

The lawyers all worked very hard to save the Emperor. They did all that was in their power as lawyers, and with their influence as men.

I asked the Emperor if he thought he would have been able to sally out of Queretaro had he not been sold by Lopez, and had the plans formed on his part been executed. He replied, "Yes." He believed that he would have been successful in reaching Vera Cruz. He observed that he had at that time, May 14th, five thousand men in Queretaro. He did not seem to have any doubt in his mind that he would have fought his way through.

While he was sitting up in bed one day, the name of Lopez came up in the conversation, and the wife of Prince Salm Salm was present, who remarked to me, "What do you think? A few days ago His Majesty heard that some man was in pursuit of Lopez to kill him, and His Majesty sent a person to inform Lopez of the fact, and to be on his guard." I looked at the Emperor, and observed, "Did Your Majesty do that?" He smiled, and blushed a little, and answered, "Yes, I did." I then said that that was more than I could have done to a man that had sacrificed me. He made some remark to the effect that he supposed but a few persons would have done it.

I asked him if I could have one of his photographs; to which he replied, "With the greatest pleasure; and you will please give me yours, with your signature on it."

He gave me one of his, observing that it was taken some time ago, but that if God spared his life he would give me a better one. I gave him my own, with my signature. He thanked me very kindly. He further said, "If God spares my life, and you go to Europe, the castle of Miramar shall be your home." I thanked him, and said I hoped we would meet there; and that if he and I lived, we should probably see each other in Europe. It was his custom, when speaking of what he would probably do if he lived, to preface the remark with the words, "*If God should spare my life.*"

His Majesty was dressed in citizen's clothes, having on black pants and vest, a dark-blue single-breasted frock-coat, black necktie, white socks, and a pair of variegated cloth slippers. His health was not very good; and frequently, when I visited him, he was sitting up in his bed, somewhat feeble.

On the seventh of June, I was sent for by General Escobedo. I called at his office. After a few moments' conversation, he observed that he had just made an order requiring all foreigners to leave the city on the following day. He further said that I was not alone included in the order. I inquired of him if any accusations had been made against me; to which he replied, "Not any." I then called upon the Emperor, and informed him of the fact; at which he was very much displeased. He wished me to say to General Escobedo that I was one of his counsel, and on that ground, to request that I could stay with him through the trial. He also desired that I should solicit Mr. Vasquez, one of his counsel, to call upon General Escobedo, and ask of him permission for me to remain. I called on Mr. Vasquez, and made known to him the desire of the Emperor. He refused to comply, saying that he had once that day called upon the general, and found him in a bad humor, and quite enraged about something. I bid His Majesty good-bye that afternoon, saying that I did not see how it was possible for me to remain any longer, as the order of the commanding officer was positive, and must be obeyed. He said to me "Good-bye" most affectionately, with a very complimentary additional remark; and then we parted. That parting I never shall forget.

Subsequently, I saw General Escobedo again, and said to him that I was one of the Emperor's counsel, and that it was his wish that I should remain with him. He replied, "Foreigners cannot practice in our courts." I might further add, that if he had the control of the nation, and the law-making power, he would not allow a foreigner to live in the country. He did say, that were it in his power to govern the rights of foreigners, he would not permit them to live in Mexico, unless they became citizens of the country. The following morning I left the city for Tacubaya.

CHAPTER XIII.

Court-martial—Accusations—Defence—Trial and judgment—Maximilian's decree of October 3d, 1865—Law of Juarez, 1862—Treaty of Miramar—Correspondence between United States and Mexico—Parts of the Mexican Constitution—Comments on the law.

BY an order of Señor Don Benito Juarez, as President of the Republic of Mexico, General Mariano Escobedo, chief of the forces at Queretaro, was commanded to form an Ordinary Council of War, which should be authorized and required to try His Majesty Maximilian, and his generals, Miramon and Mejia.

The Government of Mexico recognized Maximilian only as Archduke of Austria, and the other two prisoners as mere citizens, not acknowledging their titles as generals, but as the "*so called generals.*"

They were thus entered on the records.

General Escobedo telegraphed to the Minister of War on the 27th of May, 1867, that, in answer to his note of the 21st, he had the honor to say that proceedings had been taken toward the trial of the three mentioned persons.

In accordance with the foregoing order, General Escobedo appointed the following persons as members of that Council of War: Lieutenant-Colonel Platon Sanchez (President), Captain José Vicente Ramirez, Emilio Lojero, Ignacio Jurado, Juan Rueday Auza, José Verastigui, and Lucas Villagran.

Lieutenant-Colonel Manuel Aspiroz was appointed by the general as Fiscal, and Joaquin M. Escoto as Asesor. Both are law-officers of the Government. The Fiscal's duty is to write the accusations, take the evidence, and manage the cause on the part of the Government; in short, he is the attorney for the Government. The Asesor's duty is to examine the cause after the court shall have passed judgment, and to render his opinion thereupon, in favor or against the legality thereof; which opinion governs the commanding-officer, in his approval or disapproval of the judgment.

The Minister of War sent instructions to the Fiscal containing the main points of complaint; upon which the latter drew the accusations, which were based on the alleged violations of the provisions of the law bearing date January 25th, A. D. 1862, created by the President of the Liberal party alone.

The three prisoners were tried together, although upon separately-written charges.

The first proceeding, on the part of the Government, after the formation of the Court, was a preparatory writing, drawn by the Fiscal, containing interrogatories addressed to the Emperor, demanding of him to answer whether he was Ferdinand Maximilian, Archduke of Austria, the so-called Emperor; and for what purpose he came to Mexico. To which he answered that he was the aforesaid Archduke, and was born July 6th, 1832: that he came to Mexico at the solicitation of a large number of Mexican citizens; and that he believed that he was so called by a majority of said citizens.

A Protest, bearing date May 29th, was drawn by Señor Vasquez, the resident lawyer of His Majesty at Queretaro, signed by Maximilian, wherein was set forth that various Mexicans were desirous of establishing an empire in Mexico, and to elect him Emperor thereof; that he answered them that he wished proof that a majority of the Mexican people were of that opinion: that subsequently an Assembly of Notables presented him a document which evidenced that the people of Mexico had already adopted that form of government;

and that believing, after an examination, that the principles therein laid down were in accordance with the will of the Mexican people, he then consented to their proposition to accept the crown; that, accordingly, he governed Mexico for more than two years, recognized by the nations of Europe. Also that other facts presented themselves in favor of his cause, namely: Jesus G. Ortega proclaimed himself President of the Republic of Mexico; that he had been arrested and not yet tried, but was waiting for a high tribunal, vested with competent authority; and that he, Maximilian, was chosen Emperor while he was at Miramar, and did not, like Ortega, proclaim himself the head of the Government. Finally, the Protest closed, asking: first, that the Council of War be declared incompetent; second, that orders be given to suspend all summary proceedings against him, based upon the said law of January 25th, 1862; third, that no Ordinary Council of War be formed or installed, based upon the said law of January, the competency of which he did not recognize. The Protest had subjoined thereto the following:

"Finally, I say, that in conformity with the frankness of my character, I ought not to keep it as a secret from you, General, that a true copy of this writing is in the hands of the Hamburg Consul, in order that he may transmit the same, when he may be able, to the Diplomatic Corps, accredited near my person.

"QUERETARO May twenty-ninth, one thousand eight hundred and sixty-seven.

"MAXIMILIAN.

"JESUS M. VASQUEZ, *Counsel.*"

The foregoing Protest was handed me for examination, and for an opinion as to the points raised in favor of the defendant. I do not think it was satisfactory to the lawyers who came from the city of Mexico on behalf of the Emperor, nor to the Emperor himself.

The objections to the jurisdiction made therein were overruled by General Escobedo; and thereupon the Fiscal prepared the accusations against Maximilian in the form of interrogatories, and propounded the same in the presence of the notary appointed to take down the answers that might be given thereto.

The accusations, answers of the defendant, and statements of the notary therein, constituted the charges in full, and were embraced in one document, which was in the following language:

"Maximilian being asked if he would promise to speak the truth as to all he knew upon which he might be interrogated, responded that he would answer all questions which were not of a political nature.

"Being asked concerning the charge of having offered himself as the principal instrument of the French Intervention, to carry out the plans of said Intervention, which were to disturb the peace of Mexico, by means of a war, unjust in its origin, illegal in its form, disloyal and barbarous in its execution; and of arousing in Mexico, the political faction that has sacrificed the national rights and interests in order to satisfy their particular interest; and which faction was already reduced and unable to offer further resistance without the assistance of foreign arms: in order to destroy the constitutional Government of the nation established by the people, who were in the exercise of all its powers, and recognized by foreign nations, and even by the very powers which brought on the Intervention; in order to transform the Republic into a monarchy, which would favor the policy of Napoleon III., in opposing American democracy, and favor the base interests of the French Government and such men as Jecker, who had no other object in view than that of obtaining so base and iniquitious advantages from a war which has been called a War of Intervention, the records of which constitute the *First Charge*, and others, which are of public notoriety.

"To this Maximilian replied, that this question being a political one, he would refer them to what he had before answered.

"The Fiscal, after admonishing the defendant, repeated the charge twice to him, without receiving any other answer than the former one.

"Being asked and warned to answer to the charge of having come to second and put in practice the plans above referred to of the French Government, without any other title than that which the armed force of the same Government gave him, and a few votes, which he pretended to call the national will, notwithstanding that pretended expression of the national will is false in form and substance, as no one can deny; since the Mexican Republic being established as it was and as it is on the fundamental charter of 1857, the only legitimate expresion of the will of the people is that which is defined in the same charter, and regulated by the electoral laws in conformity with the same, it being the form established by the same supreme law and respective regulations; and the only legitimate one through which the sovereign will of the Mexicans can be made known; and not the votes of a few persons, cast in a few particular towns, and those of an incompetent minority of the 'Assembly of Notables,' who pretended, maliciously, to represent the genuine will of the people; pretending to make their acts to express the consent of the people, and transforming the Republic into the so-called Mexican Empire. And whatever might have been the cause for the proclamation of the monarchy and Maximilian, the votes obtained in the presence of an armed force cannot be considered the deliberate and spontaneous will of the people.

"The false representation of said national will was already proclaimed by native Mexican traitors and foreigners at the beginning of the War of Intervention, as it was known to the world, and protested against by the press of Europe and America; and also the plans of a few wicked Mexicans, such as Almonte, Gutierrez Estrado, and the diplomatic efforts of the cabinet of the Tuilleries, which arrived to destroy, at all costs, the Republican Government, and to found, by force, a Mexican Monarchy, at the head of which the French Government had resolved to place a prince who would accept the crown, and did, in effect, place the Prince who is present.

"Maximilian responded as he did to the prior charge, stating that his answer to other charges which might be made would be no other than already given, if they were questions of a political character. The Fiscal then repeated twice the foregoing question and charge last made, and passed on to the

"*Third Charge:* That the Archduke Maximilian accepted voluntarily the responsibilities of an usurper of the Sovereignty of a people constituted as a nation free and independent; for the acceptance of which responsibilities he is severely condemned by the legislation of all nations and various previously made laws of the Republic of Mexico, among which last is that of the twenty-fifth of January, one thousand eight hundred and sixty-two, which has ever since been in force.

"The Fiscal repeated the said charge twice, and passed on to the

"*Fourth Charge:* That of having, with an armed force, disposed of the lives, rights, and interests of the Mexican people.

"The Fiscal repeated this charge twice, and passed on to the

"*Fifth Charge:* That of having made war against the Mexican Republic, and by and in many cases under the direction of the Commander-in-chief of the French army in Mexico. Consenting to, authorizing, and committing molestations and atrocities of all kinds which could be put into practice to oppress the Mexican people, and to impose upon them the will of a Prince elected by the French Government to govern Mexico.

"Here the Fiscal caused to be read a list of the frightful number of executions by court-martial of Maximilian, of the Mexican who defended the cause of the Republic, and also of the pillage and burning of entire towns throughout the Mexican Territory, and especially in the States of Coahuila, Michoacan, Sinaloa, Chihuahua, Nuevo Leon, and Tamaulipas.

"The Fiscal here repeated this last charge twice, and passed on to the

"*Sixth Charge:* That of having made, in his own name, a fillibustering war, inviting and enlisting foreigners from all nations, principally Austrians and Belgians, subjects of Powers who were not at war with the Mexican Republic.

"The Fiscal repeated this twice, and passed on to the

"*Seventh Charge:* That of having published and of having carried into effect against the Mexicans who did not submit to his authority, the barbarous decree of October third, one thousand eight hundred and sixty-five, which gave power to all commanding officers of the so-called Imperial army to execute on the spot all prisoners, without regard to the rank or the denomination of the organized body which they formed, or the cause which they defended, and without excluding those who followed them unarmed, or citizens who aided them directly or indirectly.

"The Fiscal repeated this last charge twice, and passed on to the

"*Eighth Charge:* That of having the audacity to assume in his manifesto of the second of October, which served as a preamble to the said barbarous decree, that the person at the head of the Constitutional Republican Government had abandoned the Mexican Territory; deducing from this entirely false fact extraordinary consequences in favor of his tyranny, and for the persecution and disdaining the true patriots who were defending the flag of the Republic.

"The Fiscal repeated this last charge twice, and passed on to the

"*Ninth Charge:* That of having attempted to sustain his false title of Emperor of Mexico after the French army had withdrawn from Mexico, and when he saw the Republic rising by his side against the pretended Empire; and in support of which he surrounded himself with some of the men who, during the civil war of Mexico, became famous for their crimes; that of employing means of violence, of death, and desolation; that of shutting himself in this plaza of Queretaro, in order to check the victorious Republicans from the frontiers of the north to this place; and that he did not deliver his sword until the plaza was taken by the besiegers, and then to the Colonel of the Campana near by, and on being also assaulted, and in the fort of which Campana he took refuge with two of his Generals, and a handful of other officers, and until after his forces had been imprisoned or dispersed, leaving him no elements to prolong his defence.

"The Fiscal repeated this charge, and passed on to the

"*Tenth Charge:* That of having abdicated the false title of Emperor, so that the abdication should not take effect immediately, but only when he should be conquered; that is, at a time when he would not be able to do so by his will, but when he found himself overcome and compelled to abdicate by force of arms.

"The Fiscal repeated this, and passed on to the

"*Eleventh Charge:* That of pretending to be entitled to the consideration due to a Sovereign conquered in war, when for the Mexican nation he has not been such; not by law, because of the illegality of his title of Emperor, which he abrogated to himself, not, in fact, because he was unable to sustain his title by his own forces.

"In respect to the foregoing charge, the Fiscal read the following facts to him:

"That Maximilian was unable to establish peace under his rule, even with the assistance of the French army; that from the complete evacuation of Mexico by the French army to the time of his fall, not even three months had elapsed; that the Republican Government had sustained itself without interruption, notwithstanding the strenuous efforts of the French and Maximilian to destroy it; that the war of Mexico against the French intervention, and against the so-called Empire, the ideal of said intervention, has been maintained without cessation for more than five years, always in the name of the Republic, by the authority and under the direction of the Government of the same.

"The Fiscal repeated this charge, and passed on to make the

"*Twelfth:* That of not recognizing the competency of the Council of War, which the law of the twenty-fifth of January, one thousand eight hundred and sixty-two, establishes to try offenders guilty of the crimes therein specified; which crimes, almost in their totality, Maximilian committed, and which law he understood, and is applicable to him, because it was already in force before he came to Mexico to commit the specified crimes against the independence and security of the people, against the law of nations, against public peace and order, against individual guaranties; and which law is now in force, and has been applied, being used as an incontestable right as inherent in the sovereignty of the country, and by which law the government of the Republic has sustained itself in the defence of the national independence against the French intervention, and that of its internal sovereignty against the usurpation of Maximilian; without which there might be some reason that the law was insufficient in this case.

"The Fiscal repeated the charge twice, and passed on to the

"*Thirteenth Charge:* That of protesting against the competency of the Council of War and that of the General-in-chief to try him, when the nation has by its ancient and modern laws deposited in said council the administration of justice in time of war, in order to try those who have been conquered during it, or who, for some other reason, are subject to military law.

"The Fiscal called his attention to the consequences which he would incur by persisting in denying the jurisdiction of the General-in-chief over him, to whom he had surrendered at discretion. This was repeated twice, and Maximilian was required to answer it, as well as the rest of the foregoing charges. The Fiscal notified him again that, by the laws of the country, all the charges preferred against him would be taken as confessed, if he refused to answer and defend himself. And not having obtained any answer from Maximilian, except the one which he had previously given—that he could not answer any question of a political character, because he thought he ought not to recognize the competency of a military judge to try him—the present confession was finished and terminated, with the charges which the Fiscal and Maximilian will sign, with the notary who subscribes to the same.

"MANUEL ASPIROZ.
"MAXIMILIAN.

"Before me, JACINTO MELENDEZ."

It will not be surprising to the professional man, nor even to the layman, that the reading of such trash as the foregoing accusations and charges should have produced the remark which the Emperor made to me. He observed, "I had to put my hand over my mouth when they were read to me, to prevent laughing."

We could not expect to see such a document as that issue from among men where jurisprudence is taught as a science. And the face of Maximilian will not be the only one on which the reading thereof will have produced a smile. It will likewise cause surprise to those, at least, who have been nurtured under the benign institutions of a free government, to behold the trial of a man, for his life, under a rule of law that compels him to be a witness against himself, and if silent thereon, every accusation and charge shall be taken to be true. The humane doctrine advanced and adhered to in England and the United States is, that a man shall be deemed innocent until proved guilty; and that the temptation to perjury shall be held out to no man where his life or person is in jeopardy. And frequently in those two countries a defendant has been allowed to withdraw a plea of guilty, and to enter one of "not guilty."

What civilized country authorizes its officers to prefer charges against a man for raising a plea to the jurisdiction of its tribunals? Where Justice reigns, is a man to be chastised for presenting every point which his counsel may think valid in law? Suppose the points are overruled, is that evidence of a crime or misdemeanor?

Such a proceeding is enough to make a Republican blush, as he is told that it has been carried out under his form of government.

The Emperor desired that I should set forth my views of the law, in order that the world might know his true legal position, so far as I was able to state it, even although the Mexican authorities should overrule the positions. I did so, somewhat hurriedly. He requested me to send copies of that defence to the United States, so that it might be read by the distinguished men of that country. That defence was in the following words:

"Whereas, Maximilian is now a prisoner in the city of Queretaro, Mexico, by virtue of his surrender to the Mexican forces, heretofore, to wit, on the 15th of May, A. D. 1867; and whereas certain criminal proceedings have been ordered on certain charges and accusations against him by the Mexican authorities; and whereas the said Maximilian has, heretofore, made his solemn protest, denying the jurisdiction of the court established for the purpose of trying him on said accusations and charges: Therefore, be it known, that the said Maximilian hereby further protests against the jurisdiction of said military court or tribunal, and against the right of any military tribunal to try him; that he is only a *prisoner of war*, and was so considered and declared so to be by the Commander-in-chief of the Mexican Liberal Army, to whom he surrendered himself, as aforesaid.

"1st. He contends that he is only a *prisoner of war*, and that, according to the generally recognized usages and rules of war, that if he is to be tried by any court, or by any law, the trial should be before a competent court, and in accordance with *International Law*, as understood among civilized nations; which consists of those rules of conduct which reason deduces as consonant to justice from the nature of the society existing among independent nations, with such definitions and modifications as has been established by general consent.

"2d. That, according to the generally recognized usages and rules of *International Law*, no use of force is lawful *except* so far as it is necessary. A belligerent has therefore no right to take away the lives of those subjects of the enemy whom he can subdue by any other means. Those who are actually in arms, and continue to resist, may be lawfully killed; but those who, being in arms, submit and surrender themselves, may not be slain, because their destruction is not necessary for obtaining the just ends of war. The killing of prisoners can only be justified in those extreme cases where resistance on their part, or on the part of others who came to their rescue, renders it impossible to keep them. Both reason and general opinion concur in showing that nothing but the strongest necessity will justify such an act. See *Wheaton on the Law of Nations*, Part 4th, Chapter 2d, Section 2d.

"3d. That, if it be lawful to try him by a court-martial, the officers who compose the court established by the order of the Mexican authorities of the Liberal Party are of too low a rank, according to the usage and rules of civilized nations.

"4th. That the *internal sovereignty* of a State does not, in any degree, depend upon the recognition by other States. The existence of the State *de facto* is sufficient, in this respect, to establish its sovereignty *de jure*. It is a State because it exists. Upon this principle, the Supreme Court of the United States held, in 1808, that the *internal sovereignty* of the United

States of America was complete from the time they declared themselves 'free, sovereign, and independent States,' on the 4th of July, 1776. The same principle was recognized in the treaty with Great Britain and the United States, in 1782. See *Wheaton on the Law of Nations*, Part 1st, Chapter 2d, Section 6th.

"5th. That he, Maximilian, was Emperor and Sovereign head of Mexico for a long time, and as such Sovereign head exercised jurisdiction and control over the greater part of the territory of Mexico.

"6th. That he, Maximilian, being the Sovereign head of Mexico, and so recognized by nearly all of the nations of the world, was not and is not subject to any laws or decrees made by the President of the Liberal or any other party, although said President was recognized by the United States as President of Mexico, because said Liberal party was not the government *de facto* of Mexico, and therefore he ought not to be adjudged by any such laws or decrees.

"7th. That, according to the rules and principles of *International Law*, the Sovereign head of a government *de facto* cannot be tried or punished for making or issuing any decree or law; and while within his own government, is not amenable to the municipal laws of any other government or party. Therefore, Maximilian, upon legal principles, cannot be tried or condemned for issuing the decree known as the 'Decree of October 3d,' whatever may be the character of said decree. Every State has certain *absolute* sovereign rights; one of the most important is the right of self-preservation. This right necessarily involves all the incidental rights which are essential as means to give effect to the principal end. See *Wheaton on the Law of Nations*, Part 2d, Chapter 1st, Sections 1, 2 and 3.

"8th. The law of President Juarez of 1862, January 25th, is unconstitutional. 1st. Because it was made by the President alone, who has no authority to legislate. See *Mexican Constitution*, Title 3d, Art. 50, under the '*Division of Powers*,' which says that the supreme power of the federation is divided into legislative, executive, and judicial powers; that no two of said powers can ever be united in one person; and that *legislative* power shall *never* be deposited in *one individual*. Therefore *any law* not made by the *legislative* power is unconstitutional. 2d. Said law is unconstitutional, because it punishes a man with death for *political* crimes, contrary to Art. 23d, Title 1st, Section 1st.

"9th. The powers given to the President in Art. 29, Title 1st, Section 1st, Mexican Constitution, to *suspend* certain *guarantees* mentioned in said Constitution, do not extend to those guarantees that *secure* the *life* of man.

"10th. The word '*guarantees*' in the Constitution means *individual* guarantees or rights, and the power to *suspend* them does not *give the power* to the President *to make* laws. If the President can *make laws*, he can destroy the *form* of the government, and it would become monarchial rather than constitutional. If the President can exercise legislative power, he can likewise exercise *judicial* power, and he would then be an autocrat.

"11th. That the Congress of Mexico have no power to declare that the President can make laws. Congress cannot delegate its power to any one. If it can delegate its powers to the President, then it can do so to any other individual. Neither Congress nor the President can destroy the *form* of government by giving each other a part of their respective constitutional powers. All the powers of Congress are mentioned in Title 3d, Section 1st, Paragraph 3d, Art. 72; and there is no authority given to *delegate* the powers of Congress to the President. According to Title 6th, Art. 117, the powers which are not *expressly* conceded in the Constitution to the federal functionaries are understood to be reserved to the States. Art. 126th, Title 6th, says that 'This Constitution, *the laws of the Congress of the Union* which emanate from it, and all treaties made, or which may be made by the President of the Republic, with the approbation of Congress, shall be the *supreme law* of the Union.' It does not say that the *laws* of the *President* shall be the supreme law of the land, but, on the contrary, *none but the laws of the Congress of the Union.* And, further, under the head 'Of the Inviolability of the Constitution,' Title 8th, Art. 128th, it says, 'This Constitution shall not lose its force and vigor *even in time of rebellion.*'

"12th. The late or present war being a *civil war*, the punishment of death cannot be awarded for *political* crimes, according to the said Art. 23d.

"13th. That there is a distinction between an executive regulation and a *law.* The executive can only provide for the *execution* of the law; consequently a regulation or *decree* of the President conflicting with any existing *law*, or the Constitution, is void. *Lares*, in his *Derecho Administrativo*, page 19, says: 'Neither the judicial nor administrative tribunals are under any obligation to *obey* illegal *reglamentos*' (regulations). Such is the opinion of the writers on the Civil law which is in force in Mexico.

"14th. That if the said war is a *foreign* one, then Maximilian is not guilty of *treason*, as he is an Austrian.

"15th. That whilst a civil war, involving the contest for the government, continues, other States may remain indifferent spectators of the controversy, or may espouse the cause of either. The positive law of nations make no distinction between a just and an unjust war in this respect; and the intervening State becomes entitled to all the rights of war against the opposite party. And the fact that foreign States in Europe furnished him, Maximilian, troops and munitions of war, or whether such troops rendered him aid voluntarily, does not, according to the law of nations, change his rights as a contestant in the struggle for the supremacy of government.

"16th. That the general usage of nations regards a civil war as entitling both the contending parties to all the rights of war against each other, and even as respects neutral nations. And therefore, if the decree of Juarez, of January 25th, 1862, was legally made which punished with death prisoners of war, then Maximilian was justified in issuing the decree of October 3d, 1865, in retaliation, it being only equal in severity.

"17th. That, as a fact, the French forces under Marshal Bazaine were not subject to the control of Maximilian in regard to their military regulations, orders, and movements, as will appear by the treaty of Miramar; but only so in regard to their political government while in the Empire of Mexico.

"18th. That the said decree of October 3d, 1865, was drawn by instructions, and according to the direction of Marshal Bazaine; and that he, Maximilian, was informed that the said Marshal Bazaine enforced a part of said decree *before* it was signed by said Maximilian.

"19th. That at the time said Maximilian signed said decree, Marshal Bazaine stated to him, Maximilian, that ex-President Juarez had positively left the territorial jurisdiction of Mexico, and that he was then in the State of Texas, in the United States of North America.

"20th. That the said Maximilian, after he left the city of Mexico for Orizaba, at the Hacienda Zoquiapam, on the 21st of October, 1866, annulled said decree; but that said annulment thereof was secreted by the said Marshal Bazaine for three weeks before the same was published, although he, the said Maximilian, sent three despatches to the city of Mexico, ordering the said annulment to be published forthwith. Therefore, upon principles of natural justice and the usage of nations, the said decree of January 25th, 1862, if ever legal, should not have been enforced after the annulment of the said decree of Maximilian of October 3d, 1865.

"21st. And the said Maximilian hereby declares, as a fact, that in no single instance did he ever issue an order to take the life of any particular prisoner or prisoners; but that, on the contrary, whenever he was informed that prisoners of war were in the possession of his forces, he immediately issued orders *not* to take the life of any of them.

"22d. And further, as one of the charges preferred against him, Maximilian, is, that of contumacy in objecting to the jurisdiction of the court ordered to try him, he avers that that is a question of *law;* and that in every court in civilized nations it is the legal right of a defendant to make such objections as he may be by counsel advised.

"Frederic Hall, Of Counsel."

The foregoing points of defense were prepared on the 4th of June, and translated into Spanish. The counsel from the city of Mexico having arrived on the 5th, those points were presented to them for consideration. They observed to His Majesty, to the Diplomatic Corps, and to myself, that they fully concurred in the foregoing opinion.

On the 6th, Messrs. Ortega and Vasquez filed a petition in the nature of a plea to the jurisdiction, wherein they set forth that, according to the 128th Art. of the Constitution, in case of the observance of that Constitution being interrupted by a rebellion, and that the people thereafter should recover their liberty, the re-establishment of that instrument should immediately take place; that, in accordance with its provisions and the laws under it, the persons who rebelled against it should be tried; that the defendant, Ferdinand Maximilian, is on trial as the head of the rebellious government formed contrary to the Constitution of 1857, and therefore the 128th should govern.

That the same Constitution, in treating of the judicial power of the Federation, provides in Art. 97, that the Federal tribunals are clothed with the power, among others, to try those cases in which the Federation is a party; that the Federation is a party in all cases in which it has an interest; that it has in no case more interest than where the rights of the nation have been violated.

That it is quite clear, according to said Art. 97, and Arts. 100, 104, and 105, that the Federal tribunals have jurisdiction of the cause of Maximilian. That the Federal tribunals are the District, Circuit, and Supreme Court, as well as Congress, in certain cases; that only in such courts ought the defendant to be tried, and not in any Council of War, either ordinary or extraordinary. That, according to Art. 13 of the Constitution, no person can be tried by private laws, nor by special tribunals; that the laws of January 25th, 1862, is a private law, and the Council of War a special tribunal. That Art. 23d prohibits the punishment of death for political crimes, except against traitors in a foreign war; that the defendant, Maximilian, is a foreigner, and cannot be a traitor; that it is clear that said law of January 25th, 1862, is contrary to the said Articles 13 and 23 of the Constitution of 1857. That Art. 29 of that instrument authorizes the suspension of certain guarantees, but that it is equally clear that it does not extend to cases which secure the life of man; that no extraordinary faculties could enable the President to enact laws contrary to the Constitution; and that the Constitution can only be changed by a two-third vote of the members of Congress, and the approval thereof by a majority of the Legislatures of the States.

The petition, or plea, closes with a prayer that the Council of War be declared incompetent to try the defendant Maximilian, asking that he may be tried by the Federal tribunals; and that if the general in command does not wish to take the responsibility of deciding the question, that he consult the Supreme Government upon that point.

Such were the principal points of law raised against the jurisdiction of the court on the 6th of June; and the same being presented to the commanding general, and by him considered, were overruled, and the party ordered to trial.

The Emperor and his counsel were desirous of postponing the trial as long as possible; but were compelled to go to trial on 13th of June.

On that day, at six o'clock in the morning, fifty mounted men of the *Cazadores de Galeana* (Sharp Shooters of Galeana), and fifty infantry of the batallion called the *Supreme Powers*, formed in front of the door of the Convent of Capuchinas.

At eight o'clock, the Court, dressed in full uniform, assembled in the Iturbide Theatre,—a building which will contain about fifteen hundred persons. On that occasion the house was filled.

The Court and two of the prisoners occupied the stage. At nine o'clock Generals Miramon and Mejia entered a carriage and were conducted to the place of the court, escorted by the force above mentioned.

The Emperor was a little unwell, and did not appear in court. Had it been necessary he could have gone; but he had too much discretion to make a show of himself to a curiosity-seeking crowd. He remarked that if they intended to convict him, they would do it whether he was present or absent.

The President of the Council of War opened the court immediately after the arrival of the two aforesaid defendants, and the Fiscal commenced to read the cause. So far as the Emperor's case was concerned, no witnesses were introduced by either party. The Fiscal read some records of the shooting of General Ateaga and Colonel Salasa, who were executed by order of General Mendez, at Morelia, in the State of Michoacan, in October, 1865. It appears that they tried him for every execution that could be thought of which was made under the Empire. It certainly will be considered by the world as an anomaly in judicial proceedings. Some printed decrees and other documents, purporting to be signed by the Emperor, were introduced, without any proof that they were genuine. This evidence was supported, the Fiscal contended, by the law that permits the evidence of *public notoriety* to be adduced in proof of the acts of the defendant. Not a witness was sworn in the case to testify upon any point.

As the three cases were tried together, the reading of the charges, documentary evidence, and written arguments occupied two days. On the second day neither of the defendants were in court.

After the Fiscal had presented his views of the law, the opinion of Messrs. Ortega and Vasquez, dated June 12th, 1867, with their signatures attached thereto, was read. My name will not be found in the record of the cause: being a foreigner, the law would not permit me to make an appearance in court, nor to file any paper in the cause as counsel. But it will be observed that my views of the law, laid down in the document written on the fourth of June by me, are adopted in the petition, or plea, to the jurisdiction of the court, written by Messrs. Ortega and Vasquez, on the sixth of June. The same principles are advanced by them in their written argument of the 13th. I will state that it was my intention to have written a more lengthy opinion, had I been allowed to remain in Queretaro until the termination of the trial, and to have sustained my points by references to the authorities found in the work of Justice Story on the Constitution of the United States, and the decisions of the Supreme Court of our country—provided I should have been able to obtain them from the United States Consul's office in the city of Mexico. What I wrote were points briefly stated, as is quite apparent, upon which, thereafter, I desired to extend my argument. As the Emperor especially desired my humble opinion to be sent abroad, that the legal points, if of any value in his favor, should be known, although he might be convicted by that court; and inasmuch as I was a foreigner in Mexico, and not allowed to make an appearance in the cause, I deem it due to myself to make this statement as to my position.

It would be far more in unison with my feelings to insert herein the written argument of Messrs. Ortega and Vasquez; but its length is the reason rendered for its non-appearance. The following is given as embracing, in brief, the points of their discussion:

They presented their objections to the proceedings upon the grounds of the unconstitutionality of the law of January 25th, 1862, as contained in their plea to the jurisdiction of the court on the sixth of June; that there was no proof, either oral or documentary, that supported the charges; that under the legislation of no country is a defendant prohibited from presenting any objection to the court or proceedings which he may think valid in law; that if he does present them, it is no crime, although the decision thereon be against him; that the court is not an inquisition; that, according to the legislation of Mexico, hearsay testimony is of no value; that such testimony is contrary to the doctrine laid down in law 28th, title 16, of the 3d Partidas; that, according to the law of Mexico, two witnesses of good character who saw the alleged act committed are required for full proof (*prueba plena*); that proof of public notoriety is not allowed when witnesses can be obtained who witnessed the commission of the alleged crime. Here counsel cited the authority of Escriche, under the title "*Fama*," showing that the testimony called that of "*public notoriety*," in criminal cases, is of no value; and that Escriche says, "Notoriety, although it may be proved, is not generally full proof, because many times it is false and deceiving; as the common laws says, "*Dictum unicus facile sequitur multitudo.*" They also quoted the following from Ferraris: "*Fama regulariter loquendo de per se non facit plenam probationem . . . . . facit tamen semiplenam probatium in causes civilibus, secus autem in criminalibus, ubi requiruntur probationes indubitata et luce meridiana clariores.*" Which law clearly illustrates that the civil law does not consider public notoriety sufficient in a civil case, and much less in a criminal one. The same doctrine is supported by Febrero, in Lib. 3d, title 2d, chap. 12, num. 108, wherein he says that "public notoriety, in criminal causes, is no proof, because that ought to be clear as light, conclusive, undoubted, and not to be determined by suspicions."

The counsel further contended that, by the said law of January 25, 1862, in Art. 6, that public notoriety was sufficient to institute an inquiry, as provided by the General Ordinance of the Army and Law of September 15, 1857; but that said laws do not hold that such testimony is sufficient to convict a party; and that, according to Escriche, under title "*Callar*" (to be silent), that no one was obliged to accuse himself, and that silence is not proof that the alleged charges are true;

and that the 55th Article of the Ordinance says, that "to sustain the sentence of death, every judge ought to recollect that there must be conclusive proof of the crime, unless the defendant has confessed the crime."

That the crime must be proved as alleged, and that the criminal intent must also be shown to have existed, in order to constitute a crime.

That the decree of the Emperor, of October 3, 1865, would favorably compare with the said law of January 25, 1862.

The counsel then referred to the noble example of the United States in behalf of Jefferson Davis; that he had been conquered in 1865, and not subjected to an incompetent tribunal for trial; that when the popular crowd of Paris severed the head of Louis XVI., the impartial opinion of the world did not approve the act; that the English of the present day do not sustain the execution of Charles I.; and that Charles X. of France, in 1830, had his life respected.

Such is a summary of the points taken by the counsel in their written argument for the defence. After which, they orally commented upon the case, Mr. Ortega closing the discussion.

On the 14th day of June, the arguments being closed in the three cases, the public session was adjourned, and a private one opened, for the consideration of the case; and at the end of their deliberation, at eleven o'clock at night, a unanimous decision of guilty, with the punishment of death, was pronounced against each of the defendants.

On that night the papers in the cause were passed over to the Asesor for his examination, who, on investigation thereof, rendered an opinion that the same were valid; whereupon the commanding general, Escobedo, signified his approval, making the same final.

In order to have a complete understanding of the

Emperor's cause, it will be necessary to examine the law of January 25th, 1862; the decree of the Emperor dated October 3d, 1865; certain parts of the Mexican Constitution which are applicable to the cause; the treaty of Miramar; and the correspondence between the United States and Mexico relative to the preservation of the life of Maximilian.

The placing of the foregoing correspondence as one of the documents in the case, may produce a smile from the members of the bar; but although it was not produced on the trial as evidence in support of the issue on either side, it was so impressed upon the minds of a large number of Mexicans, that it was scarcely possible to keep it out of the scales of justice. That it had great weight in the discussions outside of the court is certain. Whether the court was entirely free from its influence remains doubtful.

It created so much excitement and discussion throughout Mexico, in connection with the fate of Maximilian, that it was considered proper and convenient to include it herein, so that the reader might not be compelled to look elsewhere to obtain a correct idea of its tenor.

Neither was the treaty of Miramar adduced as evidence; but it might have been an important feature, as showing, in respect to the direct acts of French officers, a want of criminal intention or injustice on the part of the Emperor in connection therewith, when they shielded themselves under that treaty in committing acts wholly at variance with his wishes.

The laws, treaty, and correspondence referred to, are the following:

PROCLAMATION OF H. M. THE EMPEROR.

"MEXICANS!—The cause which D. Benito Juarez defended with so much valor and constancy, has already succumbed under the force, not only of the national will, but also of the very law which that officer invoked in support of his pretensions. To-day, even the faction into which the said cause degenerated, is abandoned, by the departure of its chief from the native soil.

"The National Government for a long time was lenient, and exercised great clemency, in order to give the chance to misled and misinformed men to rally to the majority of the nation, and to place themselves anew in the path of duty. It has fulfilled its object; the honorable men have assembled under its banner, and have accepted the just and liberal principles which regulate its politics. The disorder is only maintained by some leaders carried away by unpatriotic passions, and assisted by demoralized persons who cannot reach to the level of political principles, and by an unprincipled soldiery, the last and sad remnants of the civil wars.

"Hereafter the contest will only be between the honorable men of the nation and the gangs of criminals and robbers. Clemency will cease now, for it would only profit the mob, who burn villages, rob and murder peaceful citizens, poor old men, and defenceless women.

"The Government, resting on its power, from this day will be inflexible in its punishments, since the laws of civilization, the rights of humanity, and the exigencies of morality demand it.

"MAXIMILIAN.

"MEXICO, October 2d, 1865."

"MAXIMILIAN, Emperor of Mexico. Having heard our Council of Ministers and our Council of State, *We Decree:*

"ART. 1. All persons belonging to armed bands or corps not legally authorized, whether they proclaim or not any political principles, and whatever be the number of those who compose the said bands, their organization, character, and denomination, shall be tried militarily by the courts-martial, and if found guilty even of the only fact of belonging to the band, they shall be condemned to capital punishment within twenty-four hours following the sentence.

"Art. 2. Those who, belonging to the bands mentioned in the previous article, shall be captured with arms in their hands, shall be tried by the officer of the force which has captured them; and he shall, within a delay never extending over twenty-hours after the said capture, make a verbal inquest of the offence, hearing the defence of the prisoner. Of this inquest he shall draw an act, closing with the sentence, which must be to capital punishment, if the accused is found guilty, even if only of the fact of belonging to the band. The officer shall have the sentence executed within the twenty-four hours aforesaid, seeing that the criminal receive spiritual assistance. The sentence having been executed, the officers shall forward the act of inquest to the Minister of War.

"Art. 3. From the penalty established in the preceding Articles, shall only be exempted those who, having done nothing more than being with the band, will prove that they were made to join it by force, or did not belong to it, but were found accidentally in it.

"Art. 4. If, from the inquest mentioned in Article 2d, facts are elicited which induce the officer holding it to believe that the prisoner was made to join the band by force, without having committed any other crime, or that he was found accidentally in it, without belonging to it, the said officer shall abstain from passing sentence, and he shall send the accused, with the respective act of inquest, to the proper court-martial, in order that the trial be proceeded with by the latter, in conformity with Article 1st.

"Art. 5. Shall be tried and sentenced conformably with Article 1st of this law:

"1. All those who will voluntarily assist the *guerrilleros* with money or any other means whatever.

"2. Those who will give them advice, information, or counsels.

"3. Those who voluntarily, and knowing that they are *guerrilleros*, will put within their reach or sell them arms, horses, ammunition, subsistence, or any articles of war whatever.

"ART. 6. Shall be also tried conformably with the said Article 1st:

"1. Those who will hold with the *guerrilleros* such relations as infer connivance with them.

"2. Those who voluntarily and knowingly will conceal them in their houses or estates.

"3. Those who, by words or writing, will spread false or alarming reports, by which public order may be disturbed, or will make against it any kind of demonstration whatever.

"4. All owners or administrators of rural estates who will not give prompt notice to the nearest authority of the passage of some band through the same estates.

"Those included in paragraphs 1st and 2d of this Article, shall be punished by imprisonment from six months to two years, or by hard labor from one to three years, according to the gravity of the case.

"Those who, being included in paragraph 2d, were the ascendants, descendants, spouses, or brothers of the party concealed by them, shall not suffer the penalty aforesaid; but they shall remain subject to the vigilance of the authorities during the time the court-martial will fix.

"Those included in paragraph 3d of this Article, shall be punished by a fine of from $25 to $1,000, or by imprisonment from one month to one year, according to the gravity of the offence.

"Those included in paragraph 4th of this Article, shall be punished by a fine of from $200 to $2,000,

"ART. 7. The local authorities of the villages who shall not give notice to their immediate superiors of the passage through their villages of armed men, shall be ministerially punished by the said superiors, by a fine of from $200 to $2,000, or by seclusion from three months to two years.

"ART. 8. Whatever resident of a village who, having information of the proximity or passage of armed men by the village, shall not give notice of it to the authorities, shall suffer a fine of from $5 to $500.

"ART. 9. All residents of a village threatened by any gang, who are between the ages of eighteen and fifty-five years and have no physical disability, are obliged to present themselves for the common defence, as soon as called, and for failing to do so, they shall be punished by a fine of from $5 to $200, or by imprisonment of fifteen days to four months. If the authorities think more proper to punish the village for not having defended itself, they may impose upon it a fine of from $200 to $2,000, and the said fine shall be paid by all those together, who, being in the category prescribed by this Article, did not present themselves for common defence.

"ART. 10. All owners or administrators of rural estates, who, being able to defend themselves, will not prevent the entrance in the said estates of *guerrilleros* or other malefactors; or, after these have entered, will not give immediate information of it to the nearest military authority; or will receive on the estates the tired or wounded horses of the gangs, without notifying the said authority of the fact, shall be punished for it by a fine of $100, according to the importance of the case; and if it is of great gravity, they shall be put in prison and sent to the court-martial, to be tried by the latter conformably with the law. The fine shall be paid to the principal Administration of Rents, to which the estate belongs. The provision of the first part of this Article is applicable to the populations.

"ART. 11. Whatever authorities, whether political, military, or municipal, shall abstain from proceeding, in conformity with the provisions of this law, against parties suspected or known to have committed the offences provided for in said law, shall be ministerially punished by a fine of from $50 to $1,000; and, if it appears that the fault was of such nature as to import complicity with the criminals, the said authorities shall be submitted, by order of the Government, to the court-martial, to be tried by the latter, and punished according to the gravity of the offence.

"ART. 12. Thieves shall be tried and sentenced in conformity with Article 1st of this law, whatever may be the nature and circumstances of the theft.

"ART. 13. The sentences of death, pronounced for offences provided for by this law, shall be executed within the delays prescribed in it; and it is prohibited that any demands for pardon be gone through.

"If the sentence is not of death, and the criminal is a foreigner, even after its execution, the Government may use toward him the faculty it has to expel from the territory of the nation all obnoxious strangers.

"ART. 14. Amnesty is granted to all those who may have belonged and may still belong to armed bands, if they present themselves to the authorities before the fifteenth of November next; provided they have not committed any other offences subsequently to the date of the present law. The authorities will receive the arms of those who will present themselves to accept the amnesty.

"ART. 15. The Government reserves the faculty to declare when the provisions of this law will cease.

"Each one of our Ministers is charged with the execution of this law in the part which concerns him, and will give the necessary orders for its strict observance.

"Given at the Palace of Mexico, on the 3d of October, 1865.

"MAXIMILIAN.

"The Minister of Foreign Affairs, charged with the Ministry of State.

"JOSÉ E. RAMIREZ."

LAW OF JUAREZ.

"MINISTER OF GOVERNMENT:

"The Citizen President of the Republic has been pleased to transmit me the decree which follows:

"BENITO JUAREZ, Constitutional President of the United States of Mexico, to its Inhabitants—*Know ye:*

"That in use of the ample faculties with which I find myself invested, I have decreed the following law to punish crimes against the nation, against order, public peace, and individual guaranties:

ART. I. Among the crimes against the independence and security of the nation are comprised:

"1st. The armed invasion of the territory of the Republic by foreigners and Mexicans, or by the former alone, not preceded by a declaration of war on the part of the power to which they belong.

"2d. The voluntary service of Mexicans in the foreign troops of the enemy, whatever be the character in which they accompany them.

"3d. The invitation, made by Mexicans or by foreign residents in the Republic, to subjects of other powers to invade the national territory, or to change the form of government which has been given to the Republic, whatever may be the pretext under which it is done.

"4th. Any kind of complicity to excite or prepare the invasion, or to favor its realization and end.

"5th. In case of an invasion being made, to contribute in any manner by which, in the places occupied by the invader, may be organized any shadow of a government, voting, forming meetings, making laws, accepting employment or commissions, be it from the invader himself or from other persons delegated by him.

"ART. 2. Among the crimes against the laws of nations, the punishment of which belongs to the nation to impose, are comprehended:

"1st. Piracy, and the traffic of slaves in the waters of the Republic.

"2d. The same crimes, although they may not be committed in the same waters, if the criminals are Mexicans, or if, in case of their being foreigners, they should be legitimately consigned to the authorities of the country.

"3d. The attempt to take the lives of foreign Ministers.

"4th. To induce citizens of the Republic, without the knowledge and license of the Republican Government, to serve another power, or to invade its territory.

"5th. To entice or invite citizens of the Republic to unite with foreigners who intend to invade, or who may have invaded the territory.

"ART. 3. Among the crimes against public peace and order, are comprised:

"1st. Rebellion against the political institutions, whether proclaiming their abolition or reform.

"2d. Rebellion against the legitimately established authorities.

"3d. To attempt to take the life of the supreme chief of the nation, or that of the Ministers of State.

"4th. To attempt to take the life of any of the Representatives of the nation, in the place of their sessions.

"5th. A seditious rising up, denying any proper decree of the authority, or asking that any particular law may be issued, omitted, revoked, or altered.

"6th. The formal disobedience of any authority, civil or military, to the orders of the supreme magistrate of the nation, transmitted through the channels which the laws of the ordinance of the army may designate.

"7th. Public riots and disturbances, caused intentionally, with premeditation or without it, when they have for their object disobedience or insults to the authorities, perpetrated by tumultuous meetings, with the intent to use force against any persons or the property of any citizen; contumelious shouting; introducing one's self violently into any public or private edifice; tearing down decrees from the places in which they are fixed for the information of the people; fixing in the same places subversive proclamations or pasquinades, which may in any manner incite the disobedience of any law or governmental order, which may have been ordered to be observed. In any of the cases referred to, to force the prisons, to carry arms and distribute them, to harangue the multitude, to ring the bells, and all those actions manifestly directed to augment the tumult, will be aggravating circumstances.

"8th. To fix in any public place, to distribute and to communicate openly and clandestinely a copy of any true or false order which is directed to impede the fulfilment of any supreme order. To order such publications made, and to co-operate with those that may be made, recalling their contents in places where people are assembled, or to clothe them in offensive and disrespectful expressions against the authorities.

"9th. Breaking out of prison, or place of exile or confinement, in which may have been placed by legitimate authority any citizen of the Republic, or the violation of the banishment imposed on those who are not citizens; as well as military men, who absent themselves from their quarters, station, or residence, which may have been designated by competent authority.

"10th. To assume the supreme power of the nation; that of the States or Territories; that of the districts, partidos, and municipalities, acting by their own authority, or by commission from that authority which may not be legitimate.

"11th. Conspiracy, which is the act of a few or many persons uniting together, with the object of opposing obedience to the laws or the fulfilment of the orders of the recognized authorities.

"12th. Complicity in any of the aforesaid crimes, by concurring in their perpetration in an indirect mode, by aiding in giving information to the enemies of the nation or Government, especially if those who reveal said information are public employees; by administering resources to the seditious persons or foreign enemy, whether of arms, provisions, money, baggage, or impeding those which the Government may have; by serving the same enemies as spies, post-carriers, or agents of any kind, the object of which may be to favor their undertaking or those of the invaders, or that the disturbers of the public tranquillity may realize their plans by spreading alarming and false news, or which may weaken public enthusiasm by surmising facts contrary to the honor of the Republic, or comments on them in a manner disfavorable to the interests of the country.

"Art. 4. Among the crimes against individual guaranties are comprised:

"1st. Plagiarism of the citizens or inhabitants of the Republic, in order to require them to pay a ransom. The sale, which may be made of them, or the forced letting of their services or work.

"2d. Violence exercised against persons with the object of disposing of their goods and rights, which legitimately constitute their property.

"3d. The attack, by armed hand, on said persons in the cities or uninhabited places, although the capture of said persons or their goods may not result through such attack.

"ART. 5. Every citizen of the Republic has the right to accuse, before the authority established by law to judge the crimes by it expressed, any individual who may have committed any of said crimes.

"ART. 6. The respective military authority is the only one competent to try the crimes specified in this law; for that effect, as soon as said authority has knowledge that any of said crimes have been committed, whether by public notoriety, by complaint or accusation, or by any other manner, it will proceed to make the proper examination according to the General Ordinance of the Army, and the Law of the 15th of September, 1857; and the cause, when stated, will be adjudicated before the Ordinary Council of War, whatever may be the category, employment, or commission of the person prosecuted. In places where there are no military commanders, or generals-in-chief, the governors of the States will act in their stead.

"ART. 7. The procedure will be prepared ready for the defence by the Fiscal within sixty hours; and in the space of twenty-four thereafter the defence will be completed: then the Council of War will immediately assemble.

"ART. 8. Whenever a sentence of the Ordinary Council of War shall have been confirmed by the respective military commander, general-in-chief, or governor, as the case may be, it will be executed immediately without further recourse, and as is provided for in time of war or in a state of siege.

"ART. 9. In crimes against the nation, order, the public peace, and individual guaranties, which have been specified in this law, an appeal for pardon is not admissible.

"Art. 10. The military Asesors, appointed by the Supreme Government, will necessarily be present in the Ordinary Council of War, as is provided in the Law of the 15th of September, 1857, in order to give his opinion to the members of said Council of War. The judgment which they may give to the military commanders, generals-in-chief, or governors, legally founded, must be executed in conformity with the circular of the 6th of October, 1860, since the necessary Asesors are, in fact, responsible for the advice which they may give.

"Art. 11. The Generals-in-chief, Military Commanders, or Governors, on whom is incumbent the exact fulfilment of this law, and their Asesors, will be personally responsible for any omission they should incur by their action in the national service.

PENALTIES.

"Art. 12. The invasion made into the territory of the Republic, which is spoken of in Fraction 1, Art. 1, of this law, and the service of Mexicans among foreign troops of the enemy, which are spoken of in Fraction 2, will be punished with the penalty of death.

"Art. 13. The invitation made to invade the territory, which is spoken of in Fractions 3 and 4 of Art. 1, will be punished with the penalty of death.

"Art. 14. The captains of vessels engaged in piracy or the commerce of slaves, spoken of in Fractions 1 and 2 of Art. 2, will be punished with the penalty of death; the other individuals of the crew will be condemned to hard labor for the term of ten years.

"Art. 15. Those who shall invite or decoy citizens of the Republic for the ends expressed in Fractions 4 and 5 of Art. 2, will suffer the penalty of five years imprisonment: if the deception or invitation should be made in order to invade the territory of the Republic, the penalty will be death.

"Art. 16. Those who shall attempt to take the life of the Supreme Chief of the nation, wounding him in any manner, or only threatening him with arms, will suffer the penalty of death. If the threat is without arms, and it is done in public, the penalty will be eight years imprisonment; if it is done by private acts, the penalty will be seclusion for four years.

"Art. 17. Those who shall attempt to take the life of the Ministers of State, or that of the Foreign Ministers, with a knowledge of their rank, and should wound them, shall suffer the penalty of death; and if they should only threaten with arms, the penalty shall be ten years imprisonment. It being understood always, that said Ministers have not been the first aggressors in fact, because in such cases the crime shall be considered and adjudged according to the common laws on quarrels.

"Art. 18. The attempt against the life of the Representatives of the nation, which is spoken of in Fraction 4 of Art. 2, shall be punished with the penalty of death, provided the Representative be wounded; if he should only be threatened with arms, the penalty shall be from five to eight years imprisonment, according to the discretion of the judge: it being understood always, that the said Representative may not have been the first aggressor, in which case the crime will be considered and adjudged in conformity with the common law on quarrels.

"Art. 19. The crimes which are spoken of in Fractions 1, 2, and 5 of Art. 3, shall be punished with the penalty of death.

"Art. 20. The formal disobedience, which is spoken of in Fraction 6 of Art. 3, shall be punished with the loss of employment and salary, which the guilty party may obtain, and four years hard labor; provided always that by such disobedience no losses should have resulted to the nation, in which case it will be taken in account to augment the punishment, at the discretion of the judge.

"ART. 21. Those who prepare the public riots and disturbances, spoken of in Fraction 7 of Art. 3, and those who join them, on the terms expressed in said fraction, or other similar ones, shall suffer the penalty of ten years imprisonment, or of death, in case aggravating circumstances should occur, referred to at the end of said fraction, being besides liable to respond with their property for the damages which individually they may have caused.

ART. 22. Those who may have committed the crimes spoken of in fraction 8 of Art. 3d will suffer the penalty of six years imprisonment.

ART. 23. Those who escape from imprisonment, to which they may have been reduced by legitimate authority, shall suffer double the term of their penalty; and if a second time repeated, punishment of death shall be inflicted; which shall in like manner be applied to foreigners who, once expelled from the national territory, should return without permission of the Supreme Government. Military men absenting themselves from the barracks, place of employment, or residence, which may have been designated for them, shall suffer the loss of their employment and four years imprisonment.

"ART. 24. Those who assume the public powers, spoken of in Fraction 10 of Art. 3d, shall suffer the penalty of death.

"ART. 25. The crime of conspiracy, spoken of in fraction 11 of Art. 3d, shall be punished with the penalty of death.

"ART. 26. Those who, in the perpetration of the crimes spoken of in Fraction 12 of Art. 3d, by aiding in giving news to the enemies of the nation or Government, by furnishing resources to the seditious or to the foreign enemy, whether of arms, provisions, money, baggage, or by impeding their possession by the authorities; or by serving the enemies as spies, mail-carriers, guides, or as agents of any class whatever, the object of which should be to favor the undertaking of said persons, or of the invaders, shall suffer the death penalty. Those who shall spread false or alarming news, or shall weaken public enthusiasm, by surmising facts contrary to the honor of the Republic, or commenting in a disfavorable manner on the interests of the country, shall suffer the penalty of eight years imprisonment.

"ART. 27. Those who commit the crimes specified in fractions 1, 2 and 3 of Art. 4th, shall suffer the penalty of death.

ART. 28. The criminals who shall be caught *in flagrante delicto* in any action of the war, or who shall have committed those crimes specified in the foregoing article, shall be identified, and they shall be immediately executed.

GENERAL DISPOSITIONS.

"ART. 29. The receivers of stolen property in uninhabited places shall suffer the penalty of death; those offending in like manner in populated places shall be punished by six years hard labor.

"ART. 30. The individuals who have in their possession *munition* arms, and shall not have delivered them according to the disposition contained in the decree of the 25th of last month, if they do not give them up within eight days after the publication of the present law shall, in case of their being Mexicans, be treated as traitors, and as such shall receive the punishment of death; but if they are foreigners, they shall be imprisoned for ten years.

"ART. 31. The chiefs and officers of the National Guard who may have been called into service by virtue of this law, shall receive their pay from the Federal treasury during the time of the commission which may have been given them.

"Wherefore, I order that this law be printed, published, and observed.

"National Palace of Mexico, the twenty-fifth day of January, one thousand eight hundred and sixty-two.

"BENITO JUAREZ.

"To Citizen MANUEL DOLLADO,
"*Minister of Relations and Government.*"

TREATY OF MIRAMAR.

"Napoleon, by the grace of God and the national will, Emperor of the French, to all who shall see these presents, *Greeting:*

"A convention, followed by additional secret articles, was concluded on the 10th of April, 1864, between France and Mexico, for the purpose of regulating the condition of the French troops stationed in Mexico.

CONVENTION AND ADDITIONAL SECRET ARTICLES, THE TENOR OF WHICH IS AS FOLLOWS:

"The Governments of H. M. the Emperor of Mexico, and of H. M. the Emperor of the French, animated by an equal desire to assure the establishment of order in Mexico, and consolidate the new Empire, have resolved to regulate, by means of a convention, the condition of the French troops stationed in that country, and for that purpose have appointed as their plenipotentiaries: H. M. the Emperor of the French, M. Charles François Edouard Herbert, Minister Plenipotentiary of the first class, Councillor of State, Director in the Ministry for Foreign Affairs, Grand Officer of His Imperial Order of the Legion of Honor, etc., etc.; H. M. the Emperor of Mexico, M. Joaquin Velazquez de Leon, His Minister of State without the portfolio (*sans porte-feuille*), Grand

Officer of the distinguished Order of Our Lady of Guadalupe, etc. etc.

"Who, after mutually communicating their full and written powers, found in good and due form, have agreed upon the following articles:

"Art. 1. The French troops actually in Mexico shall be reduced as soon as possible to a strength of 25,000 men, including the foreign legion.

"In order that the army may serve as a safeguard to the interests which have caused the Intervention, it will remain in Mexico temporarily, under the conditions stipulated in the following articles:

"Art. 2. The French troops will evacuate Mexico as soon as the Emperor of Mexico shall be able to organize the necessary troops to replace them.

"Art. 3. The foreign legion in the service of France, composed of 8,000 men, shall, however, remain in Mexico for the term of six years after all the French troops are called home, in conformity with Article 2.

"The said legion will pass immediately into the service of the Mexican Government, and will be paid by the same. The Mexican Government reserves to itself the right to shorten the period during which it will employ the foreign legion in Mexico.

"Art. 4. The points of territory which will be occupied by the French troops, as well as the military expeditions of these troops, if they take place, shall be determined by common accord, and directly between H. M. the Emperor of Mexico and the Commander-in-chief of the French army.

"Art. 5. In all points where the garrison is not exclusively composed of Mexican troops, the military command will belong to the French commander.

"In case of combined French and Mexican expeditions, the command shall likewise appertain to the French officer.

"ART. 6. The French commander shall have no right to intervene in any branch of the Mexican Administration.

"ART. 7. During the time the requirements of the French army necessitate every two months a service of transports between France and the port of Vera Cruz, the expenses of such service, fixed at the sum of 400,000 francs for every voyage (going out and returning), shall be reimbursed by the Mexican Government, and paid in Mexico.

"ART. 8. The naval stations which France possesses in the West Indies and in the Pacific Ocean shall frequently send men-of-war carrying the French flag into the ports of Mexico.

"ART. 9. The expenses of the French expedition to Mexico, which the Mexican Government is obligated to reimburse, have been fixed at the sum of two hundred and seventy millions for the whole duration of the expedition until the 1st of July, 1864. Said sum to bear interest at the rate of three per cent. per annum. After the 1st of July, 1864, all expenses of the Mexican army will be defrayed by Mexico.

"ART. 10. The indemnity which the Mexican Government obligates itself to pay to France for expenses, salaries, keeping and maintaining the troops of the army, commencing on the 1st of July, 1864, is fixed at the sum of one thousand francs for every man per annum.

"ART. 11. The Mexican Government will immediately remit to the French Government the sum of sixty-six millions francs in bonds of the loan at their emission value, and of which amount will be applied—fifty-four millions on account of the debt mentioned in Art. 9, and twelve millions on account of indemnities due to the French in virtue of Art. 14 of the present convention.

"ART. 12. For the payment of other war expenses

and for the extinction of the charges mentioned in Art. 7, 10, and 14, the Mexican Government binds itself to pay annually to France the sum of 25 millions in cash.

The payment shall be applied as follows:

1st. Towards liquidating sums due in virtue of Art. 7 and 10.

2d. Paying off amount of interest and capital of the sum, as stipulated in Art. 9.

3d. For indemnities due to French subjects, in virtue of Art. 14 and the following:

"Art. 13. The Mexican Government will deliver in Mexico, on the last day of every month, to the Paymaster-General of the army, the necessary sum to cover the expenses of the French troops who shall have remained in Mexico, in conformity with Art. 10.

"Art. 14. The Mexican Government binds itself to indemnify French subjects for losses which they unjustly may have sustained, and which may have been caused by the expedition.

"Art. 15. A mixed commission, composed of three Frenchmen and three Mexicans, nominated by their respective governments, shall meet at Mexico within three months, for the purpose of examining into and regulating those reclamations.

"Art. 16. A revising commission, composed of two Frenchmen and two Mexicans, appointed in the same manner, and who will reside in Paris, shall proceed with the definite liquidation of the reclamations previously admitted by the commission as designated in the last article, and will pronounce upon those submitted to their decision.

Art. 17. The French Government will place at liberty all Mexican prisoners of war, as soon as H. M. the Emperor of Mexico shall have entered his States.

"Art. 18. The present convention shall be ratified, and the ratifications exchanged as soon as possible.

"Given at the Palace of Miramar, on the 10th of April, 1864.

(Signed) "VELAZQUEZ,
"HERBERT."

To this treaty have been added the following three secret clauses, which are conceived in the following terms:

ADDITIONAL SECRET ARTICLES.

"H. M. the Emperor of the French and H. M. the Emperor of Mexico, desiring by additional secret clauses to this Convention, to explain in a complete manner their reciprocal intentions, and to clearly stipulate that, notwithstanding the events that might arise in Europe, the assistance of France will be given to the new Empire, have appointed for that purpose as their plenipotentiaries, namely: H. M. the Emperor of the French, M. Charles François Edouard Herbert, etc., etc.; and H. M. the Emperor of Mexico, M. Joaquin Velazquez de Leon, etc., etc.; who, after mutually communicating their full and written powers, found in good and due form, have agreed upon the following articles, viz.:

"ART. 1. H. M. the Emperor of Mexico, approving of the principles and promises as set forth in the proclamation of General Forey, dated June 12, 1863, as well as of the measures adopted by the Regency and by the French General-in-chief in conformity with said proclamation, has resolved to make known to his people his intentions regarding the same.

"ART. 2. On the other hand, H. M. the Emperor of the French declares that the actual effective force of the French army of 38,000 men shall, gradually only, be reduced every year, in such a manner that the French troops who will remain in Mexico, and inclusive of the Foreign Legion, shall be:

"28,000 men in 1865;
25,000 do. 1866;
20,000 do. 1867.

"ART. 3. As soon as the Foreign Legion, in conformity with the terms of Art. 3 of said Convention, passes into the service of Mexico, and is paid by it, as said Legion will continue to serve a cause in which France is interested, the general and the officers serving therein shall retain their nationality of Frenchmen, and their rights to advancement in the French army, according to *the law.*

"Given at the Palace of Miramar, on the 10th of April, 1864.

(Signed) "HERBERT,
"VELAZQUEZ."

"After perusal and examination of this Convention, accompanied by additional secret articles, we have approved and do herewith approve it, in all and every one of the dispositions which they contain. We declare the same accepted, ratified, and confirmed, and promise its inviolable observance.

"In virtue of which, we give the present, signed by our own hand, and to which is affixed our Imperial seal.

"Given at the Palace of the Tuileries, on the 11th of April, of the year of grace, 1864.

"NAPOLEON.

"By the Emperor,
"DROUYN DE LHUYS."

"NEW ORLEANS, April 6th, 1867.

"SIR:

"For reasons which are doubtless well understood by you, it has not been in my power to present formerly to His Excellency, President Juarez, my letters of credence as Envoy Extraordinary and Minister Plenipotentiary of the United States to the Republic of Mexico. The instructions of October last, under which I started on my mission, gave me a discretionary power in a certain contingency to establish my official residence temporarily at any place in the United States, or elsewhere near the frontier or coast of Mexico. For causes not necessary herein to be explained, I left Matamoras and came to this city in December last, since which time, under instructions from the Secretary of State, it has been the place of my official abode. The Government of the United States has observed with much satisfaction the withdrawal of the French expeditionary forces in Mexico, and the advance of the armies of the Constitutional Government toward the Capital of the Republic. This satisfaction has been recently disturbed by the reports it has received in regard to the severity practised on the prisoners of war taken by your armies at Zacatecas. Its fears, too, have been thereby excited that in the event of the capture of the Prince Maximilian, and the forces under him, this severity might be repeated. I have this day received by telegraph a dispatch from the Secretary of State, instructing me to express to His Excellency, President Juarez, these apprehensions in the most expeditious manner. Therefore, I communicate them by special bearer of dispatches. The Government of the United States has sincerely sympathized with the Republic of Mexico, and feels a deep interest in its success. But I have to express the belief that a repetition of the reported severities referred to, would shock its sensibilities and check the current of its sympathies. It is believed that such acts to prisoners of war as are reported, cannot elevate the character of the Mexican States in the estimation of civilized people, and may tend to bring into disrepute the cause of Republicanism, and retard its progress everywhere. The Government instructs me to make known to President Juarez, promptly and earnestly, its desire, that in case of the capture of the Prince Maximilian, and his supporters, that they may receive the humane treatment accorded by civilized nations to prisoners of war. I have the honor to be, very respectfully,

"Your Excellency's most obedient servant,

"LEWIS D. CAMPBELL.

"To his Excellency S. Lerdo D. Tejada, Minister of Foreign Affairs of the United Mexican States, San Luis Potosi, Mexico.

"SAN LUIS POTOSI, MEXICO, April 22d, 1867.

"SIR: I had the honor, yesterday, to receive the communication which you sent me from New Orleans on the 6th inst. You were pleased to inform me in it that, for reasons which are understood, you have not come to present your credentials as Envoy Extraordinary and Minister Plenipotentiary of the United States of America, near the Republic of Mexico, and that you have remained in New Orleans since December last. The Government of the Republic regrets that those reasons should have prevented you from coming to present your credentials in order to commence your official relations, since it would be very satisfactory for the Government to receive you in your character as representative of the United States.

"You were also pleased to inform me that the satisfaction with which the Government of the United States had seen the withdrawal of the French forces from Mexico, and the advance of the armies of the Constitutional Government toward the Capital, has been disturbed by information received concerning the severity with which the prisoners of war taken at San Jacinto were treated. You also mentioned that it was the desire of the Government of the United States that, in case Maximilian and his partisans were captured, they should be treated humanely as prisoners of war.

"The enemies of the Republic, desiring to produce an unfavorable impression concerning the same, have endeavored to falsify the facts and spread inaccurate information as to the care of the prisoners of San Jacinto. The greater part of them, a considerable number, were pardoned, and the punishment which the chief of the Republican forces meted out to some of them was upon the ground that they were not simply prisoners of war, but violators of the law of nations and the laws of the Republic. They had abandoned themselves to all kinds of excesses and crimes in the city of Zacatecas, because they were fighting like filibusters, without country, without flag, and as mercenaries paid to shed the blood of Mexicans, who defend their independence and their institutions.

"No small number of those foreigners taken at San Jacinto were conducted to Zacatecas, where they have been treated with much benevolence; and those taken in Jalisco have been treated in the same manner, whose acts had not so many aggravating circumstances of especial culpability.

"The invariable conduct of the Government of the Republic, and that which the chiefs of its forces have observed generally, has been to respect life, and to treat with the greatest consideration the prisoners taken from the French forces; while on their part, and even by order of their chiefs, the prisoners which they took from the Republican forces were frequently assassinated. Many times, without the obligation of exchange, prisoners taken from the French forces have been generously set at liberty.

"Many of the principal chiefs of the French forces ordered entire towns to be burnt down; others were decimated by what were called court-martials; and sometimes, for a simple suspicion, without the appearance of a trial, they killed defenceless and aged persons who were unable to bear arms against them. Notwithstanding this, the Government of the Republic and the commander of its forces, generally, far from exercising the right of reprisals, as they were provoked to do, have always observed the most humane conduct, giving constant examples of the greatest generosity. In this manner the Republican cause of Mexico has excited the sympathies of all civilized nations.

"The French forces having retired, Archduke Maximilian has desired to continue to shed unfruitfully the blood of Mexicans. With the exception of three or four cities governed by force, he has seen the entire Republic rise against him. Notwithstanding this, he has desired to continue the work of desolation and ruin of civil war without an object, being surrounded by men most known by their spoliations and grave assassinations, and the most stigmatized with the misfortunes of the Republic.

"In case these should be captured, persons on whom rest such responsibilities, it does not appear that they should be considered as mere prisoners of war; for those are responsibilities defined by the law of nations and the laws of the Republic. The Government, which has given numerous proofs of its humane principles and of its sentiments of generosity, is also obliged to consider, according to the circumstances of the cases, what the principles of justice demand, and the duties which it has to fulfil for the welfare of the Mexican people.

"The Government of the Republic hopes that with the justification of its acts it will preserve the sympathies of the people and of the Government of the United

States, who have been and are held in the highest estimation by the Government of Mexico.

"I have the honor to be

"Your Excellency's very respectful

"and very obedient servant,

"SEBASTIAN LERDO DE TEJADA.

"To His Excellency LEWIS D. CAMPBELL,
Envoy Extraordinary and Minister
Plenipotentiary of the United States,
New Orleans."

It was contended in behalf of Maximilian that the law decreed by President Juarez on the 25th of January, 1862, is in conflict with the Constitution of the Republic, adopted February 12th, 1857, which is, and has been since that date, in force with the Republican party.

It will require no very deep reflection to determine that the position assumed by the defendant was correct.

On the 7th of June, 1861, the Mexican Congress passed an Act, entitled, "*Relative to the Suspension of Guaranties for the present*," wherein it was declared that certain specified articles and parts of articles were suspended. In that Act no mention is made of Articles 23, 29, 97, nor 101.

The 10th Article of that law declares that "The suspension of these guaranties shall continue for the term of six months."

The said Article 23d declares that capital punishment for political crime is abolished, and can be extended only to the traitor to the country during a foreign war, the highway robber, the murderer, persons committing crimes under the military law, and to pirates.

The 97th Article says, that "The courts of the Federation have cognizance of all questions arising concerning the fulfilment and application of the Federal laws. Of those questions in which the Federation may be a party."

Article 101 is as follows: "The tribunals of the Federation shall decide all controversies which arise:

"I. Upon laws or acts of whatever authority which violate individual guaranties.

"Upon laws or acts of the Federal authorities which violate or restrain the sovereignty of the States."

One of the striking features of a Republic, is a division of the powers of government, so that the rights of the people may not be subject to the will of any one individual, or one body of persons. The wisdom of the framers of the Constitution of the United States provided that the division of governmental functions should be into three parts, legislative, judicial, and executive; and that each within its respective sphere should be independent. Mr. Justice Blackstone said, where the right of making and enforcing laws is vested in the same man, there can be no public liberty. It is very apparent that the liberties of the people would be in jeopardy if any one or two divisions of government could enlarge their own constitutional powers, or lessen those of a co-ordinate branch. The people only can make that change, and in the manner prescribed by the Constitution.

The Republic of Mexico followed the example of the United States in the division of its powers of government. In fact, in its organic basis it has expressed that division as clearly as human language is capable of doing. And in speaking of the three powers, it says that "No two of those powers can ever be united in one person or corporation, nor the legislative power be deposited in one individual." It would be difficult to suggest how the executive of a government thus constituted could assume legislative functions with any appearance of honesty.

Under the head, "Of the Executive Power," Section II., Article 85, the powers and obligations of the President are defined as follows:

"1. To promulgate and execute the laws made by the Congress of the Union, ordaining, in the administrative sphere, their exact observance.

"2. To nominate and remove at will the secretaries of departments, to remove the diplomatic agents and the higher employees of the treasury, and to appoint and remove at will the other employees of the Union whose appointments or removals are not determined in any other manner in the Constitution or the laws.

"3. To appoint ministers, diplomatic agents, and consuls, with the approbation of Congress, or, in its recess, of the permanent deputation.

"4. To appoint, with the approbation of Congress, colonels, and other superior officers of the national army and navy, and the superior employees of the treasury.

"5. To appoint the other officers of the national army and navy, according to the laws.

"6. To dispose of the permanent armed force, both on land and on the sea, for the internal security and external defence of the Federation.

"7. To dispose of the National Guard for the same purpose, in the manner prescribed in clause 20 of Article 72.

"8. To declare war in the name of the United States of Mexico, according to the law of the Congress of the Union previously enacted.

"9. To grant letters of marque, subject to the rules ordained by Congress.

"10. To direct diplomatic negotiations, and to celebrate treaties with foreign powers, submitting them to the ratification of the Federal Congress.

"11. To receive Ministers and other Envoys from foreign powers.

"12. To call extraordinary sessions of Congress, when the permanent deputation shall consent thereto.

"13. To give to the judicial power all necessary assistance for the dispatch of their functions.

"14. To create all ports of entry, to establish marine and frontier custom-houses, and to designate their locality.

"15. To grant, according to the laws, pardons to criminals sentenced for crimes within the jurisdiction of the Federal tribunals.

Art. 86. To expedite the business of the administrative branch of the Federation, there shall be a sufficient number of secretaries named by a law of Congress, which law shall designate the business incumbent upon each secretary.

"Art. 87. In order to be a secretary of a department, it is required to be a Mexican citizen by birth, to be in the exercise of his rights, and to be twenty-five years of age.

"Art. 88. All the regulations, decrees, and orders of the President shall be issued under the signature of the secretary of the department to which the business appertains: without this requisite they will not be obeyed.

"Art. 89. The secretaries of departments, as soon as the first session is commenced, shall render an account to Congress of the state of their respective branches.

Article 51 declares that "The exercise of the supreme legislative power is deposited in an assembly, which shall be styled the 'Congress of the Union.'"

Under Art. 72, there are 32 sections, which contain the specific powers of Congress. The last section, number 33, says that Congress has the power "To make all laws that may be necessary and proper to carry out the aforesaid powers, and all others conceded by this Constitution to the authorities of the Union."

Neither branch of government is vested by the Constitution with any special functions that conflict with the division of powers under Title 3, Article 50.

The Constitution protects all persons in certain individual rights, such as those of carrying arms for personal security; travelling through the territory without letters of security, and others therein mentioned. But in time of war, or a disturbance of the public peace, those individual guaranties may be *suspended*, if public safety require it. Article 29 provides for that suspension as follows:

"In cases of invasion, serious perturbation of the public peace, or any other events that place society in imminent danger or conflict, only the President of the Republic, conjointly with the council of ministers, and with the approbation of the Congress of the Union, and in the recess of Congress of the permanent deputation, can suspend the guaranties granted in this Constitution, always excepting those which guarantee the life of man; but it shall be done for a limited time, by means of general laws, and such suspension shall not be to the prejudice of any particular individual. If the suspension should take place, Congress being in session, it (Congress) shall grant the powers it deems necessary, in order that the executive may meet the exigencies of the situation. Should the suspension take place during a recess of Congress, it shall be summoned immediately, in order to give its consent."

The Mexican government confounds the right to *suspend* certain rights with that of making laws. The divisional lines of powers are great monuments of governmental functions that cannot be changed unless by an amendment, as provided in the Constitution.

It has been held by the Mexicans, that in time of war the Constitution loses its force and vigor. And yet they invoke that instrument whenever it supports their position; and in the same breath they deny its validity, if they desire to exercise powers not within its limits. Upon an examination of their Constitution, it is clear that some parts of it never can be of practical use except in time of war or great public danger. The very suspension of certain guaranties can only be made during such a period; but even *then*, that which guarantees the life of man *cannot* be suspended.

They declare that by the Constitution they suspend certain individual rights; and if they wish to take the life of the individual, they then hold that the Constitution has no force, inasmuch as war exists. It is convenient for a vindictive executive, who desires to have his power circumscribed by his will only, to thus argue: but the argument is an exhibition of a great poverty of reason. And further: Article 128 says that "This Constitution shall not lose its force and vigor, although its observance may be interrupted by an armed rebellion. If, in case of public disturbance, a government contrary to the principles sanctioned in it be established, as soon as the people recover their liberty, its observance shall be re-established; and those that figured in the government springing out of the rebellion, as well as those cooperating in its establishment, shall be tried according to the Constitution and the laws issuing therefrom."

After the Republican party had taken a given place from the enemy, and exercised complete control over the same, how they can seriously aver that the force of the Constitution is destroyed, when the said 128th Article still exists as a part of their fundamental jurisprudence, is difficult to understand.

To amend the Constitution, requires a two-third vote of the members of Congress present; which vote must be approved by a majority of the Legislatures of the States. No amendments having been thus made, the Constitution of 1857 was and is in force.

The President of Mexico assumes, under the provisions of Art. 29, which declares "Congress shall grant the power it deems necessary in order that the executive may meet the exigencies of the situation," that Congress may vest him with legislative function. But such is not the true construction of the language; and if it were, it would be in conflict with other parts of the Constitution. It only authorizes Congress to empower the President to make orders or executive regulations in regard to individual rights during war-time; and these orders and regulations must cease to be in force after a certain period fixed therein.

It is somewhat analogous to the principle adopted in the United States, where the Legislature authorizes the judiciary to make rules which shall govern the practice in courts. That never has been considered a power to make laws. The *laws* of Mexico can only be made by the Legislature, and that body is not compelled to specify therein how long the same shall remain in force. They will thus remain until repealed by that body; which clearly shows that there is a broad distinction contemplated by the framers of the Mexican Constitution between their laws and the orders made by the President by virtue of his powers received from the Legislature, under Art. 29.

There is one great principle of law that pervades the jurisprudence of all civilized countries, and that is, when a person has a bare power or authority from another to do an act, he must execute it himself, and cannot delegate his authority to another. It is a trust or confidence reposed in him personally. The old common-law maxim is, "*Delegata potestas non potest delegari*" (a delegated power cannot be delegated). Such is the civil law, although the language of their maxim is not the same, but is, "*Procuratorem alium procuratorem facere non posse* (the agent of one person cannot appoint another agent). Therefore, when the people of Mexico delegated their law-making power to the Congress of the Union, without authorizing that body in their Constitution to delegate the same power to another, they placed a certain trust and confidence in Congress which cannot be executed by any other person.

Efforts were made by the Legislatures of several States, of the United States, to relieve themselves of the responsibility of their functions by submitting statutes to the will of the people. Such proceedings were held unconstitutional. The New York Court of Appeals said, "The Legislature have no power to make such submission, nor had the people the power to bind each other by acting upon it. They voluntarily surrendered that power when they adopted the Constitution."

The Legislature makes, the Executive executes, and the Judiciary construes the law. The learned Chief Justice Marshall, in the Supreme Court of the United States, in the case of Wayman *vs.* Southard, 10 Wheaton, 46, observed, "It will not be contended that Congress can delegate to the courts, or to any other tribunals, powers which are strictly legislative."

As has been observed, in article 23 of the Mexican Constitution, the punishment of death for political crimes has been abolished except for treason in a foreign war, and other cases therein mentioned. It is clear then, that prisoners guilty of political crimes in a *civil* war are not subject to the death penalty. That the late war in which Maximilian figured was a *civil* war will hardly be denied. After the French left, the main body of both armies were Mexicans, struggling for their respective forms of government.

Such being the facts, and the Liberal party standing by and endeavoring to sustain the Constitution, why political prisoners taken by them should not have been protected in their constitutional rights, is not easy to be comprehended.

It is true that the executive made a law declaring that whoever should take up arms against the constituted government would no longer be considered *political* prisoners, but felons, to be punished according to the law of 1862.

The first question which legally presents itself under this head is, What are political crimes?

The adjective, "political," means that which pertains to government. Political rights are those which may be exercised in the formation or administration of government. Civil rights are those which a man enjoys as regards other individuals, and not in relation to government.

Political crimes are those acts of a person or persons in violation of the political government of the country, under the belief that he or they are justified in so acting according to their honest convictions. And the crime is as distinct from a felony as black is from white. The man who robs or wilfully kills with malice aforethought, makes no pretensions to justification, because he is acting contrary to his own conscience. Any one act as much as another against the regularly constituted government, by a dissident, is a political crime. The Constitution has made no classification of political crimes, but has declared that no person shall suffer *death* who may commit them. Undoubtedly Congress could classify such crimes, as the prohibition in the Constitution is only on the *limit* of punishment.

The Supreme Court of the United States said, in Martin *vs.* Hunter's Lessees, 1 Wheaton, 304, that "The words of the Constitution are to be taken in their natural and obvious sense, and not in a sense unreasonable or enlarged."

One of the Circuit Courts of the United States held that the words, "admiralty and maritime jurisdiction," in the Constitution of the United States, had a signification which could not be extended or curtailed by Congress.

It is manifest then, from the plain import of the Mexican Constitution:

1st. That the President has no legislative power.

2d. That the Congress of Mexico cannot delegate its powers to the President.

3d. That among the individual guaranties which may be suspended, that which affects the life of man is not included.

4th. That the powers of suspension in regard to individual guaranties do not authorize either the President or Congress to deprive the Constitutional Courts of their jurisdiction.

5th. That neither the Legislative nor Executive branch of government can change the signification of the language of the Constitution from its usual and general sense.

6th. That the Constitution provides that its provisions shall not be inoperative during the time of war.

7th. That the ordinary Council of War which tried Maximilian had no jurisdiction of the cause.

It follows from this review that the law made by Juarez, dated January 25th, 1862, upon which the accusations against Maximilian were based, is in violation of the Mexican Constitution, and therefore void.

Passing from the questions of constitutional and municipal laws of the Republic of Mexico, which have been applied to the case, it becomes necessary to investigate the rights of the parties under the law of nations. This has become quite essential, in order to arrive at just conclusions, inasmuch as the severest criticisms have been passed upon the Emperor for issuing the decree of October 3d, 1865. That decree engendered a great deal of bitterness in Mexico, and it has been alleged to be the cause of the Emperor's death. Those who were the bitterest in their denunciations of him were under the necessity of presenting some kind of an argument to support their position; and the severity of that decree was advanced as sufficient therefor. It has been so much commented upon by the Mexicans, and by their press, while they have been silent as to the terrible law of their own enactment, that the people of the United States and Europe have been inclined to attach considerable blame to Maximilian for issuing it without knowing the circumstances and facts which surrounded the Emperor, and which so clearly, in the eyes of the law, justified him in issuing the same.

When Maximilian executed that decree, he was the sovereign of the *de facto* government of Mexico, beyond any doubt. He was so recognized by several powers. The fact that the United States did not so recognize him, did not change the real condition of things in Mexico. It brings to my mind an observation once made by that distinguished American jurist, Chief-Justice Marshall, who said, "If Congress should pass a resolution, declaring that Hume never wrote the History of England, I do not think that it would change the fact."

The United States, for certain political reasons, did not wish to recognize any new Empire on the American continent, particularly in an adjacent territory. Those reasons were not based upon the true state of facts as to the actual possession of the one or the other contending parties in Mexico.

If the relative position of the two parties had been changed, the United States would not for a moment have doubted that the same facts which surrounded Maximilian would have been ample, upon principles of international law, to hold that he was the sovereign *de facto* and *de jure.*

The law of nations is governed by the state of facts which exist in a country, not what some nations may say of it. Suppose a nation declares certain ports blockaded, does the proclamation *ipso facto* render them blockaded in the eyes of the law? Will not the law inquire whether adequate physical and material force is actually on the spot to support the blockade?

The same reason applies to a nation. The question is, what party holds and exercises control over a country. Whatever party does, that is the government *de facto* of that country. If no other nation on earth had recognized the Empire of Maximilian, still the fact of its having the possession and control of the territory, made it the government *de facto* and *de jure*. The internal sovereignty of a State requires no such recognition. It is a State because it exists.

Nor did the fact that foreign troops aided the Empire change its rights. The settled doctrine of the law of nations, which was adhered to by the United States Supreme Court, is, that a weak power does not surrender its independence and right to self-government by associating with a stronger and taking its protection. It would be a singular doctrine to advance that the nationality of some of the troops of the Empire could change the rights of its Sovereign.

One of the *absolute* rights of a State is to protect itself, and to make all needful laws; and no other power has a right to dictate to it in regard to those municipal laws. And the judicial investigation and punishment of a sovereign for enacting laws within the jurisdiction of his territory, is what will not be found on the records of any nation but those of Mexico. Such an investigation may well be considered a judicial curiosity.

After the intervention ceased, and Maximilian assumed the reins of government, at the request of a large number of Mexicans, and, as he believed, in accordance with the will of a majority, the war was a civil one. Wheaton says, and it is not denied by any other writer on international law, that "the general usage of nations regards such a war as entitling both of the contending parties to all the rights of war as against each other, and even as respects neutral nations." (*Wh. on Laws of Nations*, part 4, ch. 1, § 7.)

What, then, *are the rights of war?* One among the many is that of *retaliation*. That is, one nation may apply in its transactions with another the same rule of conduct by which that other is governed under similar circumstances (*Ibid.*, Section 1st). Notwithstanding the severity of the decree of October 3d, executed by Maximilian, we fail to find less in the law of January 25th, 1862, made by President Juarez. According to said law of 1862, if any Mexican should be caught who had served in any manner the foreign troops in the country, which were the enemies of the Liberals, he would be punished with death. (See Article 2d.)

Under that law, if the Liberal party contained only one-eighth part of the whole population, and the other seven-eighths wished to change the form of government, and should attempt it, and any one of them should be caught so doing by the Liberals, he would be subject to the punishment of death.

If a Mexican boy should carry wood to build a fire for one of the enemies of the Liberal party, he would be liable to the same punishment if caught. And yet the party that promulgated that harsh and bloodthirsty law charge the Imperial ruler with cruelty in issuing the decree of October 3d, 1865.

Not only was the law of January 25th, 1862, on the statute-books of the Juarez party, but the bloody act was carried into execution.

Was not General Robles caught on the road to Vera Cruz without arms, and shot in cold blood by the Juarez party, merely because it was suspected that he was going to talk to the French forces? The shocking crimes, covered by the law of 1862, were numbered by hundreds, nay thousands, long before the decree of October 3d was issued. Will not the surprise of the reader be rather that such a decree was not issued earlier, than that it was issued at all? Was the Emperor not justified upon the principle of *retaliation*, based on international law, in issuing that decree?

Let us suppose another case for illustration. If the Liberals were composed of only one-third of the population, and possessed all of the arms in the country, and should see proper to issue decrees contrary to the Constitution, and to enforce them upon the unarmed two-thirds, and if the latter, in their defence, should invite foreign aid, in the way of men and munitions of war, and be subsequently caught by the Liberal party, they would be liable to a death punishment under the law of 1862. Such a case might well arise, because one-third of a nation well armed could hold in subjection the remaining unarmed two-thirds.

It appears, not unfrequently, by observation among men, that many persons first determine in their own minds which of the contending parties have the right side of the issue, and then conclude that that party is authorized to enact laws, however severe, which its judgment may dictate, while they deny the same right to the other party. The rule of law is, that the justness or unjustness of the war is not to be taken into consideration, when passing upon the question of the method of warfare.

There are certain principles of international law which are founded on the rights of humanity, and enforced by moral sanction; and it makes no difference what has caused the war, for when it has once commenced, certain rules based on international morality, and acknowledged by the civilized world to be just and humane, are to govern the acts of the contending parties.

And the fact that one party in a civil war is vastly superior in numerical strength, does not alter the rights of either. Nor is there any rule of international law that will support the position that, if the head of one party in a civil war be a foreigner, the rights of that party as to the method of warfare are lessened thereby. And Maximilian, as the sovereign head of the Empire, was entitled to all the rights which any Mexican would have been had he held the same position.

It would be difficult for any moral man, be he professional or layman, to advance any good reason why that principle of law, which holds that no use of force is lawful except so far as it is necessary,—and that a belligerent has no right to take away the lives of the subjects of the enemy, whom he can subject by any other means,—should not have governed in the war between the Imperialists and Liberals in Mexico.

If a man declares that he justifies the shooting of the Emperor because he is opposed to the establishment of an empire in Mexico, or because some secessionists in the Southern part of the United States favored Maximilian's policy, he would give no room for discussion, and would be rather an object of pity than of admiration, on account of his prejudices and great want of argumentative powers.

While the law of January 25th, 1862, stares the world in the face, the complaint of inhumanity against Maximilian comes with a bad grace from the lips of the Juarez party.

It will be readily admitted that there was a time in the barbarous ages, as even now among the wild savage tribes, when warriors considered it their right to take the lives of prisoners of war; but we have long indulged the hope that the torch of science had dispelled such a doctrine; and that there was a universal desire among the civilized nations of the present age to adopt measures that would mitigate that ancient practice of cruelty. And it is with no very kind feelings that we can view that people who claim a place in the great family of nations, who cannot consent to respect the principles of international morality.

As we closely review the individual acts of His Majesty, which pertain to the Empire, we shall perceive a steady aim on his part to avoid cruel treatment and to keep within the rules of warfare that are sanctioned by the general consent of mankind, as being just and humane. If we investigate the treaty of Miramar, we shall ascertain that the position of Maximilian was not an enviable one for a sovereign. Wherever there was a body of French troops or allied forces of French and Mexican soldiers, they were under the control of the French commander by virtue of that treaty. And thus, while they were acting in accordance with instructions from a French general, they were committing acts obnoxious to the feelings of the head of the nation, and upon whom was placed all the blame for the committal of those acts.

As soon as the Emperor was freed from the dictation of the French commander Bazaine, he annulled the decree of October 3d, 1865; which act took place about the 21st of October, 1866. Thus, for many months prior to the capture of the Emperor, that decree which infuriated the Liberals was not in force, while their murderous law of January 25th, 1862, was still unrepealed.

And further, even while the said decree of October was in full vigor, Maximilian never consented to its enforcement in any given case; but, on the contrary, issued strict orders to his commanders not to execute it. Wherever executions were rendered under the law, it was without his prior knowledge, and met subsequently with his disapproval. At the same time, hundreds of prisoners taken by the Liberal forces were sent to their graves under the stern provisions of the law of 1862.

Humanity, and the just principles of war, demanded that the Liberals should have ceased to carry out the law of 1862, after the annulment of the October decree, by His Majesty. Is there any rule of law or conscience that would hold the life of the Emperor responsible for every murder, or unjust act committed by French soldiers, against the will of the Emperor? The rule of law is, that the conduct which is observed by one nation toward another, will be reciprocally observed by the latter toward the former. And the moment the rigor of a law is abated by one party, the other should immediately repeal that law which was enacted by it as retaliatory of the one which was abated. Reason and good faith could not support any other doctrine.

There is a very short argument advanced by some who favored the murder of Maximilian, and that is, that he had no business to come to Mexico.

Let us examine that question in a legal and moral point of view.

The generally recognized doctrine that a people have the right to change their form of government, is expressly laid down in the 39th Art., Sec. 1, Title 2, of the Mexican Constitution, in these words: "The people have at all times the inalienable right to alter or modify the form of their government."

The Imperial party attempted to avail themselves of that right. The next question which would naturally present itself is, Did that party represent a majority of the people of Mexico? Upon that point there are two opinions in Mexico.

As I am in favor of the stability of the Republic, and against the Empire, upon principle, I hope I shall not be charged with prejudice against the Liberal party.

And as I wish to make no incorrect statement in regard to Mexico, I will not state which way the majority of the people would have decided that issue had a test vote been taken. I will give some facts from which conclusions may be drawn.

I have visited Mazatlan, Durango, Zacatecas, San Luis Potosi, Queretaro, the city of Mexico, Puebla, Orizaba, Cordova, and Vera Cruz. With the exception of Zacatecas and Vera Cruz, a large majority in those places were in favor of the Empire. That Guadalajara, Guanajuata, Puebla, and Orizaba were strongly in support of the Empire was never doubted. I have thus mentioned nearly all of the *large* cities of Mexico. The majority of the educated and refined people of those cities do not mix with the Liberals. There is also a marked change noticed by those who observed the government under both *régimes*, in regard to the activity of business and the gayety of social life; showing that progress was making headway under the Empire. When the Emperor and Empress entered the country they were greeted with unbounded enthusiasm. Many who witnessed that entrance have frequently remarked that no one could have doubted that the majority were for the Empire.

I witnessed the entrance of President Juarez into the city of Mexico, on the 15th of July last, and I was completely surprised at the want of enthusiasm. It appeared more like a funeral than a joyous reception. Several Liberal officers standing by me could not help remarking what a silence prevailed. A large portion, if not a majority of the intelligent people in Mexico, dressed in mourning for the demise of the Emperor. In consequence thereof it was difficult to obtain many articles of mourning wearing-apparel at the mercantile establishments.

As an admission from the Liberals, we take the following article from the "*La Sociedad*," May 25th, 1866;

which copied the same from the "*Revista*," of Vera Cruz, a Liberal journal.

"Before the Emperor Maximilian arrived in this country, when the Assembly of Notables in the Capital proclaimed the Monarchy, and elected him the arbiter of the destinies of Mexico, he wished to know the will of the entire country, or at least of the localities occupied by the French-Mexican army; and a call was made on the inhabitants of those localities, the only object of which call was to know the true opinion of the Mexicans.

"In fact, *in each locality* a declaration was made, which was subscribed by thousands of citizens, and among them, certainly, very few figured that were not in feeling favorable to the new order of things.

"The Archduke Maximilian, in view of these acts, which we cannot deny were numerous, accepted the imperial crown which the Mexican deputation, who were sent for that purpose, offered him at Miramar. . . . .

"We who, whatever may be our ideas, cannot deviate from the path we have marked out, *believe ourselves obliged to confess that if any ruler ever had reason to believe himself really called by the people, the Emperor Maximilian had in the highest degree.*

"And it is so far so, that we even recollect the first words which the new Emperor dictated to the Mexicans on his arrival to our shores, words which were in *complete harmony with the facts already referred to.*"

The rejoicing exhibited wherever the Emperor went in Mexico, and the foregoing admission of one of his political enemies, ought to be considered as some evidence that a large party of the Mexicans were friendly to the Empire, if not a majority of them. The admission of that Liberal journal is so strong, that it relieves the Emperor of the charge of an *intent* to act *contrary* to the *will* of the Mexican people.

The fact that the Liberals conquered the Imperialists, is no proof that the former are supported by a majority of the people. Any one acquainted with the history of Mexico, will well understand how that may be. No party can long remain in power in that country. And it is immaterial what principles are advocated by the reigning party, they are destined, sooner or later, to be overthrown. As I have in another place observed, the supreme power of a nation is always with the party who happen to have the arms in their hands, although that party may not number one-third of the whole.

Out of the whole population of Mexico, there is not a million that have anything to say about the affairs of government. The common soldier has no opinion on political matters, and knows not the difference between an empire and a republic. And the man who thinks that the soldiers volunteered in the Liberal party, never had a more erroneous idea. They were forced into the service, not by any law regulating a draft as in other countries, but by sending armed men to take them wherever they could be found. I have this information from persons who have lost their working men in that manner. I adduce these facts in support of the proposition that the numerical strength of the Liberal army is no criterion of the correct views of their political opinions.

I went to Mexico in the beginning of the year 1867, strongly impressed with the idea that the Liberal party was far in the majority—and I must confess, against my wish, I have had that opinion shaken. That the majority of the wealthy people were in favor of the Empire, I think no well-informed and unbiased man will deny.

More improvements were made under the Empire than under any President, during the same length of time.

It has been difficult for the people in Europe and the United States to obtain correct information as to the condition of affairs in Mexico. Many correspondents of newspapers have visited Mexico with a view to obtain profitable concessions from the Government, and with a view of aiding their contemplated projects: they have written highly favorable to the Administrative power. And others strongly biased, have written in opposition thereto. The poorer class care but little who governs; the rich are in favor of an empire, but do not wish to do the fighting; and the middle class, together with some of the rich, are the most energetic, and belong to the Liberal party; hence their success, added to the fact, that the Imperialists had no sufficient army of native element formed when Bazaine left.

To sum up then, it is obvious that a number so large, of the Mexican people, were in favor of Maximilian as their ruler, that he was not wholly without proof that the party was composed of a majority. The weight of evidence is in his favor sufficiently to acquit him in a moral point of view.

And further, it is too clear and conclusive to admit of a serious argument, that the law of January 25th, 1862, is in conflict with the provisions of the Mexican Constitution; and that international law cannot support the execution of Maximilian.

The sustaining of Mexico in that brutal act, is only on a par with the praise of Booth, for murdering President Lincoln. The latter was a cold-blooded murder *without* a trial; the former was murder after a farcical one.

Mexico has long witnessed calamities flowing from mutual persecutions, but it was to be hoped that in this age some benefits and improvements were to be expected from the light, and human sympathy acquired from the advancement of science. When the Mexican people formed their present Constitution, they were not unmindful of the barbarity and injustice indulged in during their many intestine conflicts; and in order to impress moderation upon their minds, and to work up to the standard of modern ideas of civilization, they wove into that Constitution certain principles in harmony with justice, and which were, that life should not be forfeited on account of political opinions, nor for any acts honestly committed in support thereof; and that confiscation of property should not take place. And yet the party that stands upon that Constitution as its political platform, pays but little respect to its prohibitory clauses.

And admitting, for argument's sake, that the law of January 25th, 1862, was in perfect harmony with the Constitution, and that the Court had jurisdiction of the cause, then it can be safely said that the judgment was fraudulent, and unsupported by the evidence presented, according to the rules of the Civil Law, which governs judicial proceedings in Mexico. Public notoriety, hearsay testimony, nor secondary evidence never were sufficient under the Civil Law, nor by the legislative laws of Mexico, to sustain a judgment of guilty in a criminal cause.

It was not from ignorance that the authorities of Mexico committed their deed of horror, nor from any mistaken notion of law and justice.

It was considered too good an opportunity to lose to show the world that Mexico was an independent nation, and that however much sympathy the adjoining Republic might have heretofore shown in the hour of need, it was by far insufficient to permit that Republic to assume an advisory position which savored in the slightest degree of dictation. Such has been given by Mexicans themselves as one reason why the executioner should have done the bloody work.

As we review all the circumstances of the case, we

cannot but conclude that they justify the suspicion that revenge and cupidity dictated their acts rather than the spirit of a manly foe.

We have seen, in this case, great questions of constitutional and international law considered and decided within a few hours by not very wise and learned men—questions that learned tribunals in other lands would have considered for days before giving a final decision. That is, although they might have considered at first blush the questions not difficult, yet the magnitude and importance of the cause would have demanded from learned jurists a complete and serious examination before the rendition of a definite judgment thereon.

Had the goddess of Justice been present during the trial of the Emperor, she would have hung her head in shame as the judgment was read.

It is apparent that the scales and beam of justice were broken into fragments, and that there was no weighing of the evidence.

The trial was the prelude to the tragedy, in order to increase the assumed dignity, and to extend the great dramatic play of the nation. It was, indeed, a bombastic farce, and the tragedy that followed a terrible one. And both are recorded as a stain on the pages of the history of the Mexican nation which can never be effaced therefrom, though steeped in the sulphurous fumes of the infernal regions.

CHAPTER XIV.

Application for pardon—Pardon denied—Sentence approved—Pardon again asked and denied—Execution postponed—Letter from Maximilian to Baron Largo — Pardon asked by Baron Magnus—Refused—Despatch from Maximilian to Juarez—Preparations for execution—Last words of the victims—Execution.

AFTER the decision of the Council of War, or court-martial, and the approval thereof by the Commander of the Division, General Escobedo, there was but one other mode to pursue on the part of the defendants—that was, to seek the clemency of the Executive. Before, and during the time of the trial, Messrs. Palacio and De la Torre, two of the Emperor's counsel, were at San Luis Potosi exercising their influence with the President and Cabinet.

The said counsel having learned that, on the 14th of June, at ten minutes past twelve o'clock at night, the three prisoners, Maximilian, Miramon, and Mejia, had been condemned to death, immediately applied for the pardon of the three, without waiting to ascertain whether the decision of General Escobedo would be in approval or disapproval of the said sentence. In answer to that application, the Minister of War transmitted to the said counsel the following note:

"Secretary of State, War, and Navy:

"You have set forth in your new petition that having notice that the Council of War assembled in Queretaro have condemned to the extreme penalty Fernando Maximilian of Hapsburg, you ask, as his counsel, the Government to grant him a pardon, or, that if even it cannot pass upon that question, that in the mean time it will order a suspension of the sentence. The Citizen-President being in possession of this new petition, has directed me to say to you, as I declared to you yesterday officially, that it is not possible to pass upon the question of pardon before knowing the condemnation of the court, there not being a condemnation that may have the effect as such, as, in the mean while, the judgment of the Council of War may not be confirmed by the military chief according to the ordinance and respective laws. And further, I am directed to say to you, also, as I stated to you officially yesterday, that the Government not having altered the provisions of the law, if in case the judgment of the Court should be confirmed, and then should be submitted within the proper time to the decision of the Government, the question of pardon, in such a case, among the considerations which the Government ought to weigh, it will remember the facts set forth in your two petitions.

"Independence and Liberty. San Luis Potosi, June 15th, 1867.

"MEJIA.

"Citizens MARIANO RIVA PALACIO, and
"Lawyer RAFAEL MARTINEZ DE LA TORRE.
"Present."

"Telegram from Queretaro for Potosi, received the 16th day of June, 1867, at one o'clock and 15 minutes of the afternoon:

"CITIZEN-PRESIDENT:

"The sentence which the Council of War pronounced on the 14th inst., has been confirmed at these headquarters, and to-day, at ten o'clock of the morning the prisoners were notified thereof, and at three o'clock this afternoon they will be shot.

"ESCOBEDO."

The Government having read the report of General Escobedo, approving the judgment of the Court, and having received another petition from the said counsel, replied thereto with the following note:

"SECRETARY OF STATE, WAR, AND NAVY.

"As to the petition presented by you of to-day's date to the Citizen-President of the Republic, soliciting a pardon for Ferdinand Maximilian of Hapsburg, who has been sentenced, in Queretaro, by the Council of War that tried him, to suffer the extreme penalty, the President has come to the following determination:

"Having examined this solicitation for pardon with all the gravity which the case requires, and the other solicitations for the same purpose, the Citizen-President of the Republic has thought proper to determine that the petitions cannot be acceded to; the gravest considerations of justice and of necessity to assure the peace of the nation being opposed to this act of clemency.

"And I communicate it to you for your information, and as the determination on your said petition.

"SAN LUIS POTOSI, June 16th, 1867.

"MEJIA.

"Citizens MARIANO RIVA PALACIO, and
Lawyer RAFAEL MARTINEZ DE LA TORRE,
"Present."

Upon an application for further time to be extended to the Emperor's life, the following despatch was forwarded to the commanding officer, at Queretaro:

"Telegram—S. Luis Potosi, June 16th, 1867. At one o'clock of the afternoon.

"CITIZEN GENERAL M. ESCOBEDO, Queretaro:

"The counsel of Maximilian and Miramon have just presented themselves, to state to the Government, that the sentence of the Council of War has been confirmed, which imposed upon them and Mejia the punishment of death; and that the execution has been ordered to take place this afternoon. Pardon has been asked for the three condemned persons, which the Government has denied, after having held the most attentive deliberation thereupon. In order that the condemned may have the necessary time to arrange their business, the Citizen President of the Republic has determined that the execution of the three condemned persons will not take place until Wednesday morning, the 19th of the present month.

"Please give your orders in conformity with this resolution, and advise me immediately of the receipt of this message.

"MEJIA."

The following reply came from General Escobedo:

"Telegram from Queretaro for San Luis Potosi—received the 16th of June, 1867, at four o'clock and one minute of the afternoon.

"CITIZEN MINISTER OF WAR:

"I am informed that the Citizen President has ordered a suspension of the execution of the three prisoners until the morning of Wednesday, the 19th. I shall comply with this supreme order.

"M. ESCOBEDO.

"SECRETARY OF STATE, WAR, and NAVY.
"SAN LUIS POTOSI, June 16th, 1867."

Baron Von A. V. Magnus, the Prussian Minister near the Imperial Government of Mexico, was also at San Luis Potosi, for the purpose of interceding in behalf of Maximilian. The Baron gave all his attention to the welfare of the Emperor. After the final conclusion of the President upon the question of pardon, the Baron became anxious to hasten with all speed to Queretaro. In order to facilitate him in that respect, the Government ordered the owners of the stage-line to make preparations therefor, as follows:

"MINISTER OF FOREIGN RELATIONS AND GOVERNMENT,
Department of Government—Section First.

"The Citizen President of the Republic has determined that you will please to so arrange immediately, that there will be provided an extra stage which will go with all possible dispatch from this city to Queretaro; and that you will place this stage at the disposition of Baron A. V. Magnus, and the persons whom he wishes to accompany him.

"I communicate it to you in order that said extra stage may be provided, at the hour which M. Baron Von Magnus may designate, this afternoon or to-night.

"Independence and Liberty. San Luis Potosi, June 16th, 1867.

"LERDO DE TEJADA.

"Señor Agent of the Stage-lines of this city, Present."

On the fifteenth of June, General Mejia had been requested to say to the Emperor, that authentic information had just reached Queretaro, that the Empress Carlota had died. The General communicated the statement to His Majesty.

In consequence thereof, he wrote that day a letter to Baron Largo, who had been ordered away from Queretaro, the 14th, by General Escobedo, and who went to Tacubaya, where he received the letter; in the postscript to which, the Emperor wrote as follows: "I have just learned that my poor wife has died, and though the news affects my heart, yet, on the other hand, under the present circumstances, it is a consolation. I have but one wish on earth; that is, that my body may be buried next to that of my poor wife. I intrust you with this, as the representative of Austria. I ask you that my legal heirs will take the same care of those who surrounded me, and my servants, as though the Empress and I had lived."

On the sixteenth, about half an hour before the Emperor's anticipatad execution, he took from his finger his marriage-ring and gave it to his physician, Dr. Samuel Basch, requesting him to carry it to the Archduchess his mother, supposing at the time that his wife the Empress was dead. Not being executed that day, he received it back again, and wore it as usual. On the next day the Emperor wrote the following letter to Baron Largo:

"Dear Baron:

"I have nothing to look for in this world; and my last wishes are limited to my mortal remains, which soon will be free from suffering and under the favor of those who outlive me. My physician, Dr. Basch, will have my body transported to Vera Cruz. Two servants, Gull and Tudas, will be the only ones who will accompany him. I have given orders that my body be carried to Vera Cruz without any pomp, and that no extraordinary ceremony be made on board. I await death calmly, and I equally wish to enjoy calmness in the coffin. So arrange it, dear Baron, that Dr. Basch and my two servants be transported to Europe in one of the two war-vessels.

"I wish to be buried by the side of my poor wife. If the report of the death of my poor wife has no foundation, my body should be deposited in some place until the Empress may meet me through death.

"Have the goodness to transmit the necessary orders to the captain of the ship de Groeller. Have likewise the goodness to do all you can to have the widow of my faithful companion in arms, Miramon, go to Europe in one of the two war-vessels. I rely the more upon this wish being complied with, inasmuch as I have recommended her to place herself under my mother at Vienna.

"Again, I give you my most cordial thanks for all the inconveniences which I cause you; and I am, with the greatest good-will,

"Yours,

"MAXIMILIAN.

"QUERETARO, in the Prison of the Capuchinas, 17th of June, 1867."

Before Maximilian's execution, he observed to some of his officers in the convent, that it was not so very hard to die after all; that he felt as though he were going into battle. He also remarked that he could forgive Lopez; but Marquez, never!

The day before his death, the captain who was to direct the execution, went to the convent to see the Emperor, and apologized, saying that he was sorry that he, Maximilian, was compelled to suffer death; that he him self was ordered to cause him to be executed, which he regretted; and that he was obliged to obey the order. The Emperor excused him from any blame, observing that it was not his fault.

Baron Magnus arrived on the eighteenth at Queretaro, from San Luis Potosi, and immediately visited the Emperor. After which, considering as he did that it was his solemn duty to do everything that was within his power, he was not inclined to remain silent, until he saw that the safety of Maximilian's life was beyond hope. He therefore again placed himself in communication with the officers of Government, as the last remedy, at a late hour that night; when he sent the following message:

"Telegram from Queretaro to San Luis Potosi, received at 9 o'clock and 30 minutes of the night, June 18th, 1867.

"HIS EXCELLENCY

"SEÑOR D. SEBASTIAN LERDO DE TEJADA:

"Having reached Queretaro to-day, I am sure that the three persons, condemned on the 14th, died morally last Sunday; and that the world so estimates it, as they had made every disposition to die, and expected every instant, for an hour, to be carried to the place where they were to receive death, before it was possible to communicate to them the order suspending the act.

"The humane customs of our epoch do not permit that, after having suffered that horrible punishment, they should be made to die the second time to-morrow.

"In the name, then, of humanity and Heaven, I conjure you to order their lives not to be taken; and I repeat to you again, that I am sure that my Sovereign, His Majesty the King of Prussia, and all the monarchs of Europe united by the ties of blood with the imprisoned Prince, namely, his brother the Emperor of Austria, his cousin the Queen of the British Empire, his brother-in-law the King of the Belgians, and his cousins, also, the Queen of Spain and the Kings of Italy and Sweden, will easily understand how to give His Excellency Señor D. Benito Juarez, all the requisite securities that none of the three prisoners will ever return to walk on the Mexican territory.

"A. V. MAGNUS."

The following reply to the foregoing was received by Baron Magnus:

"Telegram.—San Luis Potosi, June 18th, 1867, at 10 o'clock and five minutes of the night.

"SEÑOR BARON A. V. MAGNUS, etc., etc., Queretaro:

"I am pained to tell you, in answer to the telegram which you have been pleased to send me to-night, that, as I declared to you day before yesterday, in this city, the President of the Republic does not believe it possible to grant the pardon of the Archduke Maximilian, through the gravest considerations of justice, and of the necessity of assuring peace to the Republic.

"I am, Señor Baron, very respectfully,

"Your obedient servant,

"SEBASTIAN LERDO DE TEJADA."

The following despatch was sent by the Emperor to President Juarez on the 18th of June:

"Central Telegraph Line. Official telegram. Deposited in Queretaro. Received in San Louis Potosi at one o'clock and fifty minutes of the afternoon, the 18th of June, 1867.

"C. BENITO JUAREZ:

"I desire that you may preserve the lives of D. Miguel Miramon and D. Tomas Mejia, who day before yesterday suffered all the tortures and bitterness of death; and, as I manifested on being taken prisoner, I should be the only victim.

"MAXIMILIAN."

This was an exhibition of nobleness of character seldom to be met with, and which had been manifested by the Emperor all through his Mexican career.

On that night the commander, General Escobedo, visited the Emperor at half-past eleven o'clock. He asked His Majesty for his photograph, which the Emperor gave him. After a few moments' conversation they bid each other farewell, and the General left. The Emperor had retired at nine o'clock, but was restless, dozed a little, and was awake when Escobedo entered. He slept only about two and a half hours. The thoughts of the morrow were ill suited to produce slumber. He dressed at a little past three o'clock. The priest came at four, and prayers were said at about five. He gave to Dr. Basch his marriage-ring, to be delivered to the Archduchess, his mother, still under the supposition that the Empress was dead. He then wrote the following letter to the President:

"QUERETARO, June 19th, 1867.

"SR. BENITO JUAREZ:

"About to receive death, in consequence of having wished to prove whether new political institutions could succeed in putting an end to the bloody civil war which has devastated for so many years this unfortunate country; I shall lose my life with pleasure if its sacrifice can contribute to the peace and prosperity of my new country. Fully persuaded that nothing solid can be founded on a soil drenched in blood and agitated by violent commotions, I conjure you in the most solemn manner, and with the true sincerity of the moments in which I find myself, that my blood may be the last to be spilt; that the same perseverance which I was pleased to recognize and esteem in the midst of prosperity—that with which you have defended the cause which has just triumphed—may consecrate that blood to the most noble task of reconciling the minds of the people, and in founding in a stable and durable manner the peace and tranquillity of this unfortunate country.

"MAXIMILIAN."

Many of the last letters and documents signed by His Majesty were penned by Mr. Herman G. Schwesinger, who was a confidential friend of His Majesty, and who, for that friendship was imprisoned six weeks without any charges being made against him. He deserves a mention herein for his fidelity to the Emperor.

The city of Queretaro, on the 19th of June, A. D. 1867, presented one of the most solemn scenes ever witnessed, save that which the murder and burial of Abraham Lincoln produced in Washington City. For a beloved mortal, about to put on immortality, the drapery of mourning was worn by thousands, as an emblem of hearts sincerely touched with grief.

At half-past six o'clock, on that morning, stood before the entrance of the convent of the Capuchinas, three ordinary carriages, with a pair of not very elegant horses attached to each. The first one of those carriages was entered by Maximilian and Father Soria, a priest. The Emperor was dressed in a single-breasted black frock-coat, buttoned up save the last button; black vest, necktie, and pants, ordinary boots, and a wide-brimmed hat.

After the Emperor arrived at the carriage, he sent back for his physician, Dr. Samuel Basch. He desired to have some one that he believed to be his friend near him in the last moment. The Emperor sent for Dr. Basch twice, but the doctor did not appear. It was not because Dr. Basch did not wish to do him a favor; the attachment which endeared His Majesty so much to the doctor completely broke the spirits of the latter, and so unnerved him that he had not the heart to look upon the Emperor as the leaden messenger of death winged its way into his noble form. The doctor was a true friend to His Majesty: would that he had possessed more like him!

General Miramon and his accompanying priest occupied the second carriage, and General Mejia and his priest the other. In the extreme advance of their military escort were five mounted men, one of whom was a corporal, a few paces in front of the others. Next followed a company of infantry, composed of eighty men, who belonged to the regiment known as the "Supreme Powers;" in their rear were the three carriages escorted by a battalion of Nuevo Leon infantry, one half of which flanked each side of the road, parallel with the vehicles. Then came a rear guard of two hundred and fifty mounted men, called *Cazadores de Galeana* (sharpshooters of Galeana).

Soon after those carriages were thus entered, they and their escorts moved slowly on, carrying three noble men into the arms of death. What a contrast in the two pictures—that of His Majesty's entrance into Queretaro, and that of his departure therefrom! The former was a glittering procession and triumphal entry; the latter, a solemn march into the hands of the executioner,

> "Where Mexicans wrought their cruelty."

The appointed place for that work of barbarism was *El Cerro de las Campanas* (the Hill of the Bells), about one and a quarter mile northwest of the city. It was near that hill the Emperor and Mejia were taken prisoners. Are we to suppose that the conquerors were actuated by the same principles which governed the infuriated English two centuries ago?—that mob which, dethroned of reason, and wild with vengeance and hate, executed Charles I. before Whitehall, near his own palace, to show the triumph of republicanism over royal majesty. Did the Mexicans hope to overrun the cup of sorrow by presenting to Maximilian's dying view the unfortuaate spot of his surrender? The English would feign seal up that part of their history. What will Mexicans hereafter think of their own past record?

While the *cortège* advanced to the place of execution, the faces of the surrounding multitude were pictured

CERRO DE LAS CAMPANAS.

with sorrow. Crowds upon crowds rushed along, mournfully looking at the victims for the sacrifice, shedding tears, offering up prayers, and holding up the cross as the true emblem of consolation. Could one have dropped suddenly from the clouds among that gathered concourse, he would have thought that a whole nation were in mourning. If ever there was proof of true affection from a whole people for living man it was then. It was not idle curiosity that assembled that mighty host. Their actions, their expressions of grief, their contempt exhibited toward the soldiery, were too apparent to deceive the observing witness.

About twenty minutes time brought the unfortunate men to their death-ground. His Majesty stepped out of his carriage and gave his hat and handkerchief, with which he wiped his face, to his servant, to carry to his mother and brother, and looked to see if any friend came, and asked if he was alone, to which the servant on the carriage said "Yes." He stroked down his ample beard, as was his frequent habit, and walked proudly to his place; this was where the right-hand cross in the engraving herein stands, and is within about twenty feet of the wall in the rear, which is a part of the fortification erected by himself.

About three thousand soldiers stood in a square, so as to enclose the ground of execution on three sides, leaving the rear supported by the wall. The centre cross marks the spot where General Miramon stood, and the other the position of General Mejia.

The Emperor gave to Lieutenant-Colonel Margain, on the 16th, for each of his seven executioners a twenty-dollar gold piece of money, with his profile thereupon.

The victims embraced each other three times, the Emperor saying that they would meet in Heaven. He also said to Miramon, "Brave men are respected by sovereigns—permit me to give you the place of honor," placing him at the same time in the centre. Gen. Escobedo was not on the ground. He remained at his quarters.

Each of the three victims had an opportunity of delivering a farewell address. The Emperor spoke as follows:

"Persons of my rank and birth are brought into the world either to insure the welfare of the people, or to die as martyrs. I did not come to Mexico from motives of ambition. I came at the earnest entreaty of those who desired the welfare of our country. Mexicans! I pray that my blood may be the last to be shed for our unhappy country, and may it insure the happiness of the nation. Mexicans! Long live Mexico!"

General Mejia had previously requested General Escobedo to take care of his son, but at the time of his execution he said nothing: his attitude was firm and resolute.

Miramon drew from his pocket a small piece of paper, from which he read:

"MEXICANS! behold me, condemned by a Council of War, and condemned to death as a traitor! In these moments which do not belong to me, in which my life is already that of the Supreme Being, before the entire world I proclaim that I have never been a traitor to my country. I have defended my opinions, but my children will never be ashamed of their father. I have not the stain of treason, neither will it pass to my children. Mexicans! Long live Mexico! Long live the Emperor!"

Just as Miramon was finishing, the Emperor placed his hand on his breast, threw up his head, and gave the word—"Fire!" The executioners then discharged their guns. At each victim six soldiers fired simultaneously. The two Generals were killed immediately. The Emperor first received four balls, three in the left breast, and one in the right;—three passed through and came out of the shoulder. As they fired, Maximilian fell a little sideways, falling on his right side, causing a little bruise on the face and hip. And as he fell, he exclaimed, "*Hombre! Hombre!*" (O man! O man!) This statement has been disputed by Baron Magnus, but he did not stand as near the victim as some other individuals, who heard more distinctly. After Maximilian had fallen, a soldier fired into his stomach, which caused him to move slightly; then another shot sent a ball through his heart, producing instant death.

When the victims first entered the ground of execution, the officer in command of the forces present read the following order to the surrounding multitude:

"SOLDIERS:

"In the name of the nation, he who solicits pardon for the three prisoners, or any of them, will be shot."

Possibly, it may be denied that such an order was read; but nevertheless it is true. A general in the Liberal army said that the law required such an order to be read.

Thus passed away that good man, Ferdinand Maximilian I., Emperor of Mexico, from a corruptible to an incorruptible crown of glory.

He died like the bravest. And well may it be said that

"Never in moment most elate,
Did that high spirit loftier rise;
While bright, serene, determinate,
His looks were lifted to the skies,
As if the signal lights of fate
Were shining in those awful eyes!
'Tis come—his hour of martyrdom
In honor's sacred cause is come;

And, though his life hath passed away,
Like lightning on a stormy day,
Yet shall his death-hour leave a track
Of glory, permanent and bright."

It was apparent, even to a casual observer, that the spirit of revenge was running high, from the moment of the capture of Maximilian until he was murdered. The zeal and animosity engendered against a man of high rank, who had come from a foreign land, added to the raging violence of a civil war, so inflamed the minds of the Liberals that the voice of reason was unheard. Their victims were marked, the work must be done; they could not be deprived of the sight of that Imperial blood which was to tinge their soil, gratify their savage spirit, and satisfy "*justice and the peace of the nation*," as by them considered requisite.

No argument could be presented which they would admit savored of reason, if it had for its object the saving of life. The officers of the army, from Generals down, with but few exceptions, were desirous that death should embrace the victims. If they were addressed on the subject by persons in favor of leniency, they exhibited the greatest acrimony of expression which their abilities were capable of forming. You could not go among the officers without inhaling the breath of vengeance. It seemed as though they had turned around and looked the dark ages in the face, that they might bring up the same scenes then witnessed, for the review of the present century. That they equalled them in barbarity cannot be doubted by civilized nations. The ideas of toleration, the mild and charitable spirit taught by Christianity in the present age, entirely escaped their thoughts. In short, such ideas were repugnant to their sentiments of justice. A photograph of the pagan world would present a view not unlike that of to-day, within the jurisdiction of Mexico.

I desire not to be understood as applying this to all Mexicans; there are many exceptions. There are many in the Liberal party that were opposed to taking the life of Maximilian. The officers of the army were furious. The common soldier hardly expressed an opinion on the subject of his execution. I believe the majority of them were not in favor of it. One officer high in command, had been in favor of the execution of the Emperor; but, when he received a telegram stating that the execution had taken place, he observed to a friend of mine that it made him feel sick for several days. He would have gladly restored him, had such a thing been possible. When reason was brought to bear coolly, the conclusion was correct. I think that there are thousands of Mexicans who deeply regret the act. Some brutal Mexicans, near the frontier, fired cannon in commemoration of the execution. It would be a sad reflection on civilization, if the death of a man should cause rejoicing, even when every principle of law and justice would justify the deprivation of life.

Cruelty is a plant that took root in Mexico long ago, and the scythe of civilization has made but little advancement toward its destruction.

CHAPTER XV.

Order to embalm the body—Mode of embalming—Requests for the corpse—Denials—Written request granted—Corpse delivered to Austrian authorities—Departure of same for Europe.

PRIOR to the execution of the Emperor, the Government of the Republic had been solicited to permit his remains to be so prepared that they could be sent out of the country, and also to allow the transportation thereof to the family of Maximilian in Europe.

His Majesty wrote a letter to that effect, on the sixteenth of June, to Señor Don Carlos Rubio, and also one on the eighteenth, to General Escobedo, in which he requested that his physician, Dr. Samuel Basch, be permitted to embalm his body; and, in conjunction with Baron A. V. Magnus, to take it to his family relatives in Austria.

That request was not wholly acceded to; but with a view of having the body so preserved that it might be in a proper condition to convey away, provided that right should thereafter be granted, the Government forwarded the following instructions in relation thereto, to General Escobedo:

"Telegram—San Luis Potosi, June 18th, 1867. At nine o'clock of the morning:

"C. General Mariano Escobedo, Queretaro:

"The Government has been asked that, as soon as the execution of Maximilian shall have taken place, permission be granted to dispose of the body, with the intention of carrying it to Europe.

"This has not been permitted; but in consideration of the petition, the C. President of the Republic has ordered that you will proceed in conformity with the following instructions:

"*First.* After the execution of the three convicted persons shall have taken place, if the relatives of D. M. Miramon and D. T. Mejia should ask to dispose of their bodies, you will permit them immediately freely to do so.

"*Second.* You only will order what may be necessary respecting the body of Maximilian, denying anybody else the right to make any disposition thereof.

"*Third.* You will order to be made, within the proper time, boxes of zinc and wood, to preserve in a proper manner the body of Maximilian; and also those of D. M. Miramon and D. T. Mejia, if their relatives do not ask for them.

"*Fourth.* If any person should ask that he be permitted to embalm or inject the body of Maximilian, or to do anything else which may not be improper, you will refuse the right to any other person to do the same; but in such a case, you will provide, without prohibiting the presence of foreigners, that it be done by Mexicans, in whom you have confidence, and that every thing be done in proper manner, at the expense of the government.

"*Fifth.* After the execution shall have taken place, you will provide that care be immediately taken of the body of Maximilian, and also of the others, if their relatives do not ask for them, and that proper decorum be paid them after the fulfilment of justice.

"*Sixth.* You will direct that the body of Maximilian be deposited in a proper and secure place, under the vigilance of the authorities.

"*Seventh.* For the final rest of the body of Maximilian, and of the others, if their relatives do not ask for them, you will provide that the accustomed religious acts be performed.

"Lerdo de Tejada."

Baron de Largo, the Austrian *chargé d'affaires* near the Empire of Maximilian, having, among others of the diplomatic corps, been ordered away from Queretaro, went to Tacubaya, and remained until the city of Mexico surrendered. He sent the following message to the President of the Republic:

"Telegram—From Tacubaya, for San Luis Potosi. Deposited in Tacubaya the 19th of June, 1867.

"Received in Potosi, at nine o'clock and 25 minutes of the night, the 20th of June.

"C. President:

"I pray you to concede to me the body of Maximilian, in order that I may convey it to Europe.

"Baron de Largo."

The following reply thereto was given by the Minister of Foreign Affairs:

"Telegram—San Luis Potosi, June 20th, 1867, at 10 o'clock and 15 minutes of the night.

"To Señor Baron de Largo:

"The President of the Republic has directed me to say to you, in answer to your telegram of yesterday, which was received this evening, that for grave reasons the right cannot be granted you to dispose of the body of Maximilian.

"S. Lerdo de Tejada."

On the 19th, immediately after the execution of the Emperor, his body was transported back to the convent, whence it went forth with breathing life scarcely an hour before. That lifeless corpse presented a ghastly sight to the few surrounding friends that had been near it when it was the tenement of the bright soul that had already winged its flight with more than the wild lightning's speed to mingle with others around the heavenly throne. Alas! what an hour may bring forth! It was a mournful proof that there is one event unto all.

The work of preservation was forthwith commenced by Drs. Rivadeneyra and Licea, in the presence of Dr. Basch; the latter having no right to dictate as to the mode of procedure in the embalming, but only to make suggestions. The physicians had no naphtha to use in the work, but injected chloride of zinc into the arteries and veins, having taken out the intestines, heart, liver, lungs, etc., leaving the frame by itself. That operation lasted three days. During these nights the body was kept in alcohol, save the head. It was varnished twice, each time occupying two days in drying, and was hung up for that purpose. Nearly eight days were occupied in completing the process of embalming.

All the parts taken from the interior of the body were prepared by being mixed with the powder of tannin and gauls.

The body was afterward dressed in black pants, military boots, with the blue campaign coat which the deceased wore, with plain gilt buttons, buttoned up to the neck; black neck-tie, and black kid gloves. Black glass eyes were placed over his natural ones. Glass eyes of the color of Maximilian's could not be obtained. Robbing the face of a portion of its whiskers, and the head of its hair, and changing the color of the eyes, have somewhat disfigured the remains.

The coffin in which the body was placed was made of cedar and lined with zinc. Within the metallic lining was another of cambric. Under the head was placed a black velvet pillow trimmed with gold thread, with gilt tassels at the four corners. The exterior of the coffin was covered with black velvet, ornamented with bands of gold lace. The cover over the face was of glass. Near the foot of the coffin and parallel with it were two small compartments, one on each side, and about two feet in length. In the one on the left side were deposited the heart, liver, and lungs; and in the other the remainder of the substances taken from the interior of the body, all which were mixed with charcoal and chloride of lime.

The coffin thus arranged, with its contents, was placed in one of the churches at Queretaro, and subsequently moved to the Governor's quarters. For the first two or three weeks after the embalming the body looked tolerably well; but a month's time darkened it, and it soon gave increasing evidence that the work of attempted preservation had been badly done. While in the quarters of the Governor, it was seen with the glass cover cracked and spotted with candle-grease, as though stowed away like so much worthless trash.

Baron Magnus—who had been most faithful to the Emperor during his imprisonment, and was still anxious to render favors to the family of the deceased, as well as to carry out his own desires—presented the following solicitation to the Minister of Foreign Relations:

"San Luis Potosi, June 29th, 1867.

"Sir: The prisoner Prince at Queretaro, the evening before his death, expressed, in a letter signed by his hand and directed to General Escobedo, the desire that his mortal remains be confided to us, myself and Dr. Samuel Basch, physician of the deceased, in order that

Dr. Basch might accompany the body to Europe, and that I might charge myself with having the body embalmed, as well as with all that which concerns its transportation to Europe.

"In conformity with the will of the deceased Prince, which he expressed to me verbally, the transportation of his remains should be done without any ostentation, and in such a manner as may carefully avoid anything which might excite demonstrations or even public curiosity alone.

"Reiterating, in consequence, the demand which I have had the honor to express to His Excellency, to please cause the necessary orders to be given that the mortal remains may be confided to me; it would be agreeable to me, should it please the Government, to transport the body to the coast and on board of one of the vessels of the Austrian navy stationed at Vera Cruz.

"I avail myself of this occasion to repeat to Your Excellency the assurance of my high consideration.

"A. V. Magnus.

"His Excellency D. Sebastian
Lerdo de Tejada."

The minister responded to the foregoing communication with the following note:

"San Luis Potosi, June 30th, 1867.

"To Señor Baron A. V. Magnus, &c., &c., &c.

"Sir: I received the communication which you were pleased to direct to me yesterday, stating that the Archduke Ferdinand Maximilian of Hapsburg, on the evening before his death, expressed the desire that his mortal remains should be confided to you and Dr. Samuel Basch, to transport them to Europe.

"According to what I had the honor to manifest to

you before, the Government of the Republic believes that for various considerations it cannot permit the mortal remains of the Archduke to be carried to Europe.

"For this reason, I am pained to answer you, that the Government cannot give the orders which you have desired, with that end.

"I avail myself of this occasion to repeat to you, Señor Baron, that I am, very respectfully,

"Your obedient servant,

"S. LERDO DE TEJADA."

The body of the Emperor was again solicited on the part of his physician in the following terms:

"C. LERDO DE TEJADA, Minister of Government and of Foreign Relations:

"The undersigned, with due respect, has the honor to present to you, Citizen Minister, that:

"As private physician to the deceased Archkduke Maximilian, I was charged by him to carry his body to Europe, with the object of delivering it to his family.

"That such was his will is shown by the letter signed by himself, which on the 16th of June last past he directed to D. Carlos Rubio, in Queretaro, and a copy of which I have the honor to annex hereto (Sub. A), as well as the letter of the 18th of the same month, the original of which is in the hands of C. General Escobedo, as it is shown by the letter of C. Colonel Ricardo Villanueva, which (Sub. B) is found hereto annexed.

"The fulfilment of this request I consider a sacred duty, and I hasten in its performance to solicit you, Citizen Minister, to be pleased to grant that the above-mentioned body be delivered to me; supporting this solicitation by the fact that, by a superior order, the bodies of his companions in misfortune have been delivered to the families, and that never, and in no time, has the supreme government refused to deliver any corpse to the relatives who asked for it.

"I beg, finally, that you will condescend to answer my respectful solicitation, whatever that answer may be, in order that, on returning to my country, I may be able to justify myself before the family of the deceased Archduke, in having done on my part all that I could to succeed in transporting the body in question.

"Which will be received as a favor from you by

"Your most respectful servant,

"DR. SAMUEL BASCH.

"C. MINISTER.

"MEXICO, July 27th, 1867."

The above petition produced the following response:

"Minister of Foreign Relations and of Government. Department of Government, Section 1st.

"In view of your petition of day before yesterday's date, for permission to convey to Europe the mortal remains of the Archduke Maximilian, the C. President of the Republic has determined that for various and grave considerations the petition cannot be acceded to.

"Independence and Liberty. Mexico, July 29, 1867.

"LERDO DE TEJADA.

"To DR. SAMUEL BASCH."

The following message was sent by the Military Commander of Vera Cruz to the Minister of War:

"Telegram—From Vera Cruz to Mexico. Received in Mexico the 26th of August, 1867, at 7 o'clock and 29 minutes of the night.

"C. Minister of War:

"The Austrian Admiral, Tegethoff, arrived this morning at Sacrificios, in the war-steamer of his nation, '*Elizabeth.*' He sent a message to this military command, stating that he desired to pass to the Capital, and to obtain permission from the Supreme Government to carry away the body of Maximilian. I desire to know whether I must prohibit his going to Mexico.

"Zerega."

The answer sent was as follows:

"Telegram—Office of Minister of War and Navy, Mexico, August 26th, 1867.

"Citizen Military Commander of Vera Cruz:

"The President of the Republic has been informed that Admiral Tegethoff has arrived at that port, and that he desires to pass to this Capital. You can let him pass without objection.

"Mejia."

Messrs. Mariano Riva Palacio and Rafael Martinez de la Torre, two of the counsel of Maximilian, presented themselves before the Minister of Foreign Relations on the third of September, and stated to him that Admiral Tegethoff had arrived, and that he desired an interview with him, the Minister.

The request was granted, and the hour of five on that afternoon was designated for an audience.

At the appointed time, the Admiral, accompanied by the two mentioned counsel, appeared before the Minister, and said that he had come to Mexico with the object of asking of the Government of the Republic permission to carry away the mortal remains of the Archduke Maximilian.

Mr. Lerdo, the Minister, replied that he would submit

the petition to the President of the Republic; and in order that he might take it into consideration, the Minister requested the Admiral to be pleased to state in what character he made the solicitation.

The Admiral said that when he determined to come to Mexico, it was considered that it would appear better to the Government of the Republic that he should not come on an official mission from the Government of Austria; but only with a private charge from the family; for the natural feelings of affection and piety create the strongest desire to possess and honor the mortal remains of the Archduke. That in consideration thereof, he had only come with a private charge from the mother of the Archduke, and from his brother, H. M. the Emperor of Austria.

In response to an observation of the Minister, the Admiral also remarked that he had brought no written document, and that his charge was given to him verbally. He added, that were it necessary, he was ready to state in writing that he had come with such a charge.

The Minister concluded by saying that he would submit to him, on the following day, the determination of the President.

On the 4th, the same counsel and the Admiral returned to the palace; on which occasion, the Minister of Foreign Relations stated to them as follows:

"That the permission to carry away the mortal remains of the Archduke had been asked before, by Baron Largo, *Chargé d'Affaires* of Austria near Maximilian; by Baron Magnus, Prussian Minister, near him; and by Dr. Basch, physician of the Archduke. That the Government answered the three, that it had reasons for not acceding to their petition. It so answered, because the Government believed it to be its duty; that in order to decide whether it would permit the transfer to Austria, of the body of the Archduke, it would be necessary to have for consideration, either an official document from the Government of Austria, or an express one from the family of the Archduke, asking for the body, from the Government of the Republic.

"That although the Vice-Admiral, by his social position in Austria, and by his personal circumstances, is worthy of the consideration of the Government of Mexico, it cannot decide to permit the carrying away of the body of the Archduke, considering that he has brought no document in which is contained any of those two requisites necessary in the case. And that the President of the Republic has authorized the Minister of Relations to say to the Vice-Admiral Tegethoff, that when any of the two requisites are fulfilled, either by an official act of the Austrian Government, or by an express one from the family, asking for the body of the Archduke, the Government of the Republic will be ready to permit that it be transferred to Austria, being governed by the natural feelings of piety through which the petition will be made.

"That the Government ordered opportunely that the body should be embalmed, and that it should be deposited and preserved with the care and decorum which a body merits; which was done through the same natural feelings of piety.

"LERDO DE TEJADA."

Not many days had elapsed after the termination of the foregoing correspondence relative to the body of Maximilian, when the same was transported to the city of Mexico, and deposited in the San Andres Hospital. It was soon observed that decay was working so rapidly upon it, that it became necessary to make some preparation to arrest its progress. When the cloth bandages were taken off for that purpose, the smell of putrefaction issuing from the wounded places was sickening. It was bathed for some time in a solution of arsenic, which assisted in its preservation for a short while; but it was apparent that it would not long be recognizable. The face was much sunken in, and the whole features were gradually changing. There was a prevailing opinion that the Government was ashamed to let the world know the true condition of the corpse; hence the unwillingness to let any one view it. If any particular friend obtained a permit from the Government to see it, he did not succeed in so doing. The keeper gave some excuse, and it so turned out in every instance, that the seeking individual was frustrated in his plan. In fact, I was informed that the keeper in charge of the corpse had received positive orders to allow no one to see it, although the persons presenting themselves there for that purpose should bring written permission from the highest officer in the Government.

After the second process of attempted preservation of the body was completed, it was attired in a suit of black, and laid in a new coffin made of granadilla wood, which was elegantly polished, and ornamented with a few carvings.

On the 9th of November the corpse was delivered to Vice-Admiral Tegethoff by the Mexican Government, after the following official correspondence in relation thereto:

Count Beust to the Mexican Minister.

"VIENNA, *Sept.* 25, 1867.

"EXCELLENCY: A premature death having torn the Archduke Ferdinand Maximilian from his relatives, his Imperial and Royal Apostolic Majesty has the very natural desire that the mortal remains of his unfortunate brother may find their last repose beneath the vault that covers the ashes of the princes belonging to the house of Austria. The father, the mother, and the remaining brothers of the august deceased share in this desire with an equal earnestness, as likewise do all the members of the Imperial family.

"The Emperor, my august master, has the confidence that the Mexican government, listening to sentiments of humanity, will not refuse to mitigate the just grief of His Majesty by facilitating the realization of this desire.

"To that end, Vice-Admiral de Tegethoff has been sent to Mexico with orders to address to the President a petition for the delivery to him of the remains of His Imperial Majesty's beloved brother, so that they can be conveyed to Europe. On my part, I am charged, in my capacity as Minister of the Imperial Household, to request the kind interposition of your Excellency for the object of securing for the Vice-Admiral the authority necessary to that effect.

"I have the honor, Excellency, of asking that you will convey, in anticipation, to the Chief Executive the expression of gratitude on the part of the august Imperial family for the granting of this petition; and accept for yourself the expression of that same gratitude for the good offices which you may have to perform.

"I avail myself of this occasion to present to your Excellency the assurances of my high consideration.

"Beust,
Chancellor of the Empire, and Minister of the Imperial Household.

Reply of Señor Lerdo de Tejada.

"Department for Foreign Affairs,
Mexico, *Nov.* 4, 1867.

"Excellency: Vice-Admiral de Tegethoff has delivered to me the note which your Excellency addressed me on September 25 last.

"Your Excellency informs me therein that His Majesty the Emperor of Austria has the very natural wish that the mortal remains of his brother, the Archduke Ferdinand Maximilian, may find their last repose beneath the vault that covers the ashes of the princes belonging to the house of Austria; that the father, the mother, and the remaining brothers of the deceased Archduke share in this desire, as do likewise all the members of the Imperial family; and that His Majesty the Emperor having the confidence that the Mexican government will, out of sentiments of humanity, facilitate the realization of this request, has sent to Mexico the Vice-Admiral de Tegethoff to solicit of the President permission to convey the Archduke's remains to Europe.

"Fully impressed with the just sentiments set forth in your Excellency's note, the President of the Republic has not hesitated to take measures so that the natural request of His Majesty the Emperor of Austria, and of the Imperial family, may be duly heeded and carried out with distinguished consideration. In accordance with the dispositions of the President, I have made known to Vice-Admiral de Tegethoff that the mortal remains of the Archduke Ferdinand Maximilian shall be at once delivered to his care, in order to convey them to Austria, and thus accomplish the object of his mission.

"I have the honor, Excellency, to assure you of my most distinguished consideration.

"S. LERDO DE TEJADA.

"To his Excellency Count of BEUST, Chancellor of the Empire, and Minister of the Imperial Household of Austria, Vienna."

On the 10th of November, Vice-Admiral Tegethoff, several other Austrian officers, and a Mexican force of a hundred men, escorted the remains of Maximilian from the city of Mexico, and reached Vera Cruz on the 25th, at four o'clock, P. M. The Ayuntamiento of Vera Cruz met the *cortége* at Potrero, about two miles distant from the city, and returned with it. The coffin was deposited in the Parochial church until six o'clock the next morning, whence it was removed to the Austrian war-steamer *Novara, en route* for Vienna. The saloon was draped in mourning; in the centre of which, a table covered with black cloth, supported the coffin. At the head was erected an altar bearing a cross with the image of the Saviour; on the right, hung the Austrian flag; on the left, the Mexican;—both with drapery of black drooped upon the coffin—over all which laid a sword. Around the coffin stood six large silver candlesticks, supporting each a large lighted wax-candle. Two armed sentinels stood near by, day and night.

At about nine o'clock that morning, religious service was performed; and at one o'clock, P. M., the *Novara* steamed from the Mexican coast for Havana, arriving there on the first day of December. The Cuban Government had made extensive preparations for imposing obsequies, and communicated with Admiral Tegethoff in relation thereto. The Admiral replied that his instructions would not permit him to allow any funeral pomp.

The *Novara* remained in that port until six o'clock, P. M., of the 4th, when she weighed anchor and sailed for Austria.

Large crowds of people had gathered upon the wharves, in little boats, and at the windows, long before the hour of departure. At half past five, the bands on the two Spanish war-steamers *Gerona* and *Tetuan*, commenced to play funeral marches. On ships and forts, waved at half-mast the Austrian and Spanish colors, wreathed with black crape. And as the *Novara* ploughed the water out into the sea, all the Government bands united to freight the air with martial funeral notes. The Austrian fleet in the Levant have been ordered to return to escort the *Novara* as she nears the Austrian coast.

It will be remembered that the *Novara* carried Maximilian and Carlota to their new home when both were in blooming health and in high spirits, as the elected Sovereigns over many subjects.

But how changed! That Emperor is now a subject of "Death! great proprietor of all." The humble clay of that once noble chief has crossed the bounding main to his native land again, where father, mother, brother, and others of imperial and royal blood, await its coming in mourning and sorrow; where the heaving sigh and moistened cheek can but faintly attest the depth of smothered grief; where the monumental stone shall mark the final rest of MAXIMILIAN I.

"Deep for the dead the grief must be,
Who ne'er gave cause to mourn before."

THE END.

UNDINE AND SINTRAM. From the German of THE BARON DE LA MOTTE FOUQUÉ. 1 neat vol. 12mo. cloth, $1.50.

——— The same, in red edges, $1.75.

THIODOLF THE ICELANDER: A Romance From the German of THE BARON DE LA MOTTE FOUQUÉ. 1 neat vol. 12mo, cloth, $1.50.

——— The same, in red edges, $1.75.

1. **HOW TO GET A FARM,** and where to find one. Showing that Homesteads may be had by those desirous of securing them. By the author of "Ten Acres Enough." 1 vol. 12mo. Cloth, $1.75.

   It is known that foreigners are now seeking this country in larger numbers than for several years past. This coming stream of immigration promises to expand into greater volume than ever. Multitudes of these are ignorant of our true condition, and need correct information. The majority are in search of land. Even our own citizens are deplorably ignorant of where to find the most eligible, and how to secure it. The facts contained in these pages have been collated with especial reference to the wants of both these classes of inquirers.

2. **TEN ACRES ENOUGH:** A practical experience, showing how a very small Farm may be made to keep a very large Family. 1 vol. 12mo. Cloth, $1.50.

   "That this is a fascinating book a five minutes' examination will convince almost any one. It urges with force the idea embodied in its title, the author confining himself almost entirely to his own experience, which he relates in such a winning manner as to tempt the weary resident of the city to change employment without delay. The book will be invaluable to those interested in the subject."—*The (Boston) Congregationalist.*

3. **OUR FARM OF FOUR ACRES,** and the money we made by it. 1 vol. 12mo. Cloth, $1.

4. **CHRISTIAN ASPECT OF FAITH AND DUTY** By J. J. TAYLER. With an Introduction by Rev. H. W. BELLOWS, D. D. 1 vol. 12mo. Cloth, $1.25.

5. **THE PROBLEM OF HUMAN DESTINY.** By Rev. ORVILLE DEWEY, D. D. 1 vol. 8vo. Cloth, $2.25.

www.ingramcontent.com/pod-product-compliance
Lightning Source LLC
LaVergne TN
LVHW020214110826
845151LV00003B/718

* 9 7 8 1 4 2 5 5 3 3 6 8 7 *